Understanding
Devotion
A LOGICAL PERSPECTIVE ON HANUMAN CHALISA
❖
Br. Ramanandamrita Chaitanya

An attempt to grasp the practical essence

of Bhakti through Amma's teachings,

as exemplified by Lord Hanuman

Understanding Devotion

A Logical Perspective on Hanuman Chalisa

Br. Ramanandamrita Chaitanya

Published by:
Mata Amritanandamayi Center
P.O. Box 613
San Ramon, CA 94583-0613
USA

Acknowledgments and credits:
With deep gratitude to Swami Amritaswarupananda Puri for his unwavering support and insightful contributions.

Deeply grateful to the following people for their careful proofreading, greatly enhancing the quality of the book:

Vinay (Dan) Marshall, Shakti Fleisher, Bri. Amrita Chaitanya, Dr. S Krishnamoorthy, Dr. Keshavan Varadarajan, Dr. Vidya (Elizabeth) Corley, Dr. Shivesh (Rajagopalan) Rameshbabu.

Cover Design & Book layout: Br. Harikrishnan, Arun Raj S R, Ratheesh N R, Amrita Office of Communications

Her Holiness Sri Mata Amritanandamayi Devi
My guiding light and inspiration

O Amma, how can I seek devotion towards you
when you are the very embodiment of true devotion?
Bless me to remain your child, filled with innocence and truth

Table of Contents

Preface:
Author's Note

Let us imagine a scenario: we are standing before the beautiful sanctum sanctorum of the temple of our most beloved deity. A dedicated and sincere priest waves lit camphor before the deity, filling the space with light and fragrance. Our mind is absorbed in appreciating the beauty of the altar, remembering the greatness of the deity, and expressing heartfelt prayers, saying, "I have no one but you to take refuge in." This is a good example of a moment filled with devotion.

But can this "good example" be transformed into a "perfect example?" What if, in addition to appreciation, adoration, prayer, and thoughts of surrender, we rather focus on the burning camphor and remind ourselves: For my prayers to be fulfilled and for me to become deserving of my deity's grace, my ego must burn like the camphor—sublime in the fire of wisdom and knowledge—leaving no residue behind. This sincere effort to overcome the ego should be my true offering to the deity.

In this way, when our dedication is complemented with the proper understanding and wisdom, we elevate the experience from good devotion to perfect devotion.

This book attempts to grasp the practical and logical essence of bhakti (devotion) as exemplified by Lord Hanuman in the Hanuman Chalisa, through the lens of Amma's life, work, and teachings. Bhakti is often discussed from stereotypical perspectives, wherein logic takes the backseat. It is frequently given a mystical flavor, with devotees expecting miracles from the Divine. Moreover, bhakti contains within it an element of surrender, that is sometimes misinterpreted as leaving everything up to the Divine without focusing on our responsibilities. Practiced without proper understanding, it can also carry an element of blind belief, wherein one may develop a fear of a punishing God.

In its essence, the path of devotion is much more profound, evolving from fearing God to loving God. This book attempts to understand bhakti as a simple yet profoundly transformative, practical, and logical path of spiritual pursuit. While we are not outright dismissing the common stereotypes associated with devotion, we will try to understand the meaning and reasoning behind such beliefs. We aim to reinterpret and understand them through a lens of logic and practicality.

Lord Hanuman, the epitome of devotion, is perhaps the greatest inspiration for a spiritual seeker—not just for those on the path of bhakti, but also for those pursuing the paths of jnana (knowledge), karma (selfless action) or other major spiritual disciplines. The *Hanuman Chalisa*, a collection of forty verses praising Lord Hanuman, highlights his virtues and pivotal role in the *Ramayana*'s critical moments. Lord Hanuman serves as the ultimate role model for a spiritual seeker, exemplifying how one can transcend the ego by becoming nothing and, in doing so, becoming one with everything— the ultimate goal of any spiritual pursuit, regardless of the path one follows.

Meanwhile, Amma's teachings are strikingly simple and yet profoundly practical. They make perfect sense not only to a spiritual seeker but also to an agnostic individual. Amma's teachings are rooted deeply in the ancient principles of Sanatana Dharma (the ancient Indian tradition) but, at the same time, are practically molded for today's context. They transcend boundaries and appeal universally. Amma's teachings are not merely conveyed through words; her very life is her greatest lesson. She leads by example, literally giving herself selflessly to others. Spending anywhere from 10 to even 22 hours a day giving darshan, Amma remains seated in one place, forgoing basic needs like food, rest, and even nature's call as she listens to people's problems, receives them with a motherly embrace, consoles them, offers guidance, and inspires them. This is not an isolated event but a daily routine for Amma, which she has kept for the last 50 years. Through her teachings and example, Amma inspires and resonates with an aspiring bhakta (devotee) on the path of bhakti, an aspiring jnani (seeker of wisdom) on the path of jnana, an aspiring karma yogi (selfless doer) on the path of karma. In fact, I have seen that even atheists and rationalists have no argument with Amma's tangible example of selflessness.

Amma's practical wisdom as expressed in her life, work, and teachings, combined with Lord Hanuman's exemplary life as elucidated in the Hanuman Chalisa, offer the perfect guidance for a spiritual seeker to grasp the true essence of bhakti. The heart of this book is a close reading of the *Hanuman Chalisa*, in which we reflect on each verse and work to decipher the ways in which Hanuman exemplified being a true bhakta in every situation he faced. These reflections will draw on several sources, for which I have included a visual key: Amma's teachings (🐘), stories and episodes from the Puranas and epics (📖), scriptural references (🗡), and intriguing facts (💡).

I do not claim this is the only way to understand or practice bhakti. However, exploring bhakti from a practical perspective is undoubtedly worthwhile, and it is essential to recognize that this path is in no way inferior to any other. Bhakti is a path for the brave, as it demands the tangible relinquishment of ego in every situation encountered.

Br. Ramanandamrita Chaitanya

sā tvasmin parama prema rūpā |2.2|
amṛta svarūpā ca |2.3|

~ Narada Bhakti Sutra

That (bhakti) is indeed the embodiment of Supreme Love (untainted, wise and selfless), and verily the nature of the nectar of immortality.

|| *Aum* ||

Introduction:
The Essential Unity of Bhakti and Jnana Yoga

In July 2023, the Indian Space Research Organisation (ISRO) launched a successful lunar exploration mission — the first ever to land near the south pole of the Moon. The mission was the result of years of meticulous effort by some of the top scientific minds in the country. This remarkable achievement was lauded across the globe by governments and space agencies alike. Interestingly, the mission was accomplished on less than half the budget of a Hollywood movie about space exploration — a testament to India's innovation and resourcefulness. Without the brilliance and precision of these scientists, such a feat would not have been possible.

Now, you may wonder why I am opening a book about bhakti with an anecdote about the Indian space agency's successful launch. A few days before the launch, Indian news channels aired images of some of the lead scientists visiting a famous temple in South India, offering prayers and seeking divine blessings for the mission's success. Setting aside the usual political commentary and media debates, I was personally heartened to see them seeking grace from the Divine. And yet, a question lingered in my mind: What was the rationale behind such accomplished scientists choosing to visit a temple just days before the launch? Why were minds so oriented toward logic seeking divine intervention?

Not long after the mission was underway and the spacecraft was en route to the Moon, one of the top scientists involved in the mission came to meet Amma. I had the opportunity to interact with him and decided to ask him that very question. "Why did your team choose to visit the temple just before the launch?" His response was precise. "We did our part the best way we could," he said. "We went to the temple to make sure the rocket didn't launch before it was supposed to." Though brief, his words carried deep meaning. They had given their all on the scientific front, and their visit to the temple reflected a deeper recognition — there are countless factors beyond human control that influence the outcome of any endeavor. It was their way of aligning with something greater, preparing themselves inwardly for the days ahead. A simple yet powerful act of humility and surrender.

Curious, I asked another question: "What is your reason for visiting Amma?" He smiled and replied: "Though the rocket launches high into the sky, I still want to stay grounded here on Earth. I want to learn from Amma's wisdom." That, too, was a striking insight. Our achievements may carry us to great heights, but true wisdom lies in remaining humble and grounded. In staying calm under pressure. In holding our nerve. In being patient, centered, accepting, and wise during the most critical moments of our lives. Their devotion gave them the inner grounding needed during the challenging moments to come.

This is the essence of bhakti, a path that uplifts us beyond anything we could have imagined, yet keeps us deeply rooted within. It prepares us to face every situation, favorable or otherwise, with an attitude of equanimity, and helps us cultivate the inner maturity to accept whatever outcome unfolds.

Bhakti is often a trivialized path of spiritual pursuit. But as we shall see in the pages to come, it is one of the most effective and practical approaches to spirituality, especially in today's uncertain world. In fact, its vastness is masked by its outward simplicity. Bhakti is often seen through a stereotypical lens, where logic takes a backseat. It is by turns wrapped in mystique, tied to favor and miracle-seeking, and mistaken for blind surrender that ignores personal responsibility and fears a punishing God. And yet, devotion is not limited to ritualistic worship or singing the praises of the Divine. It is far more profound and expansive, grounded in selflessness, humility, and wisdom.

Bhakti is a comprehensive journey from the "me" to the "Me" — a shift from the ego-bound self to the higher Self. In fact, to say "I have an understanding of bhakti," is almost an oxymoron. One who truly understands and practices bhakti no longer has the "I" to make such a claim. A true devotee transcends the ego, rising above personal likes and dislikes, attachments, judgments, and the sense of "I" and "mine." The beauty of this path lies in its practicality. These profound spiritual ideas are not left as abstract concepts. Rather they are brought into daily life through simple, tangible practices. Bhakti gently transforms our thoughts, words, and actions, making them purposeful and meaningful.

This book explores the *Hanuman Chalisa*, a forty-verse tribute to Lord Hanuman — to his wisdom, virtues, and unwavering devotion to Lord Rama. Lord Hanuman is given the highest regard, the utmost respect, and the deepest reverence for how a true devotee should be. Lord Hanuman embodies the ideal spiritual seeker, exhibiting the courage and strength to transcend ego to become "nothing." In doing so, he becomes one with "everything," the essence of every spiritual path. Throughout these pages, we delve into bhakti as a spiritual path with a transformative power that reveals an inherent logic all its own. We shall seek to understand the roots of bhakti through reason and practicality. Rather than dismissing stereotypical beliefs, we explore their significance through Amma's teachings, interpreting episodes from the *Puranas* and epics, referencing scriptures, and uncovering intriguing insights that illuminate the depths of devotion.

Why is Lord Hanuman an Inspiration?

As individuals committed to spiritual development, it is vital to appreciate what real bhakti looks like, and no one illustrates it more clearly than Hanuman. His humility and devotion did not stem from helplessness or a lack of abilities — on the contrary, he possessed immense strength and wisdom. Yet, despite his extraordinary capabilities, he remained immensely humble, always maintaining the attitude of a devoted servant. This is a lesson we, too, should embrace. For many of us, even the slightest reason can cause our ego to swell beyond measure. Hanuman, then, serves as the ultimate inspiration for overcoming our vastly inflated sense of self.

Bhakti Yoga vs Jnana Yoga

Given that this book's title underscores the comprehension of devotion through logical inquiry, it is imperative to begin by considering two fundamental avenues of spiritual pursuit: bhakti yoga, which centers on devotion, and jnana yoga, which emphasizes logical contemplation.

Scriptural texts are often associated with deeply philosophical Vedantic principles — whether dualistic, non-dualistic, or variations thereof. This is the common stereotype we attach to them. However, the *Hanuman Chalisa* stands apart in its simplicity. It narrates Lord Hanuman's various deeds and the contexts in which he acted, and can be read as a devotional text without a deeper philosophical meaning. Yet, as is the case for all the devotional texts of Sanatana Dharma, beneath its straightforward storytelling, the essence of its teachings remains firmly rooted in Vedantic principles.

There is a reason for this Vedantic underpinning. For though the paths of bhakti and jnana have different flavors, their essence is the same. Amma says bhakti and jnana are like two wings of a bird, complementing each other. It is impossible to fly with one wing alone; we need both to soar in the sky. Similarly, we need both bhakti and jnana to tread on our spiritual path and grow. Focusing solely on the path of knowledge or devotion alone will lead us nowhere; we need both to achieve our spiritual goals.

To achieve a goal, domain knowledge is crucial. Let us consider the example of the Apollo 11 space project. This project required expertise in mechanical engineering, aerospace engineering, atmospheric science, meteorology, computer science, electrical engineering, medicine, psychology, and many more disciplines. However, just having expertise was not enough. The team members also needed to be equipped with qualities like hard work, perseverance, patience, faith, and trust, along with the ability to put domain knowledge into practice. Both the knowledge the project team members had acquired, and the virtues they had cultivated as part of their character, were equally essential to the project's success.

Renowned Irish rugby player Brian O'Driscoll once remarked, "Knowledge is knowing that a tomato is a fruit. Wisdom is knowing not to put it in a fruit salad." Likewise, raw knowledge, when cooked with the experiences and maturity that life situations provide, becomes more palatable and applicable.

Knowledge alone is insufficient for our spiritual journey. Much like the Apollo 11 team members, we too are embarking on an ambitious and at times, difficult project. In order to be successful, we must develop good qualities like dedication, perseverance, patience, faith, and trust. Bhakti yoga helps us develop these qualities, while jnana yoga provides the proper understanding of what we need to do. Both paths are equally challenging and important. Choosing a path only means prioritizing one while using the other as support.

Bhagavad Gita, Chapter 12 is dedicated to the topic of bhakti. Lord Krishna elaborately describes what a true devotee is like. The verses 13 and 14:

adveṣhṭā sarva-bhūtānāṁ maitraḥ karuṇa eva cha
nirmamo nirahankāraḥ sama-duḥkha-sukhaḥ kṣhamī || 13 ||

*One who is free from ill thoughts towards everyone and
everything, who beholds the attitude of friendship, compassion,
and the like; One who is free from thoughts of "me and mine"
and lets go of egotism; one who is equipoised in happiness
and distress, and is ever-forgiving and patient.*

santuṣhṭaḥ satataṁ yogī yatātmā dṛidha-niśhchayaḥ
mayy arpita-mano-buddhir yo mad-bhaktaḥ sa me priyaḥ || 14 ||

*One who is ever content, steadfast in the path, self-reliant,
firm in resolve, and committed; one who submits one's
mind and intellect unto me is my dearest devotee.*

The verses underscore that becoming a true devotee is not a trivial task. The qualities expressed above aren't possible to exhibit and exercise unless one has overcome one's self-centered thoughts and deeds based on true wisdom. Thus we need both the proper knowledge and the commitment to put the values gained into practice.

The primary objective of both the path of jnana and the path of bhakti is to overcome our ego and realize our true self. In jnana yoga, we logically negate our ego to discover our true self. In bhakti yoga, we surrender our ego to a higher force, such as our guru or a deity, using them as a reference point. To achieve this shared goal, we will need to embrace aspects of both paths, to appreciate the complementary nature of these paths, and avoid feelings of superiority of one path over the other.

Concluding a strenuous tour of the US and Japan in 2024, Amma arrived in Amritapuri early one morning in mid-August. Amma had not slept for the past 48 hours, and it was expected Amma would not be coming for the evening bhajans. However, as the unexpected often happens around a mahatma, Amma arrived to everyone's pleasant surprise for the evening bhajans. In between the bhajans, Amma interacted with the tiny tots of the ashram, as she hadn't seen them for several weeks. She asked one of the ashram children what she had been doing while Amma was away. The girl replied that she was learning the *Srimad Bhagavatam*. Amma inquired whether she liked the *Bhagavad Gita* or the *Srimad Bhagavatam*. Ashram kids are known for being ardent students of the *Bhagavad Gita*, and this cute little girl was particularly known for quoting verses from the *Bhagavad Gita* during her talks and interactions. The little girl responded that she liked both, as the *Srimad Bhagavatam* focuses on bhakti. At the same time, the little girl reflected, the *Bhagavad Gita* embodies the essence of the Vedas (jnana), and both are needed for spiritual growth. Amma appreciated her response and added that Veda Vyasa, after compiling the Vedas and writing the Brahma Sutras (the aphorisms of the Vedas) and other Vedantic texts, ultimately wrote the *Srimad Bhagavatam*, which is rooted in bhakti, and in so doing, pointed out that bhakti is one of the most practical and effective paths to reach the ultimate state. Since jnana yoga involves the intellect, Amma reflected, the Vedanti (student of Vedanta) often becomes deluded and grows egotistical. Simply proclaiming the vedantic principles without practicing them is useless to us or those around us.

Amma was recollecting an incident in the old times at the ashram. One of the early brahmacharis (celibate monks), who was studying philosophy, was contemplating philosophical thoughts while sitting outside the old temple. He was writing on a piece of paper, "I am the Supreme Brahman," repeatedly. Amma, sitting elsewhere, sent him a note with the word "honey" written on it. The note also said, "Please lick this piece of paper and see whether it tastes sweet." Amma meant to teach the brahmachari that the vedantic principles in mere words alone are of no use. They need to be put into practice. And once put into practice, it becomes inevitable to integrate and merge the path of bhakti and jnana into one. One who puts into practice the principles learned from the scriptures is indeed practicing the path of bhakti. One who devotes himself to a cause with the proper understanding and wisdom is indeed practicing the path of jnana. Both paths converge, complementing each other.

Bhakti yoga is the means to dedicate oneself to a form of the Divine, imbibing the inspiring qualities and characteristics (saguna rupa), to become one with the form; and jnana yoga is to contemplate on the aspectless Divine (nirguna rupa), trying to go beyond characteristics and realize the oneness with that Supreme Soul.

Jnana Yoga - An Overview

The path of jnana involves three main steps: shravana, manana, and nididhyasana. The literal meaning of shravana is to listen. In this context, listening means perceiving knowledge in every way possible from every source available. We should learn as much as we can and remain open to knowledge as it comes to us, receiving it as well as we can.

The second step is manana, which means to contemplate. It's not enough to simply let information pass through one ear and out the other or to boast about our knowledge without truly understanding it. Once we have grasped the knowledge, the next step is to contemplate it and organize it in our cognitive system to properly utilize what we have learned.

The third step is nididhyasana, where we assimilate everything we have learned and contemplated. We then put them into action. We can see the concept of nidhdhyasana brought to life most vividly in Amma's vision for research at Amrita University; Amma always insists that research be done with an aim toward materializing a tangible benefit to society, especially for people in need.

In my own case, I have wondered what is the point of Amma asking me to do my PhD in Computer Science if all I am doing as a monk is giving talks, leading scriptural discussions, singing bhajans, doing pujas, and ashram administration. I have asked Amma why she made me do my PhD if this is the role I had to play. Amma told me I had a prarabdha (karma) of higher studies and mentioned that my biological mother strongly desired all her children to do a PhD.

Surprisingly, my biological mother hadn't revealed her hidden desire to any of us until much later. In this way, Amma made me go through the process of burning out my prarabdha and then, though discharging the duties of a monk, did not let me abandon my computer science knowledge. Amma always reminded me that the PhD work should directly impact and benefit society. Although I am not directly involved in computer science research, Amma has found ways to keep me passively involved in research through my PhD students. In the first few years after my studies were completed, I happily and conveniently forgot about my PhD. Around 2016, when Amma found that I was not guiding any PhD students or, at the very least, even helping students with research, she ensured that I had at least a few PhD students to guide at Amrita University in Amritapuri, India. Amma mentioned that all the effort to secure a PhD should not go in vain and should be of benefit to others. What is the use of all the knowledge we have grasped and contemplated if we don't assimilate it and put it into action? That is the essence of nididhyasana.

Bhakti Yoga - An Overview

Srimad Bhagavatam, canto 7, chapter 5:

> śravaṇam kīrtanam viṣṇoḥ smaraṇam pāda-sevanam
> arcanam vandanam dāsyam sakhyam ātma-nivedanam
> iti pumsārpitā viṣṇau bhaktiś cen nava-lakṣaṇā
> kriyeta bhagavat-yaddhā tan manye-dhītam uttamam

Listening to and singing the glories of the Supreme (Vishnu), constant remembrance, worshipping His holy feet, offering with surrender, salutations, service, cultivating a bond of friendship, and complete self-surrender — when an individual offers these with sincere devotion to the Divine, it becomes a true offering. I consider this the highest wisdom learned.

The path of bhakti is usually described as having nine steps. The first is shravana, which begins with the same idea as in jnana yoga. Listening to the glory of the beloved deity or guru helps us realize that our inflated ego is in vain.

The second is kirtana. It's not just about listening; we should also repeat it and make it a practice. We should call out all the qualities of the Divine or our beloved deity that we focus on. Singing or calling out the glory of the Divine gives us direction to the ultimate state we look upon.

The third step is smarana, which, simply put, means not only outwardly expressing devotion but also internalizing it. Our actions, thoughts, and words should all be enveloped in devotion and love for the deity or central point.

The fourth step is pada sevana, which is worshiping the feet of our beloved deity. This act isn't merely about the physical feet; it symbolizes the admirable qualities and virtues that the guru embodies. For instance, Amma says she is not in the least interested in having her feet worshiped, but allows it as a long-standing tradition. Amma would rather have us clean a gutter, a park, or a public place to benefit others. And while we follow Amma's wish, we also preserve the tradition of worshipping the guru's feet because of the deeper meaning behind it. When we focus on the guru's or deity's feet, we worship all the great qualities they walk through life with. Reflecting on these qualities and imbibing them in ourselves is the true essence of pada sevana.

The fifth step is archana, which typically involves offering flower petals. In essence, it means offering everything to the deity — our prayers, desires, worries, goodness, negativities, especially our ego, and shortcomings — at the lotus feet of the deity and being open to growing. The term used for the flower's fragrance is called vasana in some Indian languages. Interestingly, vasana is also the term used for the tendencies we have. As part of archana, we need to offer our negative tendencies, along with the flowers.

The sixth step is vandana, which means to pay obeisance. It involves always considering the focus point, our guru or deity, as being in a higher state and looking to reach that level. A guru is like a surgeon cutting into our mind and removing our ego. In the process, our hurt ego may sometimes even start questioning the guru. Thus, maintaining an attitude of vandana remains critical in our spiritual pursuit to keep our ego at bay.

The seventh step is dasya, which means to be of service. The guru or deity doesn't need our service, but doing so helps us cultivate an attitude of humility. Amma always says that service to humanity is the best service we can offer her.

The eighth step is sakhya, which means developing a bond or friendship with the deity. This bond helps nullify all other attachments. It is similar to displaying a "Stick No Bills" sign on a wall to prevent other unnecessary posters from being stuck there. This unique attachment — sakhya with the guru or deity — helps overcome other meaningless attachments.

The ninth step is atma-nivedana, which means surrender. Surrender doesn't mean giving up; it means developing an attitude of acceptance. We should do our best and give our all, but complement our efforts with the attitude of acceptance of whatever the outcome is.

In conclusion, the steps of bhakti — shravana, kirtana, smarana, pada sevana, archana, vandana, dasya, sakhya, and atma-nivedana — are meant to purify our thoughts, words, and actions. They help us develop humility and overcome our ego.

Awaken Children Vol. 1, page 151

A group of devoted women were sitting around the Amma.
A few of them had taken a course on Vedanta. Mother told them,
"The goal is Jñana, and the means is bhakti. Children, bhakti
is the path to Jñana. Devotion with love for God should arise.
In this age, more concentration is gained through kirtan than

dhyana (meditation). The present atmosphere is always filled with different kinds of sound. Because of that, dhyana will be difficult. Concentration will not be gained easily. This can be overcome if kirtan is performed. Not only that, the atmosphere will also become pure. Innocence will arise if one travels on the bhakti marga (path of devotion). All can be seen with the attitude of brotherhood.

A few years ago, during Amma's North American tour, we were traveling from Los Angeles, California, to Albuquerque, New Mexico. As always, Amma was traveling by road with all the tour staff. There were several buses carrying approximately 250 to 300 people traveling with Amma. As is tradition, in the evening, Amma stopped to serve chai and dinner to everyone.

During the stop, Amma posed a question to everyone about bhakti. Different people had various things to say, and the topic of the gopis of Vrindavan came up. Amma talked about how the gopis are given the highest regard as bhaktas. Their attitude towards Lord Krishna was one of complete dedication. They would forget everything else, including their and their families' needs, and focus entirely on Lord Krishna. They would drop everything to be with him if they found that Krishna had come out of his house and was doing Rasa Leela (divine play). Many humorous episodes in different texts mention gopis running to Krishna with ladles in their hands or even with their children straight from the shower.

The gopis were unconcerned with their ego and purely devoted to Lord Krishna. It is widely believed that the seers and sages of ancient times, despite all their tapas (penance), could not attain the level of access to the Divine that the gopis had. These sages were believed to be reborn as the gopis in Vrindavan to live a life dedicated to Lord Krishna, where they could be near him in his human form as a cute little boy whom they adored with pure bhakti. We can palpably feel this same phenomenon in Amritapuri today when Amma steps out of her room, and thousands are thronging around Amma, regardless of the activity in which they had been involved when Amma appeared.

Returning to the conversation of bhakti with Amma during the dinner stop, Amma mentioned that while the gopis' bhakti is highly revered, Hanuman's devotion is considered even a step beyond that. This is because Hanuman's bhakti was based on knowledge, understanding, and wisdom. He was ever-wise in his devotion, not merely driven by spontaneous emotion.

Amma likened Hanuman's bhakti to the situation we often experience around her. When there is a rumor that Amma will sing after giving darshan, many of us rush to be near her, sometimes forgetting our duties and even the people we were talking to. This is similar to the gopis' dedication, driven by a desire to be close to the divine. In contrast, Hanuman's bhakti involved thinking about others, and about the comfort of the Divine. He would consider whether crowding around Amma would cause her discomfort and whether others around her would get the opportunity to be with Amma. He would sacrifice his desire to be near her for others' sake. Amma jokingly inquired how many around her thought like Hanuman as they tried to find space to sit in Amma's close proximity then. Amma said Hanuman had unwavering dedication towards Lord Rama, and importantly, this devotion was founded on knowledge, wisdom, and maturity. We will try to focus on this aspect of Hanuman's devotion as we discuss the 40 verses of the *Hanuman Chalisa.* .

Kamya and Nishkamya Bhakti

Bhagavad Gita, chapter 7, verse 16:

> chatur-vidhā bhajante mām janāḥ sukṛitino-rjuna
> ārto jijñāsur arthārthī jñānī cha bharatarṣhabha

O best amongst the Bharatas (Arjuna), four kinds of pious people
engage in my devotion - the distressed, seekers of material gains,
the seekers of knowledge and those established in knowledge.

Bhakti can be of two different types, kamya bhakti and nishkamya bhakti. Kamya bhakti refers to devotion that arises out of need or desire. As Amma mentions, many people first meet her when they are facing difficult situations in life, praying to Amma to alleviate their situation. You may have heard Amma mention that many people living in Amritapuri ashram initially asked for help with their relationships, jobs, finances, health, and other personal issues. Eventually, they reached a level of giving up their desires and started living in Amritapuri, engaging in selfless service at the University or in various ashram projects.

Kamya bhakti starts with a desire for something. It's like a person going to an exam hall, stopping by a temple to pray for success in the exam, and making promises of offerings if they pass. If they fail, they may go to the temple to blame the deity saying, "I knew you would not help me." Then why go to the temple and pray? This kind of devotion is transactional, which is not the essence of true bhakti.

There is a funny story about a little boy named Somu, who was not well-mannered and often got into trouble. He wanted a bicycle and asked his mother for one. She told him he needed to improve his behavior first. She suggested he write down all his mistakes, take the letter to the Krishna temple, and promise to be a good boy next year. Somu took time to write a long letter but quickly returned from the temple without leaving it there. He then hardly spent a few minutes in his room, wrote a new letter, and returned to the temple. Curious, his mother followed him and later retrieved the letter he left at the temple. The letter simply said, "I have kidnapped Radha. If you want her back in the temple, make sure my mother gets me the bicycle." This story humorously illustrates the transactional nature of kamya bhakti.

However, bhakti should not be about getting things but about giving up things. Kamya bhakti is the devotion that arises out of desire or need. It is essentially transactional. One may start with kamya bhakti, but we need to upgrade to nishkamya bhakti — selfless devotion, not driven by any desire for personal gain. This form of bhakti doesn't arise out of craving but rather out of contentment. A good analogy would be how an uncontrollably hungry person would handle a yummy piece of mango mousse compared to someone else who is there just to enjoy the mousse. The former would just shove the dessert down their throat, not enjoying the taste of the dessert. The priority there is to quench hunger, and that's it. On the other hand, the latter can relish every bite of the dessert as there is no other objective to satisfy.

Bhakti can be expressed in five bhavas (attitudes):

1. Shanta bhava: Shanta means peace and silence. Here, the expression of devotion towards the Divine is through silence. There is nothing external about it. The devotee expresses devotion by just meditating on the Divine. It's about internalizing spiritual values and silencing the mind. Every thought, word, and action, every moment, is directed towards the Supreme. This bhava is the basis of all the other bhavas. Irrespective of any bhava a devotee chooses, they must eventually evolve into this state of emotional detachment.

2. Sakhya bhava: The expression of bond or companionship. The attitude of friendship towards the beloved deity is like Arjuna's relationship with Lord Krishna, being cousins. Of course, his attitude towards Krishna evolved to be that of an ardent disciple after Krishna advised the *Bhagavad Gita* to Arjuna on the Kurukshetra battlefield. But being a companion, you can open up and pour your heart out with abandon. I have known many youngsters who bonded with Amma and shared their problems and secrets with Amma, as they would confide in a friend.

3. Vatsalya bhava: Compassion, like the attitude of a mother. Mother Yashoda had this attitude towards baby Krishna, caring and

nurturing him. Sometimes, in bhajans that we sing, we consider the Divine Mother or Lord Krishna as a baby, bathing, feeding, caring for them, and singing a lullaby, expressing this motherly affection.

4. Madhurya bhava: Sweet, unconditional love, like Radha's love for Krishna. This love is not about bodily attraction but is much higher. It is about unity and becoming one with the Divine. Amma often shares the story of Lord Krishna's consort Rukmini asking him about Radha. She tells him she has heard so much about Radha and is curious. She requests Krishna to draw Radha's face for her. Krishna obliges. Looking at the picture, Rukmini asks Krishna not to play the fool with her and draw Radha's image because Krishna ended up drawing his face. As often as he tries, he draws his own face. He finally tells Rukmini that he is helpless, because Radha and Krishna are one. There is no duality in the ultimate state of union. The form of ardhanarishwara also depicts this exalted state of unity. Also known as the form of shiva-shakti-aikya, this combined form of Shiva and Shakti with half masculine and half feminine form underscores how one cannot be removed from the other.

5. Dasya bhava: Devotion in the form of service, exemplified by Hanuman's selfless service to Lord Rama. Despite all his abilities, Hanuman practiced humility by serving the Divine. This attitude of bhakti involves putting the needs of the deity and others before one's own, with the conviction that what the deity wants will benefit others and the world.

As we explore the 40 verses of the *Hanuman Chalisa*, we will explore the facets of the dasya bhava that Lord Hanuman exemplifies and inspires us with.

Setting the Context:
Tulasidas, Hanuman Chalisa and Ramayana

Before we delve deeper into the topic of bhakti, it will be helpful to first understand the context in which we are discussing it. Our primary focus is the *Hanuman Chalisa*, authored by Tulasidas Goswami, with references to Lord Hanuman's pivotal role in the great epic *Ramayana*. Examining these aspects will provide a holistic understanding of how Bhakti is a central force in addressing life's problems and challenges.

Tulasidas Goswami

Goswami Tulasidas, the author of the *Hanuman Chalisa*, was a great poet and philosopher from the 16th century. "Goswami" is a title given to someone highly spiritually evolved and revered. Goswami is also sometimes pronounced as Gosai in regional languages.

Awadhi
अवधी

By birth, his name was Rambola, meaning "one who always has the name of Ram on his lips." It is believed that when he was born, he did not cry but was in a state of bliss and constantly uttering the name "Ram" thereafter. Some believe that Tulasidas is a reincarnation of Sage Valmiki, who composed the *Ramayana* and is referred to as Adi Kavi, the first poet in the world.

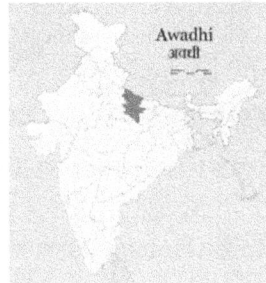

Tulasidas was ever devoted to Lord Rama from childhood. He would organize plays and skits based on various episodes of the *Ramayana*. He was a scholar in Sanskrit and Avadhi (a regional language in Uttar Pradesh). His compositions in Avadhi, including the *Hanuman Chalisa*, captured people's hearts because they made the teachings of the scriptures accessible to the masses.

Tulasidas spent most of his life in Varanasi (Banaras or Kashi), the abode of the famous Lord Shiva Temple, Kashi Vishwanath Temple. Kashi is a holy city where many people, after fulfilling their life's responsibilities, attain liberation by spending the dusk of their life there. Tulasidas wrote many of his works on the banks of the River Ganga in Kashi.

It is believed that Tulasidas had a vision of Lord Shiva and Parvati, who instructed him to write the *Ramayana* in Avadhi for the benefit of the local people. He traveled to Ayodhya, the birthplace of Lord Rama, and spent several months composing the *Ramcharitmanas* (*Ramayana* in Avadhi). When he returned to Kashi, he wanted to place the text in the Kashi Vishwanath Temple per Lord Shiva's instructions. However, the Sanskrit scholars of the time did not appreciate his work in a local language and placed the *Ramcharitmanas* beneath other Sanskrit texts. The following day, when the temple was opened, the *Ramcharitmanas* was found on top of the other texts as if someone had read through them during the night. The scholars realized their mistake and apologized to Tulasidas. This event increased his fame, and his work positively influenced more people.

It is also believed that Tulasidas was once arrested and imprisoned by the guards of the Mughal Emperor Akbar. The reasons for his imprisonment vary: some say that the emperor felt that he failed to respect him, while others say that because he was promoting a different religion than the emperor, he was jailed at the fort in Fatehpur Sikri. During the forty days in jail, it is believed that he composed the *Hanuman Chalisa*, 40 verses in praise of Lord Hanuman. Miraculously, upon completing the *Hanuman Chalisa*, it is said that an army of monkeys descended upon the kingdom of Akbar, causing havoc everywhere, including the emperor's royal dwelling. Even the so-called mighty Mughal army was rendered helpless and no one could contain the monkeys. The emperor was advised by a Hafiz (a scholar of the Holy Quran) that the events unfolding in the kingdom were a manifestation of divine play, resulting from the wrongful imprisonment of a devotee of the Lord.Realizing his mistake, Akbar sought forgiveness from Tulasidas for the grave mistake committed by him. Upon Tulasidas's release, the monkeys miraculously disappeared.

Benefits of Hanuman Chalisa

The *Hanuman Chalisa* is highly regarded by the devotees of Lord Rama, Lord Vishnu, and Lord Hanuman, especially in northern India. The 40 verses of the *Hanuman Chalisa* praise Lord Hanuman, especially in the context of various episodes in the *Ramayana*, highlighting his critical roles. Although Hanuman is honored in these verses, from a spiritual point of view, there is much to learn from how he conducted himself in various situations. We will discuss these lessons as we approach each verse.

The basic lesson is how Hanuman, with all his abilities, conducted himself with humility, restraint, and control over his mind and senses. Despite his appearance as a monkey, an embodiment of restlessness, he demonstrated how one could be completely focused and dedicated. Monkeys are known for their constant movement, yet Hanuman's form illustrates how one can be centered and devoted. It is a message for us to bring our monkey mind under control.

Devotees of Hanuman and Lord Rama strongly believe that chanting the *Hanuman Chalisa* brings physical and mental strength. In fact, many bodybuilders in India are traditionally devotees of Lord Hanuman (Bajarang Bali - the one who is as strong as an unbreakable diamond) because they believe praying to Hanuman helps them build physical strength. The *Hanuman Chalisa* is widely thought to provide the strength needed to be a bold individual.

This belief can be interpreted in two ways. First, by chanting the *Hanuman Chalisa* regularly, one receives the grace and guidance of Lord Hanuman. With this divine grace, one automatically gains the strength to face every moment. This is the faith-based perspective of bhakti.

The second, more logical perspective is that you will develop mental strength by not just mechanically chanting the *Hanuman Chalisa* but also imbibing its teachings and the examples set by Lord Hanuman into your character. Hanuman is the embodiment of mental and physical strength. By trying to emulate his qualities, you will naturally be able to face life's challenges better and develop the strength you need.

From a very young age, I feared being alone in the dark, a fear that persisted for many years. I often tried to escape this feeling by avoiding situations where I would be alone in the dark. Unfortunately, as fate would have it, I found myself alone in the newly inaugurated Washington, D.C. ashram, a four-story, 16,000-square-foot building. Living in such an isolated place, where the neighboring buildings are not visible from any of the windows, heightened my fears. I tried convincing Amma about not making me stay there alone as I was scared. But Amma was resolute in her response: "Nothing to do with fear. You have to face the situation and overcome it as soon as possible. Rather than trying to escape situations, face them and overcome the hurdles." I had no choice but to face my fear. I can list out many instances and experiences wherein I felt so scared and did crazy things to deal with the situation. I would call out to Amma to be with me, but with the condition that she shouldn't appear in front of me to protect me. I would have been all the more scared seeing her appear before me.

My biological sister, who used to chant the *Hanuman Chalisa* often, introduced me to it when I was young, telling me how *Hanuman*

Chalisa gives you strength. Every time I chanted it, I felt a sense of courage and boldness. It would make me sense Amma's presence. It made me realize that Amma's presence was always there. After all, it was Amma's ashram. But chanting *Hanuman Chalisa* would clear my mind of unnecessary anxiety and fear, thus helping me become aware of Amma's presence. Having that mindset helped me to slowly start facing the situations one by one and exploring the sound or experience that scared me. I started realizing that in each case, there was a tangible reason behind the sound or experience. I realized that the fear was all based on my unnecessary imagination. For example, I used to regularly hear footsteps near the kitchen whenever I was having dinner. With it happening only at night, I was initially convinced that the deceased previous owner of the property was taking a walk in the house and, based on the sound, that she was wearing high-heeled shoes. Maybe, I thought, she was too attached to the house. She would always take slower steps first and then up her speed eventually as if running towards the kitchen. As I would hear her run towards me, I would drop everything and run to my room upstairs and lock myself up. Once when I heard her take a walk during the daytime, I mustered up the courage to find out what the lady was up to. Did I find her in the adjacent room? Of course not. So I started exploring where the sound of footsteps came from after all. Later I realized that it was just the sound produced by the ice maker in the kitchen, dropping ice cubes onto the tray beneath. It started with a few cubes dropping first and then increasing frequency. It seems funny now and sounds nothing like footsteps once I discovered what created the sound.

Chanting the *Hanuman Chalisa* developed a mindset that helped me face the situation, reason out my fears, and slowly overcome them. Chanting the *Hanuman Chalisa* and trying to imbibe its teachings in our lives will help us develop positive qualities and naturally dispel the negativities within.

Ramayana

Before we begin our close reading of the *Hanuman Chalisa*, it will be helpful to familiarize ourselves with the high-level sequence of events in the *Ramayana*, depicting Lord Rama's life. Considered the oldest poem ever written, *Ramayana* was composed by Sage Valmiki to record the major incidents in Lord Rama's life.

Titi Banda: Lord Rama and the monkey army build the bridge to Lanka - Indonesia

A play depicting the battle from Ramayana, Thailand

Even today, thousands of years after his time on earth, Lord Rama is revered worldwide. The influence of Rama's rule and his personality extended beyond India to eastern neighbors such as Bangladesh, Myanmar (Burma), Laos, Thailand, Indonesia, and Cambodia. In Bali, Indonesia, Lord Rama is still celebrated with devotion, and traditional art forms depict episodes from the *Ramayana*.

Cambodia, located in Southeast Asia, has a massive temple dedicated to Lord Vishnu, of whom Rama is an incarnation. This temple, known as Angkor Wat, is the largest religious monument in the world, spanning over 400 acres. Built by the Khmer Dynasty, it became a place of worship for both Hindus and Buddhists over the centuries.

As we approach the story of Lord Rama's life, we can begin with the Ikshvaku dynasty, with its capital city of Ayodhya, ruled by King Dasharatha. Ayodhya, located in the northern Indian state of Uttar Pradesh, was part of the powerful and widespread Sun (Surya) Dynasty.

Angkor Wat Temple, Cambodia

King Dasharatha had three wives: Kausalya, Kaikeyi, and Sumitra. Despite this, he did not have a child and was concerned about who would succeed him. To resolve this, he performed the Putra Kameshti Yagna, a fire ceremony and sacrificial ritual aimed at having a child. The presiding deity of the yagna emerged with a bowl of sweet pudding (payasam) and instructed Dasharatha to have his wives consume it. Kausalya and Kaikeyi each received half of the pudding and shared portions of their halves with Sumitra.

As a result, Kausalya gave birth to Lord Rama, the seventh incarnation of Lord Vishnu. Kaikeyi gave birth to Bharata, and Sumitra gave birth to Lakshmana and Shatrughna. The four brothers — Rama, Bharata, Lakshmana, and Shatrughna — were very close, with Lakshmana being exceptionally devoted to Rama.

Due to his noble character, Lord Rama was adored by everyone. All three mothers, the citizens, and his father, King Dasharatha, loved him dearly. As he grew older, Rama was rightly declared the Crown Prince, destined to succeed his father. Kaikeyi, upon hearing the news, was ecstatic and even gave away a precious necklace in celebration to the person who conveyed the news to her.

However, Kaikeyi's maid, Manthara, manipulated her by arguing that Kaikeyi's son Bharata would suffer under Rama's rule. Despite initially dismissing Manthara's claims, repeated attempts eventually influenced Kaikeyi. She approached King Dasharatha to claim two promises he had made to her in the past for saving his life on a battlefield. Kaikeyi demanded that Bharata be declared king and that Rama be exiled to the forest for 14 years. Dasharatha was heartbroken by Kaikeyi's demands, which brought a significant and negative change to the kingdom. Her actions, influenced by the bad company and counsel of Manthara, led to severe consequences for the royal family and the entire kingdom.

I remember singing a Malayalam poem as part of a skit we enacted when I was studying at Amma's school. The poem referred to Kaikeyi as the "blind one," blinded by her selfish thoughts, unable to see the truth in front of her. She spoke to the king while intoxicated by her selfishness. The term used, "Matā," basically means intoxicated — intoxicated in selfishness, blinded to the truth, acting without hesitation and in haste. She spoke in haste, and very soon after, she repented. Acting in haste, being intoxicated by selfishness, and being blinded by bad company or negative influence led to severe consequences.

Devastated, King Dasharatha commanded Lord Rama to go into exile. Bharata was not present in Ayodhya at that moment and learned about it later. He was utterly shattered by this development and harshly reprimanded his mother for her wrongdoing, demonstrating the deep love the brothers had for each other.

Contrary to how things might unfold today, where even a simple command from our parents like turning off the TV or putting away mobile phones might be met with rebellion, Lord Rama humbly accepted his father's command to go into exile for 14 years. He had no hesitation despite the hardship of living in the forest without any comforts. He even went to console Mother Kaikeyi, telling her not to worry and that he would be completely fine, showing no hatred or anger towards her. This exemplified the deeply virtuous character that people, especially Lord Rama, had at that time. Lord Rama was the personification of perfection.

Lord Rama set out from Ayodhya, which is in the northern part of India. Though they had no compulsion to leave the comfort of the palace, Lord Rama's wife, Mother Sita, and his devoted brother Lakshmana, decided to accompany Rama to the forest. The map below traces the various places where they stopped along the way, all the way to the southern tip of India. It is during this exile period when Lord Rama and Lord Hanuman meet. It seems the whole exile episode was meant to be for a larger purpose, and indeed Rama eventually annihilated the demon king Ravana in this process and freed the region of Ravana's tyranny.

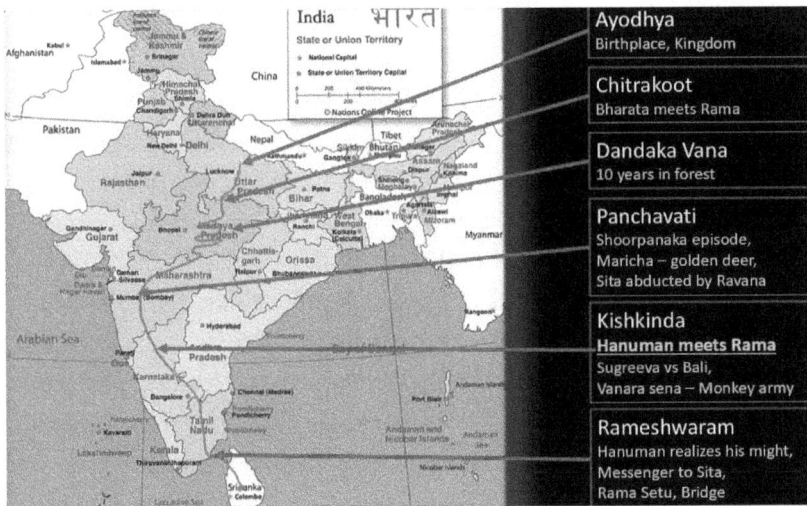

Place	Description
Ayodhya	Birthplace, Kingdom
Chitrakoot	Bharata meets Rama
Dandaka Vana	10 years in forest
Panchavati	Shoorpanaka episode, Maricha – golden deer, Sita abducted by Ravana
Kishkinda	**Hanuman meets Rama** Sugreeva vs Bali, Vanara sena – Monkey army
Rameshwaram	Hanuman realizes his might, Messenger to Sita, Rama Setu, Bridge

High-level sequence of Ramayana

Ramayana, which means Rama's voyage, starts from Ayodhya, which is in the state of Uttar Pradesh, and he first goes to Chitrakoot, which is on the border of the states of Uttar Pradesh and Madhya Pradesh. This is where Bharata comes to meet Lord Rama. Bharata insists that Lord Rama should disregard Mother Kaikeyi and return to Ayodhya as he was the kingdom's rightful ruler. Lord Rama, however, remains firm and says, "No, we must follow our father's directions as he commanded us. You should be the king, and I will return in 14 years." This demonstrates Bharata's love and respect for his brother and Lord Rama's dedication to duty and adherence to dharma. Bharata agrees to return but refuses to be the king. Instead, he takes Rama's sandals, places them on the throne, and rules as a steward king, showing his detachment and disinterest in power.

Lord Rama then moves to the central part of India, to the Dandaka forest, where he spends the next ten years helping sages and seers by protecting them from demons. Eventually, he moves to Panchavati, where a significant episode occurs with Shurpanakha, Ravana's sister. Enamored of Lord Rama, she proposes to him, but when he declines, she attacks Sita. Lakshmana intervenes and punishes her, leading her to flee to Lanka and incite Ravana.

Ravana, influenced by Shurpanakha's description of Sita's beauty, decides to abduct her with the help of Maricha, a demon who creates an illusion of a golden deer to lure Rama away. Sita is greatly attracted to the golden deer and demands that Lord Rama brings it for her. Despite Rama's warning, Sita insists on having the deer, and Rama sets out to capture it. Maricha mimics Rama's voice, calling for help, which prompts Sita to send Lakshmana after him. Some adaptations of *Ramayana* even mention that Lakshmana draws a line of protection (lakshmana-rekha), advising Sita to remain within the line to remain safe. Ravana, disguised as a sage, tricks Sita, abducts her and takes her to Lanka. Jatayu, a devoted vulture, tries to rescue Sita but is mortally wounded. Before dying, he informs Rama about Sita's abduction.

Rama and Lakshmana then move southward, reaching the kingdom of Kishkinta, ruled by the monkey king Vali and his brother Sugriva. After helping Sugriva regain his throne, Rama allies with Sugriva and his minister, Hanuman. The monkey army joins Rama in his quest to rescue Sita. They travel to Rameshwaram, where Hanuman leaps across the Indian Ocean to Lanka. He finds Sita, delivers Rama's ring as a token, and reassures her of Rama's impending rescue. Hanuman encounters Vibhishana, Ravana's righteous brother, and influences him positively, eventually leading him to become a devotee of Lord Rama.

Caught by Ravana's soldiers, Hanuman warns Ravana of the consequences of his actions. Ravana sets Hanuman's tail on fire, but Hanuman uses it to set Lanka ablaze before returning to Rama with news of Sita. Hanuman sent a strong message to Ravana: Your beautiful kingdom is burning by just setting ablaze the tail of Rama's servant - so think of what will happen when Lord Rama arrives here to rescue Mother Sita.

Rama, with the help of the monkey army, builds a bridge to Lanka, defeats Ravana, and rescues Sita. They return to Ayodhya, and Rama assumes his rightful place as king.

This entire sequence, listed briefly, demonstrates the virtues of Lord Rama, including his adherence to duty, humility, and ability to inspire devotion and loyalty in others. The story also illustrates the consequences of actions influenced by selfishness and bad company, as seen in the character of Kaikeyi when influenced by Manthara.

An important point to note is that the battle between Rama and Ravana was part of a divine plan. Jaya and Vijaya, the gatekeepers of Lord Vishnu's abode, were cursed to be born on earth as enemies of Vishnu. When given a choice, they chose to be born three times as Vishnu's opponents rather than seven times as his devotees. They chose the former so they would be done with the curse earlier. Lord Vishnu assured them that he would incarnate in each of their births to liberate them from their curse. In their second birth, they were Ravana and Kumbhakarna, and Vishnu incarnated as Rama to liberate them from their curse.

Rama and Hanuman meeting for the first time

We discussed how when Lord Rama walked from Central India to Southern India, he came to the northern part of South India in today's state of Karnataka, specifically to the monkey kingdom of Kishkinda. Kishkinda was ruled by the Monkey King Vali (Bali). He had wrongfully ousted his brother Sugriva from the kingdom. Sugriva went into hiding in the Rishyamukha mountain. A curse prevented Vali from going to the Rishyamukha mountain. The very special event of Lord Rama and Lord Hanuman's meeting happens in this context. As Sugriva sees two able warriors approaching their hideout, he wonders whether they were sent by King Vali to kill him. Hanuman was asked to go in disguise as a hermit to find out who Rama and Lakshmana were.

Hanuman's meeting with Lord Rama is not easily expressed in words. Various texts beautifully explain how this meeting was meant to be: for the welfare of creation, forming a bond that defines the highest standard of bhakti. The moment that the demi-gods, sages and seers were eagerly awaiting finally happened.

The original *Ramayana*, written by Sage Valmiki, narrates how Hanuman approaches the brothers and politely asks them who they are. At the very sight of Hanuman's appearance, conduct, and controlled command over his speech, Lord Rama recognizes that he isn't just a mere hermit. He asks him, "Who are you? With your conduct and command over your speech, you don't seem to be a mere hermit. Please reveal your true identity." Hanuman reveals his true form and explains the situation of the kingdom of Kishkinda. Eventually, Lord Rama helps Sugriva defeat Vali and Sugriva rightfully re-ascends the throne of Kishkinda.

Ramcharitmanas, the version of the *Ramayana* written by Tulasidas, offers a moving account of this momentous occasion. Both Rama and Hanuman recognize each other as someone special beyond their outward appearances. They inquire about each other's true identities. Rama tells Hanuman, "We are the sons of King Dasharatha — Rama and Lakshmana. We are in the forest at our father's command and are now searching for my wife, Sita, who was abducted by a demon." Hanuman immediately realizes who stands before him. In that instant, he recognizes his Master, his Lord Rama. He stands still, overwhelmed with joy, his hair standing on end as a wave of emotions overpowers him. Unable to contain his bliss, Hanuman clasps the Lord's feet and exclaims, "O Lord! My question to you was born from my ignorance, as I was swayed by the spell of your maya (illusory power) and failed to recognize you. But you, the omniscient Lord — how could you ask me who I am as if you did not recognize me?" Tears stream down Hanuman's cheeks as he offers himself in devotion. The innocence, sincerity, and dedication Hanuman had towards Lord Rama, mentioned above, is succinctly highlighted by Tulasidas in the verses from Kishkinda Kand (canto), Chapters 1 and 2. These verses aren't just inspiring but palpably moving.

Some versions of the *Ramayana* say that Lord Hanuman and Rama met much earlier. According to some *Puranas*, Lord Shiva had once expressed his desire to become Lord Vishnu's devotee and worship him, having heard so much about Lord Vishnu's incarnations and the blissful experience of his devotees. Lord Vishnu also expressed his desire to worship Lord Shiva as a Shiva linga.

Thus, Lord Shiva incarnated as Lord Hanuman, known as an amsa (part) of Shiva. This incarnation is not considered a complete (poornavatara) but rather a partial incarnation (amsavatara). Lord Vishnu incarnated as Lord Rama. Based on their plan, Lord Shiva, as Hanuman, was supposed to meet Lord Vishnu, as Rama, much later

— after Lord Rama grew up, went into exile, and spent ten years in North and Central India before coming to South India.

But in some versions of this telling, Hanuman, being a monkey, couldn't wait and wanted to meet Lord Rama earlier. These versions suggest that Lord Shiva disguised himself as a sage or beggar to meet Lord Rama but couldn't due to the guards around the prince. Finally, as a little monkey, Hanuman accompanied a madari (monkey trainer) who entertained the royal princes, including Lord Rama. This version suggests that Hanuman and Rama met when they were both cute little children, well before their destined meeting in the South during Rama's search for Sita.

When they reached the southern tip, Rameshwaram, Lord Rama desired to worship Lord Shiva before crossing over to Lanka for war with Ravana. Lord Rama requested Hanuman to fly to the north and bring a Shiva linga made out of the rock of a particular mountain. However, Hanuman took a long time, and Lord Rama made a shiva lingam with sand with his own hands, and worshipped it. When Hanuman returned and was surprised to see that Lord Rama had already performed the puja on a Shiva linga, Lord Rama gave him a boon that both the Shiva lingas would be worshipped for ages to come. Even today, two Shiva lingas are worshiped at the famous Rameshwaram Temple. The one built by Rama is called the Rama Lingam, and the one brought by Hanuman is called Vishwa Lingam.

This story highlights the deep connection and mutual respect between Shiva and Vishnu, as both deities worshiped each other.

With all these back stories, the bond between Rama and Hanuman is profound and supremely inspiring. Amma reminds us that the bond with the guru plays a pivotal role on the spiritual path. I feel that amid my strengths and weaknesses, moments of praise and moments of blame, moments of pure happiness and what felt to me like extreme crises, throughout every up and down, what has grounded and guided me is my bond with Amma. It has always cushioned what could otherwise have been hard falls.

The spiritual perspective of Ramayana

Let us revisit the above sequence of the *Ramayana* with a focus on the negativities we should be mindful of and avoid, as well as the virtues we should strive to cultivate.

Following Lord Rama's journey from the north of India down to Lanka to rescue Mother Sita, we went over the major episodes of *Ramayana*. We considered the various characters who played pivotal roles in shaping the epic. We saw the negative influence of bad company, such as Mother Kaikeyi's association with her maid Manthara, which led to Kaikeyi's selfishness and hasty actions. Despite preordained reasons for these events, they resulted in mistakes, misdeeds, and consequent sorrow. Lord Rama was sent into exile, creating sorrow, and Kaikeyi soon regretted her actions.

We also talked about Sita's obsession with the golden deer, which led to her abduction by Ravana in disguise and Sita inadvertently crossing over the line of safety. This event highlighted the consequences of acting on obsession and desire, crossing limits, and falling prey to deceit. Ravana's rude and disrespectful treatment of Hanuman in Lanka further exemplified negative qualities.

On the positive side, we discussed how Lord Rama, despite being sent into exile, was forgiving and dutiful. Bharata, upon discovering the injustice, showed deep love and respect for his brother. The brothers' adherence to dharma, their sense of duty, and selflessness were inspiring. Lakshmana and Lord Rama emphasized the importance of discipline and limits, while Hanuman demonstrated clarity, humility, maturity, self-confidence, and positive influence on Vibhishana.

The episodes of *Ramayana* illustrate that life is a mixture of good and bad qualities, both externally in the world and internally within our minds. This duality maintains the equilibrium of nature. When negativity prevails, like in Ayodhya's loss of Lord Rama, the Supreme's grace and guidance are lost. Mother Sita's desire-driven actions led to her separation from Rama, symbolizing the separation of the individual soul (jivatma) from the Supreme Soul (Paramatma).

However, Hanuman, representing devotion and dedication, played a crucial role in reuniting Sita and Rama. This symbolizes how devotion can elevate us spiritually, helping us realize the oneness of the individual soul with the Supreme Soul. With the negativities in us gaining the upper hand, we are lured into the ephemeral nature of the world, forgetting our true Self. The individual soul is distanced from the Supreme Soul. The story of the *Ramayana* conveys the message that life comprises dual experiences. Still, with devotion, we can achieve the ultimate state of non-duality (Advaita), realizing the oneness of jivatma and Paramatma.

The Hanuman Chalisa
A verse-by-verse commentary

Initial Doha (prelude verse)

Guru - the first and foremost

śrī guru charaṇa sarōja raja	श्रीगुरु चरन सरोज रज
nijamana mukura sudhāri ǀ	निजमनु मुकुरु सुधारि।
baraṇau raghuvara bimala jaśu	बरनउँ रघुबर बिमल जसु
jō dāyaku phalachāri ǁ	जो दायकु फल चारि।

śrī guru - the most revered guru, the embodiment of auspiciousness; charaṇa - holy feet; sarōja - lotus; raja - dust; nija - one's own; mana - mind; mukura - mirror; sudhāri - cleanse; baranau - describe; raghuvara - Lord Rama, belonging to the Raghu dynasty; bimala - untainted, pure; jasu - glory; jō - who; dāyaka - giver; phala - fruits (of actions); chāri - four;

Cleansing the mirror of my mind with the dust from the Lotus-feet of the guru, I describe the unblemished glory of Lord Rama, which bestows four fruits of Righteousness (Dharma), Wealth (Artha), Pleasure (Kama), and Liberation (Moksha).

buddhihīna tanu jānikai	ǁ बुद्धिहीन तनु जानिके,
sumirau pavana kumāra ǀ	सुमिरौं पवन-कुमार।
bala buddhi vidyā dēhu mōhi	बल बुद्धि बिद्या देहु मोहिं,
harahu kalēśa bikāra	हरहु कलेस बिकार ǁ

buddhi hīna - ignorance, lack of intelligence; tanu - body; jānikai - having known; sumirau - remember (in praise); pavana kumar - son of the Wind God (Vayu/Pavana); bala -

strength; buddhi - intelligence/discernment; vidyā - wisdom/
knowledge; dēhu - provide; mōhi - me; harahu - annihilate;
kalēśa - tendencies/emotions; bikār - imperfections;

Humbled, realizing that this body lacks wisdom, I pray to
Lord Hanuman to bless me with strength, intelligence and
knowledge and cure my tendencies and internal conflicts.

Goswami Tulasidas begins the *Hanuman Chalisa* with salutations to
the guru. Any important deed we venture into should start with seeking
the blessings of the spiritual master. The spiritual master plays a vital
role in our spiritual journey. Whether we follow the path of devotion
or knowledge, the common goal is to let go of the ego and understand
our true Self. In the path of devotion, we try to surrender our ego to
the guru or the beloved deity. However, surrendering the ego is never
an easy task. It becomes possible only when we have tremendous
confidence in someone who has already reached the state of perfection,
such as a Sadguru.

The presence of a guru is indispensable in the path of devotion, as the
guru helps us let go of our ego. Imagine us trying to fight against our
ego without Amma in the picture. It would be much harder to let go of
our ego. For instance, consider two people in a satsang who are on bad
terms and cannot even face each other. However, we see such people
in Amma's presence, standing beside each other to do crowd control
or food seva, as best friends. The presence of the guru makes letting
go of the ego much easier.

Tulasidas highlights the importance of the guru in the very first line of
the *Hanuman Chalisa*: sri guru, the auspicious guru. He then mentions
charana saroj, which translates to the guru's lotus feet. The lotus flower
signifies complete blossoming, opening up to creation, and achieving
a state of complete acceptance and understanding — the state of
Oneness, where everyone is but me, and I am but everyone.

The lotus flower also represents blossoming amidst filth. Even in a filthy pond full of algae and other impurities, a lotus blossoms beautifully. When the lotus flower blooms, all the filth around it fades into the background. Our focus shifts to the beauty of the lotus flower. Similarly, the guru helps us highlight and express the positive aspects of our life, bringing beauty and meaning to life despite its negativities and shortcomings. This is why we refer to the feet of the guru as "lotus feet," symbolizing the qualities of the lotus flower. The guru brings meaning to life despite our challenges.

Saroj raj translates to "dust on the lotus feet." The element of dust is chosen carefully here; possibly the most insignificant thing associated with the guru's feet is the dust that may have settled on them. Even that is enough to cleanse the mirror of the mind. It highlights the exalted state of the guru. Even the mere dust on the guru's feet is so sacred and significant. This emphasizes the importance and significance of a true Sadguru, a realized Master.

Here also, the mind is equated to a mirror, reflecting our true Self. Although in sanatana dharma and other Eastern traditions, we often think of the mind negatively, it is not inherently negative. How we use the mind is crucial. One of the many positive purposes it serves is as a mirror, or put another way, as our inner conscience. The mind can reflect our true potential, but we often fail to see or realize that potential.

During Krishna Jayanti celebrations at Amritapuri, the atmosphere transforms into a joyous celebration reminiscent of Vrindavan. In the afternoon, Amma comes out to play the game of Uriyadi with the children. In this game, a pot is suspended on a rope through a pulley, and children try to break the pot with a stick. Children line up, taking turns running towards the suspended pot and swinging towards it with their stick, as a person on the other end of the rope pulls the pot just out reach, causing the children to leap into the air to strike it. The pot may sustain many blows before a lucky winner finally breaks it, releasing a shower of candy and other treats. The joy and energy in the scene are palpable, and Amma laughs and enjoys the moment, bringing happiness to all.

One particular year, as the game began with the tiny tots, I specifically remember three children. Each child was given a stick. One child started hitting everyone with the stick, creating fear among the children and anger among the onlookers. Another child kept throwing the stick up in the air, trying to break the pot, causing it to drop on people's heads, which was not well-received. A third child, very small and dressed like a Gopa (cowherd of Vrindavan), used the stick as a flute and struck various Krishna poses. This child created a feeling of attraction and charm amongst everyone.

This scene reminded me that the mind is similar to those sticks. How we use the mind is very important. The *Amrita Bindu Upanishad* states:

Manah ēva kāraṇam manuṣhyāṇām bandha mōkṣhayōh

The mind verily is the cause of both bondage and liberation for human beings.

Depending on how we use the same mind, it can lead to attachment or detachment. It's not the mind's fault but how we perceive and use it. The layer of filth (dust), which is our ego and selfish attitudes, prevents the mind from reflecting our true self. This layer shrouds the mirror and stops it from reflecting our true self. Thus, we are not able to understand our true selves.

It's like the fairy tale of Snow White. The Evil Queen always wanted to be the most beautiful person in the world. She had a magical mirror that would speak to her. She would stand in front of the mirror and ask, "Mirror, mirror on the wall, who is the fairest of them all?" The mirror would reply, "You are the most beautiful." Hearing this, she was pleased and walked away. She would repeat the same process every day. As Snow White, her stepdaughter, grew into a beautiful woman, one day, the mirror said, "Snow White is the fairest of them all." The Queen was utterly taken aback and upset. Filled with rage, she sent her confidant to execute Snow White in the forest. However, he loved Snow White, finding her virtuous, and couldn't bring himself to kill her. He left her in the forest, telling her not to return to the palace. Snow White then settled with the Seven Dwarfs. Assuming Snow White was dead, the Queen asked the mirror again, "Mirror, mirror on the wall, who is the fairest of them all?" The mirror replied, "Snow White." Realizing Snow White was still alive, the Queen disguised herself and tried to poison and kill her but ended up getting killed in the process.

Here, the mirror always gave the correct answer, but the Queen's ego refused to accept it. Similarly, we have this shroud of ego. When our conscience gives us the right decision, our ego can turn a "no" into a "yes" and a "yes" into a "no." Our selfish thoughts refuse to understand what our mind and conscience tell us.

The guidance from a realized master, the Sadguru, is critical when we deal with our ego. Taking refuge at the guru's feet signifies the readiness in us to bow down, to reach down to the feet, letting go of our ego. The Sadguru's presence and example teach us how to get rid of the ego, which is the biggest blemish on the mirror of our mind. Walking the talk, a true Sadguru will live every moment, inspiring us with the virtues we need to develop. Sometimes, when we hold on to our ego dearly, the guru will have to force us to let go of it, like a mother has to push her child to let go of the toy and do something more meaningful. Thus, Tulasidas begins with "sri guru charan saroj raj," emphasizing that the first step is to cleanse our mind with the grace of the guru.

Tulasidas then praises Lord Rama in the verse, describing his glory, his jasu. Tulasidas says, "I call out to the glory of Lord Rama, which is unblemished and untainted." Before calling out to the disciple Hanuman, Tulasidas first invokes Lord Rama, the master, again highlighting the importance of the guru.

He then says, "When I call out to Lord Rama, he bestows upon me the phala chari," or the four fruits, which are the four aims of life: dharma (our responsibilities and righteousness), artha (wealth), kama (desires), and moksha (liberation).

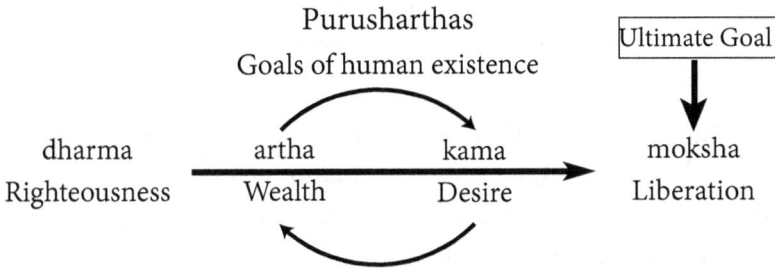

Purusharthas

Goals of human existence

Ultimate Goal

| dharma | artha | kama | moksha |
| Righteousness | Wealth | Desire | Liberation |

Sanatana Dharma does not ask us to avoid accumulating wealth or to have no desires, as that is not practical. We naturally have tendencies to desire and accumulate wealth. As we accrue wealth, we desire more wealth. It's essential to avoid being stuck in the vicious cycle of desire. Desire leads to the accumulation of wealth, which in turn fuels even more significant desires. Instead, we should use dharma as a foundation and aim for moksha. The primary purpose of life is to break out of this unending cycle. We need to marry dharma and artha. That is to say, we should gain wealth through righteous means (dharma) and use it to protect and uphold dharma. Similarly, we should channel our desires in a way that ultimately leads us towards liberation. Initially, we may desire mundane things, but over time, our desires should evolve towards higher pursuits, culminating in the desire for liberation.

Letting go of desire is difficult, but we can start by channeling desires in the right direction. Like the mind, which can lead to either liberation or bondage, desires, when properly directed, can aid in our spiritual growth. Many of our volunteers in the ashram or Amma programs utilize their tendencies for the greater good. For example, someone who loves real estate and civil engineering may be assigned a seva by Amma related to the construction of houses after disasters or the building of a college, school, or hospital. Their interest in construction and real estate is meaningfully channeled selflessly here. While their desires remain the same, their attitude and purpose have transformed, leading to growth. Tulasidas is seeking Lord Rama's grace so that rather than our natural tendency to incline towards desire (kama) for wealth (artha) alone, we seek all four fruits of dharma (righteousness), artha (wealth), kama (desire) and moksha (liberation), thus making life meaningful and complete.

After the guru and Lord Rama, Tulasidas invokes Lord Hanuman, the deity in focus in the *Hanuman Chalisa*. Before we worship Lord Hanuman, we remind ourselves of an important fact. The verse speaks about the body and intellect. "Buddhi" means intellect or wisdom, and "heen" implies lacking it. So "buddhi hina" means lacking intellect or wisdom. "Tanu" refers to the body. As we invoke the son of the wind god, Lord Hanuman, we remind ourselves of our limited existence.

Why do we say the body is "buddhi-hina"? We often take great pride in our physical selves, closely identifying with the body. True worship involves letting go of this unnecessary identification. While we shouldn't ignore the body — and should care for it as the abode of the Divine within us — we also shouldn't be bound by it. We must remember that the body is inert; it is the soul (atma) that brings life to it. In Sanskrit, a dead body is called shava (lifeless), while shiva refers to the Supreme Being. The soul in every individual (jiva-atma) is considered an infinitesimal part of shiva, the Supreme Soul. Thus, the body without shiva is merely shava. By "buddhi-hina," we are simply reminding ourselves of the limitations we embrace when we identify solely with the body and what it can do.

Awareness that the body is impermanent is the first and last step on the path of devotion. We begin by recognizing this and end by realizing it. Recognizing and realizing are two different things. It's the Self that makes the body unique and capable. So, we first recognize the self within us.

Once we recognize the self within, we remember Lord Hanuman and pray to him, calling out for his blessings. We ask for strength, wisdom, and knowledge and seek his help in overcoming tendencies that create internal conflicts and confusion.

How do we worship Lord Hanuman?

The second part of the verse says: "sumirau pavan kumar" - worship or praise Lord Hanuman, the son of Wind God. Hanuman himself is an exemplary personification of devotion. How do I worship such a being? His devotion to Lord Rama is unparalleled. His devotion to Rama was pure and selfless.

There is a verse in Sanskrit:

akṛtvā parasantāpam agatvā khalanamratām ।
anutsṛjya satāṃ vartma yat svalpamapi tadbahu ॥

Not taking actions that bring sorrow or torment to others, not becoming submissive to negativity, and not abandoning the right path — even a tiny amount of these efforts can go a long way.

Even if we put a small effort into these three things, it is significant enough. Lord Hanuman embodied this, living his devotion towards Lord Rama. His dedication is celebrated today because he lived it. Every moment of his life became an act of worship to Lord Rama. Every thought and every word he spoke was meaningful and aligned with these principles.

A deity doesn't need worship; they have reached a state where they don't require it. A realized master like Amma doesn't need our worship either. It makes no difference to them. We worship a realized master to purify our thoughts, reflect on what they inspire us with, and try to imbibe that. True worship is making our lives meaningful and aligned with these higher principles. The phrase "Sumirau Pavana Kumar" emphasizes this. How do we worship Hanuman? We should ensure that our actions do not hurt others, that we not allow ourselves to be subjugated by negativities, and that we always remain on the right path. Even a little effort in this direction is significant and will take us a long way. This is perhaps why Amma says, "When you take one step towards me, I'll take a hundred steps towards you." The sincerity of our effort is what matters most.

For me, Lord Hanuman has always been an inspiration. Chanting the *Hanuman Chalisa* has given me mental strength, especially in times of fear. I don't have a favorite deity, but Lord Hanuman has been a guiding example of being a good disciple. When I strive to be a good disciple, I become beneficial to others and, in turn, to myself. Worshiping Lord Hanuman means embodying his qualities in our actions. That is the best way we can worship him.

We pray for Bala (strength), Buddhi (wisdom), and Vidya (knowledge). Give me strength, wisdom, and knowledge to face any situation in life. As Amma says, never try to escape a situation; that's never a solution. Instead, face it the way it should be faced. To do so, we need strength — primarily mental strength. Even if we fail in our efforts or are overcome by a challenge, the effort to face it with the right attitude will never have been wasted and will certainly help us to bear the situation with equanimity.

Bhagavad Gita, chapter 2, verse 13 states:

mātrā-sparśhās tu kaunteya śhītoṣhṇa-sukha-duḥkha-dāḥ
āgamāpāyino 'nityās tans-titikṣhasva bhārata

O son of Kunti, the contact between the senses and the sense objects gives rise to ephemeral perception of happiness and distress. These are impermanent and just come and go, like the winter and summer seasons. O descendent of Bharata! One must learn to forbear and face them without being disturbed.

Lord Krishna tells Arjuna about the nature of life. He says that through our senses' contact with sense objects (seeing, smelling, hearing, touching, tasting), we have experiences, dual in nature; like shita (cold) and ushna (hot); sukha (pleasant) and dukha (unpleasant). But we need to understand that they are agamapayina (they come and go) and anitya (impermanent). Any experience, whether good or bad, is impermanent. By understanding their impermanence, we can forbear and face our circumstances with the right attitude. Lord Krishna tells Arjuna to face every situation with the understanding that it is temporary.

When we encounter sorrow, we often prefer to avoid it. However, if we understand that even sorrow is temporary, we gain the strength to face it. This is the strength we pray for — the strength to face challenges with the right attitude.

But strength alone isn't enough. Strength without wisdom can sometimes cause trouble. Strength should be complemented by wisdom. True wisdom involves understanding oneself, one's strengths — including knowing where, when, how, and with whom to use them — and one's shortcomings.

William Shakespeare said, "The fool doth think he is wise, but the wise man knows himself to be a fool." If we deceive ourselves by only acknowledging our strengths and ignoring our weaknesses, we may encounter problems. A person who believes they are only wise can be revealed as the biggest fool in challenging situations.

Socrates, the great Greek philosopher, said, "The only true wisdom is in knowing you know nothing." Aristotle, another great Greek philosopher, said, "Knowing yourself is the beginning of all wisdom." We need to know our true Self. The body is inert on its own, and recognizing our true self is where devotion begins. It ends with realizing it. The whole process is the path of bhakti (devotion).

When Lord Hanuman was asked by Lord Rama to go to Lanka as his messenger to deliver a message to Mother Sita, informing her that they were making preparations to rescue her, he was faced with the challenge of crossing the Indian Ocean. Of course in those times, there were no Air India or Sri Lankan Air, so Lord Hanuman had to figure out how to cross the ocean to reach the island kingdom of Lanka. He initially thought he couldn't do it and questioned his ability. It was Jambavan, the wise king of the bears in *Ramayana*, who reminded Hanuman of his abilities and the many boons he had acquired when he was young. Hanuman had received these boons from the Devas, the various demigods, but being a young and immature monkey, he was cursed to forget his abilities until he matured and developed wisdom. At this crucial moment, Hanuman was reminded of his strengths and skills. With this newfound awareness, crossing the small strip of the Indian Ocean between India and Lanka was a trivial task for him. This part of the *Ramayana* illustrates the importance of wisdom in recognizing our true potential. Throughout Hanuman's life we see examples of how maturity and wisdom help us realize both our strengths and shortcomings, enabling us to translate this understanding into meaningful action.

We gain wisdom through knowledge — knowledge from the scriptures, the teachings of our guru, and their guidance. A guru guides with examples rather than mere words. By taking inspiration from this knowledge and transforming it into wisdom, we develop a character that is mature and insightful. With this wisdom, we recognize our strengths and shortcomings, allowing us to act wisely.

I remember a satsang from Amritapuri given by a devotee from Singapore who had been living in Amritapuri throughout the pandemic. It was a very candid satsang where he talked about how he was once a gangster in Singapore, involved in gang fights and gangster activities. He narrated a few incidents where he almost got killed. In one such incident, he recalled how he was almost killed by one of the opposing gang members and at the last moment he told him I am sparing you because of the t-shirt you are wearing. He was wearing an Amma t-shirt, and the attacker felt something that made him decide not to hurt him. The devotee had had mental and physical strength to do whatever he wanted in life, but as he pointed out in his satsang, he lacked wisdom. His strength led him in the wrong direction. When he met Amma, it took some time for him to grasp her magnanimity. However, once wisdom began to dawn within him, his attitude towards his abilities completely changed. He is no longer a gangster; he now spends most of the year in Amritapuri. This transformation illustrates that just having strength is not good enough. Strength needs to be supplemented with wisdom, which we grasp through vidya (knowledge) from the scriptures and the life of our guru. Now, his life is such that he uses all his strength to do seva, even tasks that require a lot of physical strength. By doing this, he benefits society, and, ultimately, himself. This is the beauty of selfless acts — they benefit not only others but also our own selves.

That's the prayer Tulasidas is offering to Lord Hanuman in the initial doha (prelude verse) — bestow upon me the mental strength to face situations grounded in true wisdom that we gain through knowledge from scriptures and the guru's teachings and examples.

Insights on the Path of Bhakti from the prelude verse:

- The guru is an indispensable part of our spiritual pursuit, and the guru's grace is critical. Even the insignificant dust on the guru's feet is significant for the disciple.
- The mind is like a mirror reflecting our true self if cleansed and conditioned correctly.
- Acknowledge and understand the limitations of our physical existence; seek the strength, intellect, and knowledge to grow.

Verse 1

Abode of wisdom and qualities
Illuminator of the three worlds

jaya hanumāna jñāna guṇa sāgara । जय हनुमान ज्ञान गुन सागर।

jaya kapīśa tihu lōka ujāgara ॥ 1 ॥ जय कपीस तिहुं लोक उजागर॥

jaya - victory (to); hanumāna - Lord Hanuman; jñāna
- wisdom/knowledge; guṇa - virtues; sāgara - ocean;
jaya - victory (to); kapīśa - lord of the monkeys; tihu
- three; lōka - world(s); ujāgara - illuminator;

Victory to Hanuman, who is the ocean of Wisdom and Virtues.
Victory to the king of Monkeys, who illuminates the three worlds.

Victory to Hanuman

We begin with Jai Hanuman — Victory to Hanuman. Why call out victory to the Divine? Does Hanuman need victory? Hanuman is already in that ultimate state of victory over the mind and the senses. When we say "Victory," it's about awakening the Amma in me, the Hanuman in me. It is an external and explicit trigger to awaken the Divine in us. When we take an X-ray image of our body, it is highly likely that we won't find Hanuman in us. Then why refer to the Hanuman in me? The "Hanuman in me" refers to the virtues and qualities that he represents. Amma says we also have those qualities, but we haven't kindled or awakened them yet. We need to awaken those qualities.

So when we say "Jai," we are trying to awaken these qualities within us, or at least remind ourselves that we need to awaken these qualities. And, most importantly, the best way to call out for victory to Lord Hanuman is to live up to his example — emulating his qualities, virtues, and wisdom — all that Lord Hanuman stands for. That is the true victory of Hanuman.

The Ocean of Wisdom and Virtues

Jai Hanuman, Gyan Gun Sagar — Victory to Hanuman, the ocean of wisdom and virtues. Hanuman, as we know, is the very embodiment of virtues. As discussed in the previous chapter, during one of the dinner stops on a US tour, Amma highlighted how Hanuman embodied complete innocence blended with wisdom. The innocence we see in children is often out of ignorance. But Hanuman's innocence was out of egolessness. Amma said that this combination made his devotion all the more inspiring and meaningful.

Lord Hanuman had a great sense of wisdom. As a child, he had a desire to learn and acquire ultimate knowledge from the best preceptor possible. He was directed to Surya Deva, the Sun God. Learning from Surya Deva was like getting into an Ivy League school. He wouldn't accept a disciple so easily. When Hanuman approached him, Surya Deva initially declined, explaining that he was too occupied with his duty of sustaining life on Earth. Constantly moving across the the world, shedding light on different regions, he claimed he had no time or space for Hanuman.

Hanuman's response was quick and sharp. One simple response addressed both the issues of time and space. Hanuman said, "All I need is refuge at your holy feet. I would just be a speck in the expanse of your compassion and wisdom. Why should I be bothered about space then? And are you really traveling around the world? You are rather static, established as the source of divine light. The world revolves around you, seeking your light. So, you have enough time to enlighten me." Hanuman's words were very deep. Why bother about space when we have the Divine or the guru's holy feet to take refuge in? And to take refuge at the holy feet, we need to think beyond the confines of our ego. Though it seems the sun revolves around us on Earth, the fact remains that we revolve around the mighty sun. Our ego always misleads us into thinking that we are the center of the world. Surya Deva was so impressed by Hanuman's clarity in his thoughts and words that he immediately accepted him as his student.

As we discussed earlier, Lord Rama's first meeting with Hanuman, Lord Rama immediately recognized that Hanuman was not just a simple alms-seeker. Similarly, when Hanuman saw Lord Rama, he realized he was not an ordinary warrior. They both felt a deep connection. When Hanuman asked why they were there, Lord Rama commented to Lakshmana, "This person's words are so full of clarity, and so are his actions." Just as Surya Deva had recognized Hanuman's clarity, Lord Rama did the same.

Hanuman's clarity in words and actions was evident. Words are our primary mode of communication. They reflect our wisdom, maturity, and level of awareness. What we speak, how we speak, to whom we speak, where we speak, and when we speak are all important. Properly understanding and accounting for these factors make the experience pleasant, and failing to do so makes the experience unpleasant. Hanuman was a perfect example of maturity and awareness.

I remember an incident a few years ago wherein two very dedicated satsang members got into an argument when they had some difference of opinion during a meeting. They were arguing about how a particular issue was to be handled. And one told the other, "Don't act like a child. Act a little more mature." This comment created a lasting negative impact on the second person. The person carries the hurt feelings in his heart even today. It may have seemed to be just a simple comment telling someone not to act childish, yet those few words have created a long-lasting impact. This shows the power of our words, and the importance of choosing our words carefully.

Assessing our performance in different situations is a good factor for gauging our spiritual growth. We need to ask ourselves, "Was I able to speak and act maturely? Was I able to express myself with wise and mature words and actions? Was my conduct meaningful?" Whether others involved in the situation were right or wrong, the most critical question we need to address is whether we acted maturely.

There is a text called Manusmriti, where the great emperor Manu put forth many do's & don'ts for leading a meaningful life. One of the verses from the text goes as:

satyaṃ brūyāt priyaṃ brūyānna brūyāt satyamapriyam |
priyaṃ ca nānṛtaṃ brūyādeṣa dharmaḥ sanātanaḥ ||

Speak the truth; speak sweet words; do not speak harsh truth
that may hurt someone. Also, do not speak untruth that may
be pleasing and sweet. This is eternal dharma (law).

Perhaps when the satsang member said, "You are childish," it might or might not have been true. That is secondary. What is important is that it didn't fit into this equation as specified in the verse. You needn't speak the truth if it is unpleasant; you can always present it in a different way. Strive to steer clear of statements that may be factual but could hurt someone, or, while pleasing, are not true. Put simply, avoid unnecessary praise or criticism. This is where wisdom plays a role.

What we speak is important, and Lord Hanuman exemplified this. His words immediately gave Lord Rama the impression that he was not an ordinary being but one endowed with true wisdom. I know certain people personally who possess many great qualities, but many people are uncomfortable around them. The primary cause is their speech. What they speak, how they speak, where they speak, when they speak, and to whom they speak are not guided by wisdom. Though they may have a lot of goodness in them, others are not able to see or harness that goodness because they don't exercise wisdom in their primary mode of communication: speaking.

Amma always says that the distance between the brain and the mouth, or the time between thoughts and speech, should include a filter of wisdom. When words pass through this filter, they become meaningful and helpful. Wisdom is understanding our strengths and weaknesses as well as those to whom we are speaking, and deciding what to say, when to say it, to whom to say it, how to say it, and in what context.

For example, a boxer is wise when he uses all his strength and boxing abilities inside a boxing ring because it satisfies all the criteria of what, when, where, how, and to whom. However, if the same boxer tries to use his abilities in a courtroom with a judge, it won't help him or anyone else, and he might end up in jail. Or, if he is in the wild facing a hungry lion and tries to box with it, he'll likely get killed. In such a situation, he must recognize his own weaknesses and find ways to protect himself.

This reminds me of a story about two friends in the wild who encounter a hungry cheetah. Realizing the cheetah is going to attack, one friend says he is going to run. The second friend asks if he thinks he can outrun the cheetah. The first friend replies, "I don't know if I can outrun the cheetah, but I know I can outrun you, so I'm going to be safe." He analyzed the strengths and the weaknesses of the cheetah, his friend, and himself and decided on his course of action.

Lord of the Monkeys

Jai kapis! Victory to the Lord of Monkeys! "Kapi" in Sanskrit translates to "monkey". The suffix "Isha" is often used in Sanskrit to denote a lord or master, as seen in terms like "Isha," "Ganesha," "Sarvesha," "Mahesha," and "Paramesha." The term "Kapis" is a regional variation influenced by the Avadhi language, where "Isha" becomes "is." Thus, "Kapis" refers to the lord or leader of the monkeys — Hanuman.

Although Hanuman was not the literal king of the monkeys, he was referred to as "Kapis" in part because he was a king-maker. Hanuman's influence and qualities were such that having him on one's side assured success. In a spiritual sense, this means that embodying the qualities that Hanuman represents ensures that one will face success in life. Even in episodes of failure, these qualities can transform setbacks into challenges or stepping stones to future success.

Hanuman was always a king-maker in this way. When he supported Sugriva, Sugriva eventually became the king. When he was on Vibhishana's side, Vibhishana became the king of Lanka. Rama had Hanuman on his side when he finally ascended to the throne of Ayodhya. While Rama did not need Hanuman in a literal sense, the message is clear: we need to embody the qualities Hanuman represents to succeed in life.

Hanuman is also called the king of the monkeys because he ruled not over a kingdom like Sugriva or Vali, but over people's hearts, which is a much more difficult feat. Mahatmas, or great souls, like Amma are revered because they dwell in and rule our hearts, which requires displacing the ego — a challenging task. To enter someone's heart, especially by overcoming their ego, is far more complicated than ascending a throne and ruling a kingdom. This is why Hanuman is referred to as "Kapis," the lord of the monkeys or the best among them.

So, when we say "Jai Kapis," we are proclaiming victory to Hanuman and the qualities he embodies, and invoking the Divine to rule over our own heart.

Illuminator of the Three Worlds

Sri Lalita Sahasranama has names that refer to the three worlds: 626. Tripura (one who predates the three worlds), 787. Tripureshi (the goddess of the three worlds), 875. Tripura Malini (one garlanded with the three worlds), 976. Tripurambika (the mother of the three worlds). The term "Tri" translates to the number 3, and "pura" signifies place (world).

In Sanatana Dharma, the number three holds great significance. We chant "Om" three times, and similarly, "Shanti" is chanted three times, each time corresponding to one of the three worlds. These three worlds can be understood in various ways:

- Goals or Desires of Life: dharma (righteousness), artha (wealth), and kama (desire)
- Physical Worlds: The Earth, the immediate outer space (atmosphere), and the outer space beyond
- Time: the past, present, and future
- Day: morning, afternoon, and night
- Gunas (Qualities): sattva (purity, wisdom), rajas (activity, passion), and tamas (inertia, darkness)
- Bodies: sthula sharira (gross body), sukshma sharira (subtle body), and karana sharira (causal body)
- States of Existence: jagrat (wakefulness), swapna (dream), and sushupti (deep sleep)
- Creation: Creation, sustenance, and dissolution
- Lokas (Worlds): bhuloka (the earthly realm), swargaloka (heaven), and patala (netherworld)

- Factors: atmika (pertaining to the individual), bhautika (pertaining to the people and things around, in the physical realm), daivika (factors beyond)

These various aspects of three — whether they refer to time, states of existence, or the different bodies — point to the importance of balance and integration in Sanatana Dharma.

In this first verse, Hanuman is called "ujagar," one who illuminates or enlightens all three worlds. This means that Hanuman brings clarity and light to all these realms of existence through his wisdom and control over his mind and senses. When people master their mind and senses, they can bring balance and understanding to all three states of existence.

A folklore tale about cute little Hanuman is relevant here. As an innocent child, Hanuman was full of energy and joy. He wanted everyone around him to be joyful too. Whenever he saw Mother Anjana worried or sad, he would innocently ask why she was upset and try to cheer her up. Anjana would tell him, "Such is life. At times, it gives you reasons to be worried and sad." But Hanuman didn't want his mother to feel that way. He asked her what would make her happy. She replied, "The smile on my baby's face always brings me joy, even in the toughest of times." Hanuman sweetly responded, "Then I will always keep a smile on my face to bring joy to my mother. We can play joyfully when I'm awake, and still play in my dreams when I'm asleep." From that moment on, to keep Mother Anjana happy, Hanuman smiled when awake, in his dreams, and even in deep sleep.

Though a simple story, Hanuman's innocent decision to wear a smile illuminates the three worlds in many ways. He smiled in all three states of existence — waking, dreaming, and deep sleep. His smile brought joy across time — past, present, and future — and throughout the day — morning, afternoon, and night. It brought light and joy to all aspects of life: to himself, to those around him, especially to his beloved mother, Anjana and beyond. He truly was "tihu lok ujagar" — the illuminator of the three worlds. Drawing inspiration from Hanuman, let us remember that even the smallest of our acts can bring great joy and light. Let us seize every opportunity to bring joy to both ourselves and those around us.

Insights on the Path of Bhakti from verse 1:

- Remain open to learning from all sources, whether seemingly significant or insignificant.
- Our conduct should be such that we illuminate all three worlds with our virtues.

Verses 2 and 3

Be a Messenger
Unparalleled strength

rāmadūta atulita baladhāmā | रामदूत अतुलित बल धामा।
añjani putra pavanasuta nāmā ‖ 2 ‖ अंजनि-पुत्र पवनसुत नामा ‖

rāmadūta - Lord Rama's messenger; atulita - incomparable;
bala - strength; dhāmā - abode; añjani putra - son of Anjana;
pavanasuta - son of the Wind God; nāmā - one who is named;

*You are the messenger of Rama (to Sita). You are the abode of
incomparable power. You are also known by the names of 'Anjani
Putra' (Son of Anjana) and 'Pavana suta' (son of wind god).*

mahāvīra vikrama bajaraṅgī | महावीर विक्रम बजरंगी।
kumati nivāra sumati kē saṅgī ‖ 3 ‖ कुमति निवार सुमति के संगी ‖

mahāvīra - supremely courageous; vikrama - a person of
valor and great deeds; bajaraṅgī - one who has a body as
strong as the diamond; kumati - ill-minded; nivāra - cleanse;
sumati - good-minded; ke - of; saṅgī - companion;

*O mighty and valorous one, whose body is as strong as vajra (the
precious stone/diamond). Please remove the negativities of my
mind, for you are the companion of those with pure heart.*

Messenger of Rama

Hanuman is known as Lord Rama's messenger. As mentioned earlier, after Jambavan, the wise king of the bears, reminded Hanuman of his power, he was able to easily leap across the Indian Ocean to reach Lanka.

According to the *Ramcharitmanas*, Hanuman searched for Mother Sita in Lanka. As he encountered various women, he would think, "No, this doesn't seem like Mother Sita — it doesn't feel quite right." Finally, he came across someone and heard "Ram, Ram." He followed the sound and finally saw Mother Sita, constantly chanting Rama's name. Hanuman was wonderstruck by the charm of Mother Sita. Hanuman, who always saw himself as an innocent son to Mother Sita, was deeply moved by her devotion.

Hanuman hid in the trees, watching over Sita. It was during this time that Ravana approached Sita. Ravana had tried to make Sita his wife, but she was so devoted to Rama that she wouldn't even enter the palace. Instead, she lived in the Ashoka Vana, the Ashoka Garden, leading a hermit-like life, waiting for Rama, confident that he would come to rescue her. Hanuman watched Sita from the trees, hiding behind the leaves, as Ravana came to see her. Hoping that Sita's suffering might cause her to change her mind and agree to marry him, Ravana had made these visits a daily ritual. However, Hanuman watched as Sita remained steadfast as she did every day and throughout her period of captivity. Sita told Ravana to leave, assuring him that her Lord, the master of the world, would soon come to rescue her.

Hanuman was overjoyed to hear the glory of Lord Rama from Sita's own lips. Ravana, once again rejected, returned to his palace, unable to convince Sita to waver from her commitment to Rama. As per the Ramcharitmanas, overcome with feeling, Hanuman accidentally dropped Lord Rama's ring, which he had brought with him as a token. The moment Sita saw the ring, she recognized it immediately. There was a mix of emotions — happiness because she was reminded of Rama; sadness, for the same reason; and worry, wondering how this precious ring, which had never parted from Lord Rama, had come to be here. She thought, "Either Lord Rama is here, or someone has taken it from him," but both possibilities seemed implausible.

As Sita looked around in wonder, Hanuman finally revealed himself, dropping down from the tree and retrieving the ring. Hanuman had to convince Sita and make her understand who he was. Once Hanuman revealed his true self and explained the sequence of events to Sita, she was convinced that Lord Rama's messenger was indeed there. Hanuman was like an innocent child in front of Mother Sita. After all the serious business is over, he reverted to his innocent nature, asking Mother Sita, "Now that I've conveyed the message, I'm very hungry. I want fruits to eat. I haven't eaten for so long, and I see beautiful fruits up there on the tree." Mother Sita, concerned, replies, "I'm not sure whether you should do that because if you start plucking those fruits, the guards around will find you. You have no idea how strong these demons are, and you may not have the strength to face them." At this point, Hanuman reveals his actual Virat Rupa — his all-powerful form, which is why the verse says, "One who is full of strength." Mother Sita realizes that he is not a mere monkey, but rather a divine being. She permits him to have the fruits.

Some interpretations of the *Ramcharitmanas* suggest that Hanuman initially came with the attitude of being a messenger of Lord Rama. However, upon witnessing Mother Sita's unwavering devotion to

Lord Rama, his attitude shifted. He decided, "I am no longer just a messenger of Lord Rama; I should be his servant." His ego dissolved altogether, and he took on the role of a humble servant without any sense of position or pride.

After seeking Mother Sita's permission, Hanuman starts shaking the tree violently, causing the fruits to fall. He creates a scene that was anything but discreet — quite the opposite of what one might expect from someone sneaking into a secret place. He uproots trees and makes a ruckus that attracts the attention of the soldiers, who eventually capture him. Was Hanuman so weak that he could be easily captured by the soldiers? Of course not. This was because his second responsibility as Lord Rama's messenger was to confront Ravana.

His first objective was complete: he came as Lord Rama's messenger to Sita, conveyed the message, and convinced her. Then, his next destination was Ravana. Hanuman thought, "I need to warn him that I'm just the trailer; the blockbuster is yet to be released. Wait for it — you're going to be taken to task." The best way to reach Ravana was to allow himself to be captured. And while the soldiers were no match for the mighty Hanuman, finally Indrajit, Ravana's son, captured him.

Hanuman was put in chains and taken to Ravana's court. Despite introducing himself as Lord Rama's messenger, Ravana insulted him. There's a saying, "Never shoot the messenger," which means that a messenger should always be respected, even if they are from the enemy camp.

We see an early version of this expression in the *Ramayana* itself, when Ravana's younger brother Vibhishana tries to politely advise him:

dūtān avadhyān samayeṣu rājan sarveṣu sarvatra vadanti santaḥ

The wise have declared that the emissaries should not be killed anywhere, at any time, by any means.

However, Ravana did not accord Hanuman the respect due to a messenger. He didn't even offer him a place to sit. To convey Lord Rama's message, Hanuman then coiled his tail, elongating it until it became much taller than Ravana's throne. He sat above Ravana, teaching him a lesson. Sitting much taller than Ravana, Hanuman warned him, "You better let go of Mother Sita in a dharmic way, or you'll have to face the wrath of Rama, who is on his way. He'll be here in no time."

Ravana dismissed Hanuman's warning and insulted him further. He ordered his soldiers to bind Hanuman in chains and set his tail on fire as punishment for his so-called "disrespect" of the king. Hanuman, unfazed, thought, "You think you're punishing me by setting my tail on fire? Just wait and see. You'll regret this."

Hanuman flew across the kingdom, setting fire to everything in his path with his burning tail. He created complete havoc, leaving the kingdom in ashes. None of the soldiers could match his strength or valor; he was unstoppable. After wreaking havoc, Hanuman returned to Lord Rama. In this way, Hanuman served as a messenger to not only Sita but also Ravana, hinting at what was in store for him.

Most importantly, Hanuman is Lord Rama's messenger to each of us. He has a message for us to learn, teaching us what a true disciple should be like. This is the most important spiritual aspect we need to take away from the notion of Hanuman as messenger. Inspired by Lord Hanuman, we should also strive to be the best messengers of Amma. Being a true messenger of Amma doesn't mean constantly singing Amma's praises;

rather, it means embodying Amma's teachings in every moment of our lives — in what we do, think, and say. That's when we truly become Amma's disciples.

I remember when I first came to the U.S., one of the instructions Amma gave me was to always try to be independent. It's not possible to be completely independent in a new country, but she advised me to try to be as independent as possible and to be as little a burden on others as I could.

I recall Amma's first North American tour after I had come to the U.S. During Amma's darshan, as I was standing behind Amma, she asked me, "How's everything? Tell me how you're finding it here." I used that time to boast about myself, saying things like, "I went to all these cities to do programs, so many people attended, and they were impressed with the quality of the program." I also mentioned that I was invited to give a guest lecture as part of an undergrad course on interfaith at the University of Maryland, where I talked about the traditions of Sanatana Dharma. I was trying to give her all these updates, but Amma stopped me and said, "It's okay. I just wanted to know how you were doing. I didn't want to know what you were doing." The message was clear: don't boast about yourself.

Later on that tour, I remember a family coming for Amma's darshan and telling her I had visited their home and cooked for them. That lit up Amma's face. They mentioned how delicious the food was and how I had made two or three dishes. Amma was so happy and immediately asked me what I had cooked, what the ingredients were, how spicy it was, and how much salt I added. She was asking all these mundane questions. She was not interested when I talked about all the programs I did, the satsangs I conducted, and the classes I taught at the University of Maryland. But here she was, extremely interested in the details of my cooking. She even gave me tips like, "When you add too much salt, add some lemon juice to negate the effect of the salt," and so on. The message was clear. Amma wasn't interested in me boasting about myself, but when it came to being of service to others, though seemingly insignificant, Amma took so much interest and sought all the details. We can be a good Amma messenger or ambassador if we can do at least a little bit of service compared to Amma's monumental effort for others.

This experience reinforced Amma's earlier instruction to me when I came to the U.S.: to try to serve others. That's the best way we can be Amma's messengers, and we can learn or grasp this message from Hanuman as Ramaduta. He is a messenger to us from Lord Rama, teaching us how a true disciple should be — someone who benefits others and is not at all preoccupied with their own abilities, achievements, and recognition.

This inspiration helps me in many ways. I try to minimize, as much as possible, the instances where people cook for me; I try to cook for myself. Still, there are so many people who show love by bringing food once in a while, which I gratefully accept as Amma's blessing. I also try to take public transit whenever possible. Sometimes in the U.S., it's just not feasible, but wherever it is, I take public transit and offer rides to others when I can. When someone comes to D.C., I try to offer them a ride to their place of stay or to the nearby transit station or bus stop. These are little things, but we can draw inspiration from Hanuman and see how much we can give to others. That's the best way we can be Amma's messengers — offer our service to others and be a model of the ideal way a child of Amma should act in the world.

Son of Anjana and Vayu (Wind God)

Hanuman is the son of Anjana (also referred to as Anjani) and Vayu, the Wind God. Anjana was Hanuman's biological mother. The story goes that there was once an apsara (celestial being) named Punjikasthala, who was deeply pious and devoted to the Divine. She often served Brihaspati, the guru of the devas, in the heavenly realms. One day, she was overcome with an unusual desire for an apsara — the longing to experience family life. She shared her thoughts with Brihaspati, who advised her to rise above such worldly desires. However, as time passed, she found it increasingly difficult to let go of this yearning and continued to pester Brihaspati about it. Eventually, exasperated, Brihaspati blurted out, "In that case, may you be born on earth to become a mother!"

This was an extraordinary fate for an apsara, as they were not meant for earthly births or married life. Brihaspati himself was puzzled by what he had said, wondering why he uttered something so contrary to an apsara's nature. He concluded that there must be a divine purpose behind it — a higher reason linked to her devotion to the Divine. Thus, Punjikasthala was born on earth as Anjana, a vanara (monkey being), and was later married to a monkey chieftain named Kesari.

Meanwhile, in Ayodhya, King Dasharatha performed a sacred fire ritual known as putra kameshti yajna, in the hopes of begetting children. As a result, he received a bowl of blessed pudding or payasam from the presiding deity, sent by the demi-gods. He shared it among his three queens, which eventually led to the birth of Dasharatha's sons Rama, Lakshmana, Bharata, and Shatrughna.

According to legend, the demi-gods knew that Hanuman's birth was also essential for the divine purpose of serving Lord Rama and aiding in the welfare of the world. The Wind God Vayu was entrusted with the task of carrying a portion of the payasam from Dasharatha's ritual to Anjani. He placed it in her palms, and upon consuming it, she gave birth to Lord Hanuman. Thus, while Kesari was his biological father, Hanuman is widely known as the son of Vayu. In the *Hanuman Chalisa*, Kesari is mentioned later, but Hanuman is most often referred to as the son of Anjani and Vayu, hence the names Anjani Putra and Pavana Suta.

Even today Rama Navami (the birthday of Lord Rama) and Hanuman Jayanti (the birthday of Lord Hanuman) fall six days apart from each other on the Indian lunar calendar.

Abode of Unparalleled Strength

Verse 2 says that Hanuman possesses unparalleled strength, and verse 3 refers to him as Mahavir and Vikrama. Mahavir refers to the great courageous one and Vikrama means one who is valorous, or someone who performs great deeds. Bajrangi is another epithet for Hanuman. It translates to "one whose body is as strong as a diamond," making it very difficult to cut or break.

We've already discussed two episodes highlighting Hanuman's strength: his leap across the Indian Ocean, which only an all-powerful person could achieve, and his encounter with Ravana's army, in which he created havoc in Ravana's court and returned unscathed.

Another beautiful episode illustrating Hanuman's strength is found in the Mahabharata. The Pandava brothers are central figures in the epic. Bhima, the second Pandava, is also the son of Vayu and is thus called Vayu Putra. Bhima was mighty, capable of defeating multiple elephants by himself, and proud of his strength.

During the Pandavas' exile in the forest, a fragrant saugandhika flower was carried to them by a breeze. Draupadi, the wife of the Pandavas, was infatuated with the flower and asked Bhima to bring her more. Bhima, confident in his abilities, set off to find the flowers. He eventually reached a garden where the flowers grew, but an old monkey lying across the entrance blocked his path.

Bhima respectfully asked the monkey to move, but the monkey, claiming to be old and helpless, said he couldn't. Bhima, not wanting to step over the monkey disrespectfully, asked again for him to move. When the monkey didn't comply, Bhima became agitated and prideful, boasted about his strength, and threatened to move the monkey himself. The monkey then asked Bhima to simply move his tail, which should create enough space for Bhima to pass.

To Bhima's surprise, he couldn't even move the monkey's tail an inch, no matter how hard he tried or what weapons he used. Completely baffled, Bhima realized that this was no ordinary monkey. He humbled himself and asked the monkey to reveal his true identity. The monkey then transformed into Hanuman, revealing himself as Bhima's elder brother since both were sons of the Wind God.

Hanuman explained that he had come to teach Bhima a valuable lesson: not to be proud of physical strength alone. True strength also includes mental strength, and one must control one's emotions, mind, and senses to harness one's physical power truly. This episode from the Mahabharata beautifully illustrates the importance of humility and inner strength, with Hanuman, the elder brother, teaching Bhima what true strength is all about.

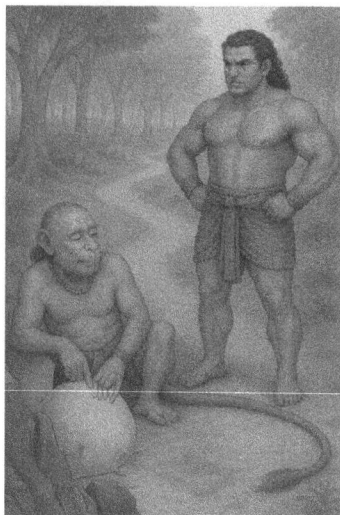

Hanuman, as much as he represented physical strength, also exemplified immense mental strength. Amma often highlights Hanuman's viveka (discernment) as one of his greatest qualities — the ability to distinguish right from wrong, and to choose wisely between what should and should not be done in any given situation. He was as strong in mind as he was in body. Even when he met Mother Sita during her captivity in Lanka, Hanuman told her that he had the strength to carry her back to Rama. He said, "I have the power to reduce this kingdom to ashes and easily carry you away." But he added, "I will not do so because my Lord has instructed me to come here as a messenger, not as a savior." In doing so, he upheld his dharma. Similarly, when Hanuman stood before Ravana and was insulted, he had all the power needed to destroy the entire kingdom and defeat Ravana then and there. But he restrained himself, saying, "I am here as a messenger, not as the vanquisher of Lanka. I will not act beyond my dharma. I have come to warn you that my master is on his way, and he will bring an end to your tyranny." To deliver that message, Hanuman created just enough havoc — setting the city ablaze — to give the people of Lanka a glimpse of what was to come: If the messenger alone could do this, imagine the might of the master.

Who else could have done that? In situations where we are insulted, most of us would instinctively use all our might to teach the other person a lesson. But Hanuman had complete control over his mind. He knew he had the power to act, yet he chose not to because that wasn't his dharma at that moment. This reflects his immense mental strength. He was never swayed by attraction, nor did he act impulsively. He remained steadfast in dharma under all circumstances. Moreover, the island kingdom of Lanka was protected by numerous traps and illusions as part of its defense. A temperamental individual would have easily fallen prey to them. To navigate such dangers and return safely — especially while on a mission like Hanuman's — one had to be equipped with both physical and mental strength. Hanuman possessed both in abundance.

That's why the last part of the third verse talks about intelligence — our mental ability. The prefix "ku-" adds a negative connotation, while "su-" adds a positive one. So "kumati nivar" means one who removes ill or wrong thoughts, while "sumati" refers to a mind endowed with positive qualities and virtues. Hanuman embodies this wisdom: to let go of negative qualities (kumati) and to nourish positive qualities (sumati).

The third verse teaches us to gauge the dharma of any given situation, understand our abilities and shortcomings, and then act accordingly. This is true wisdom and mental strength, which Hanuman represents.

In summary, Hanuman is all-powerful — not just physically but also mentally. He is the one who befriends good qualities and helps us let go of negative ones.

Insights on the Path of Bhakti from verses 2 & 3:

- Be the messenger of the Lord or the guru (Amma). Set the right example.
- Exercise mental strength and face every situation with confidence.
- Everyone has positives and negatives. We can find our inner strength by:
  - Confronting the negative tendencies of our mind
  - Befriending our positive tendencies

Verses 4 and 5

Spread the light of wisdom and compassion
Constant chanting and remembrance
Being self-sufficient

kanchana varaṇa virāja suvēśā ।
kānana kuṇḍala kuñchita kēśā ॥ 4 ॥

कंचन वरन विराज सुवेसा ।
कानन कुण्डल कुंचित केसा ॥

kanchana - gold(en); varana - color; virāja - resplendent;
suvēśā - beautifully attired and good appearance; kānana -
ears; kuṇḍala - earrings; kuñchita - curly; kēśā - haired;

One with golden effulgence, resplendent in your grand
attire, adoring beautiful earrings and curly hair.

hātha vajra au dhvajā virājai ।
kāndhē mūñja janēyū sājai ॥ 5 ॥

हाथ बज्र औ ध्वजा बिराजै ।
काँधे मूँज जनेऊ साजै ।

hātha - hand; vajra - the powerful vajra weapon; au - and; dhvajā
- flag; virājai - seated, situated; kāndhē - on the shoulders; mūñja -
specific kind of grass; janēyū - sacred thread; sājai - rests (adorned);

Vajrayudha (a special mace made out of the powerful
vajra) and flag are shining in your hand. The sacred
thread made of munja grass adorns your shoulder.

Golden Hue

The verse describes Lord Hanuman as one with a golden hue around him, resplendent, well-presented, and good-looking, with beautiful earrings and curly hair.

Starting with the golden hue: We discussed how Jambavan, the king of the bears in the *Ramayana*, reminded Hanuman of the strength he had forgotten due to a curse. When Jambavan explained Hanuman's strength, he referred to him as "hema-shaila," meaning golden mountain, one whose body has a golden effulgence and is vast like a mountain.

This golden aura is also linked to Hanuman's time spent in proximity to the Sun God, Surya Deva. As an ardent student of Surya Deva, Hanuman absorbed the sun's radiance as he learned from him. Additionally, many may be familiar with an earlier episode in Hanuman's life when, as a little boy, he mistook the sun for a fruit and went to gobble it up. (We willl discuss this story in detail later, in a different context). It is said that this act also contributed to his golden effulgence, as gobbling up the Sun symbolizes Hanuman imbibing the extraordinary qualities that the Sun God represents.

When we are in complete darkness, naturally we cannot see or comprehend anything. In fact, we are even unsure of our own appearance in complete darkness. Yet, the slightest light is enough to dispel that ignorance, allowing us to perceive the world around us. This why, in Sanatana Dharma, darkness represents ignorance, while light symbolizes the wisdom that removes ignorance. Depicting Hanuman as effulgent signifies his ability to embody and express wisdom at every moment. And it's not just any light — it is a golden hue, the most precious of colors. Gold, as a metal, does not rust or tarnish. Similarly,

Hanuman's golden radiance symbolizes the highest level of wisdom and the untainted, unwavering nature of his compassion for others.

It is also believed that when Lord Hanuman was entrusted with the responsibility of crossing the Indian Ocean to reach Lanka in search of Mother Sita, Lord Rama gave him a ring as a token of identity, in case Hanuman succeeded in finding her. Of all the ways he could carry it, Hanuman chose to keep the ring in his mouth. He did this for two reasons. First, he believed the mouth was the safest place to secure the ring without the risk of losing it. Second, the ring had "Rama" inscribed on it. And what better place is there for the Lord's name than the mouth itself? One should always remain immersed in the chanting of the Lord's name and remembrance. It is said that when Hanuman placed the ring in his mouth, he became enveloped in a golden hue.

Amma always reminds us to keep chanting our mantra as much as possible. In Amma's own life, when she was little, she would constantly chant Krishna's name. If she ever missed chanting Lord Krishna's name while walking, she would take several steps back from where she had forgotten and then walk forward again, chanting Lord Krishna's name. Amma set an example for all of us, even as a child, to always keep the Lord's name in our minds. Amma says that chanting the mantra is one of the best ways to keep our minds focused and one-pointed because the very nature of the mind is to keep jumping around like a monkey. Hanuman exemplifies how the monkey mind can be brought under control through shama (control of the mind) and dama (control of the senses). So, let us always keep the Lord's name upon our tongue.

Sage Narada is one of Lord Vishnu's ardent devotees. He is considered to be among the greatest of all sages. In movies and TV series related to ancient epics, he is always shown entering the scene chanting "Narayan, Narayan," showing that he is ever in remembrance of Lord Vishnu. But once, Lord Narada happened to overhear Lord Vishnu praising someone on Earth as his best devotee.

Narada was taken aback - how could someone be a greater devotee than him? He confronted Lord Vishnu and asked, "Who is this person?" Vishnu replied, "Go and see for yourself. You will see that he is indeed very devoted to me." Narada went down to Earth and observed this person, who was a farmer. The farmer woke up in the morning, chanted Lord Vishnu's name, did his morning ablutions, and then went about his day working on his farm from sunrise to sunset, constantly chanting Lord Vishnu's name. Narada, however, was unimpressed. He thought, "He's just chanting Vishnu's name, nothing special." He returned to Lord Vishnu and asked, "What's the big deal? I see him chanting your name, but other than that, he's just going about his normal life."

Lord Vishnu then said, "Okay, I'll put you through a test, and then we'll discuss this afterwards." He handed Narada a vessel filled to the brim with water and told him to carry it across the world without spilling a single drop. Narada, focused on the task, carefully carried the vessel all around the world and returned to Vishnu, jubilant that he had succeeded without spilling a drop. Vishnu praised him and then asked, "But tell me, during this process, how many times did you chant my name?" Narada realized that not even once had he chanted Vishnu's name. He had been so focused on the water that he forgot. Lord Vishnu then explained, "For the farmer, life is like carrying that vessel of water. A single mistake on his farm could ruin his entire year, leaving his family and those who depend on him hungry and suffering. Despite this, he still chants my name. It wasn't about glorifying the devotee; it was a lesson for you. Even you, with all your devotion, have shortcomings."

The point here isn't whether Sage Narada was great or not. It's about setting an example for us, ensuring we don't become complacent in our spiritual growth. The story also emphasizes the importance of chanting the divine name, keeping it on our tongue as much as possible.

Returning to Hanuman's story, it is said that when he placed the ring in his mouth, he was enveloped in a golden effulgence — a glow of euphoria that filled him with strength and energy. This light dispelled the darkness around him, guiding him through the unknown as he journeyed forward. Spiritually speaking, this symbolizes the light of knowledge dispelling the darkness of ignorance.

This verse teaches us that continuous chanting of the mantra or the divine name is crucial in the path of devotion (bhakti yoga). Doing so keeps our minds focused and one-pointed, automatically lighting the lamp of knowledge and wisdom, which dispels the darkness within and around us. Hanuman, who had that golden hue, is a profound example of this truth.

The Enchanting and Good-looking One

Viraja suvesa - one who is resplendent in that golden hue; suvesa - one who is well dressed, well-presented, and good-looking. Associating monkeys with good-looking is probably debatable, the fact that Hanuman is indeed described as good-looking is yet another reminder that he was no ordinary monkey.

As a matter of fact, the canto from *Ramayana* in which Lord Hanuman is the central figure is called *Sundara Kanda* - the canto of the beautiful one. Sundara means "beautiful," and Kanda means "Canto." And who is referred to as Sundara? Lord Hanuman. It seems that when Hanuman was born, his mother, Anjana, referred to him as Sundara, the beautiful one. Sage Valmiki, recognizing that Hanuman played the primary role in this part of the *Ramayana*, named the Canto after Hanuman as *Sundara Kanda*.

When we talk about beauty, one's external appearance is definitely a form of beauty, and we don't need to disregard that. Amma encourages even the monks in the ashram to be well-presented when they go out for official events, meetings, and such. However, while external beauty is significant, we must recognize and understand that it is not permanent. Aging changes it; an accident can change it; a disease can change it. By its nature, external beauty will depreciate or diminish over time. Therefore, external beauty cannot be the "real" beauty. True beauty is internal beauty, which, rather than depreciating, is enhanced as we grow. Internal beauty can always grow if we put in the effort. Meanwhile, external beauty, even with effort, will fade.

So what does it mean to be internally beautiful? Our internal beauty is the expression of our virtues, habits, nature, and maturity in different situations. This is what makes us truly beautiful. Lord Hanuman was known for his internal beauty, virtues, and maturity in handling situations. So here, when we encounter the term "good-looking" in this verse, we should read it as referring to more than just physical appearance. Good-looking is about to what extent we are able to see goodness in everything and everyone. How well we look for goodness in others determines how good-looking we are.

Various versions of the *Ramayana*, including the one composed by Tulasidas Goswami, describe how Hanuman searched through Ravana's palace in his quest to find Mother Sita. As it was the middle of the night, everyone was asleep. He saw Ravana sleeping in his chambers, and his wives and other women resting in various rooms of the palace. Each time he saw a woman, he paused and wondered, "Could this be Mother Sita?" But his conscience would always respond, "No," as he could not believe that Sita Devi would have betrayed Lord Rama and succumbed to Ravana's invitation. As he continued searching through the royal quarters, he eventually came upon a chamber filled with signs of Lord Rama and the sound of his name being chanted. This place belonged to Vibhishana, Ravana's brother. Unlike the rest of the asura (demon) clan, he was devoted to dharma. It is in this context that Hanuman gently advises Vibhishana that simply chanting Lord Rama's name is not enough — one must also actively serve Rama's cause and uphold dharma. Hanuman then explains the purpose of his journey to Lanka: to find Mother Sita. Hanuman confides that in his search every woman he encounters begins to seem like Sita to him, but he is troubled by the thought of having intruded upon the private spaces of women unknown to him. Vibhishana reassures him, saying, "That is your greatness, O Hanuman. Your gaze and your heart are so pure that you see only Mother Sita in every woman. There is not the slightest blemish in your attitude." Vibhishana then directs Hanuman to the Ashoka garden where Sita was held captive.

This resonates with advice Amma sometimes gives us, especially the monks in the ashram: "See the divine mother in everyone." One of Amma's senior disciples had an experience during his early times with Amma, when he had to stay away from Amma for some time while in Mumbai. He was so dejected that he couldn't see Amma, and it would cause him to cry at times. Once, while traveling on a bus, a young woman sat next to him, which disturbed him. He got up and moved to another seat, but the woman followed and sat beside him again, disturbing him even more. He eventually got off the bus. Later, when discussing this incident with Amma, she told him, "I came to you and sat next to you on the bus. You refused to recognize me. You refused to accept me. What can I do? See Amma in every woman you encounter."

Similarly, Hanuman saw Mother Sita in everyone, which helped him realize that he wasn't doing anything wrong in his search for Sita. This attitude reflects his internal beauty. Subesa, meaning "one who is well-dressed," when discussed in this context, can be interpreted to mean one who is "internally well dressed." What is the internal dress or clothing we can wear? It is the clothing of maturity and purity. And the clothing of having control over our senses and thoughts is the best way we can adorn our inner self. There is an interesting term in Sanskrit - dharana. It has several meanings. At the physical level, it translates to "wearing, carrying/holding." At the level of the mind, the term also has the meaning, "notion, assumption". Our notions and assumptions condition the mind and influence our thoughts. They are like the clothing of the mind that influences its appearance. Interestingly, dharana is also used as a term to convey what the mind should focus on and prioritize. The term conveys to us that the beauty or good appearance of the mind is based on its focus and priorities. A one-pointed and aware mind will always be beneficial and appealing for others, and ourselves too.

When discussing attraction and beauty, we often think of various celebrities — actors, singers, dancers, and even athletes — who have large followings. People throng around them and follow them everywhere. But as they grow old, lose their abilities, and their physical appeal diminishes, their following naturally decreases.

Imagine a woman in her 70s sitting on a chair, meeting with people — not for one or two hours, but for 15 or more, sometimes even 22 hours at a time — just sitting there, talking to each person who comes to her. Hundreds, sometimes thousands of people sit there, just gazing at her, forgoing sleep and food, simply to watch her. This is probably the best example of what true beauty is. And unlike those celebrities, the number of people who come to see her only increases as Amma grows older. It's remarkable how so many people are drawn to just watching Amma for hours. This is a testament to Amma's inner beauty.

I remember that my fellow brahmachari brothers and I followed a trend where we decided we would wait until Amma finished giving darshan before we went to bed. In the initial days it was fine as darshan didn't go too late in the night. I must admit, however, that I did come to regret making that decision as darshan started going until very, very late at night. Sometimes I wonder, why am I forgoing dear sleep to sit here, watching Amma? Upon reflection, it's this divine captivating beauty that inspires me to forgo sleep — one of the most cherished things in life — just to watch Amma.

One with the Earrings

Kanana kundala — the one adorned with earrings in his ears — again describes the appearance of Hanuman.

There are various accounts of how Hanuman came to wear the pair of earrings he is known for. One version describes how Mother Anjani gifted him the earrings as a symbol of protection. They carried her blessings, ensuring that Hanuman would be safeguarded in any adverse situation he might face. The earrings were believed to be infused with the spiritual strength she had gained through her penance and devotion.

Another account speaks of a time when the ruling monkey king of Kishkindha felt threatened by the prophecy of the mighty Hanuman's birth. Fearing a challenge to his throne, he plotted to kill Hanuman even before he was born, while he was still in Mother Anjani's womb. In one version, the king fired a special weapon crafted from panchaloha, a sacred alloy of five metals (gold, silver, copper, iron and zync), aimed directly at her womb. In another version, he deceived Mother Anjani into consuming poison made from the same five-metal combination. But the plan failed. In this telling, rather than being harmed, Hanuman was born wearing earrings forged from those very five metals.

These earrings became a symbol of his divine armor and invincibility — a mark of his mother's penance, love, and determination to protect her child. They represent the compassion that transforms even a threat into protection. Thus, the term kanana kundala refers to Hanuman — one whose inner purity is so powerful, so sacred, that even the venom of negativity is transformed into an ornament.

Amma says, "Let us trace our eyes with the anjana (kajal or traditional eyeliner) of compassion. Let us adorn our hands with the henna of good deeds. Let us bless our minds with the sweetness of humility. Let us fill our hearts with the light of love for God and all of God's creation. In this way, may we transform this world into heaven."

In light of Amma's words, the earring that Hanuman inspires us to wear is the ability to listen with awareness — to be inquisitive, to learn and grow, and to filter out the unnecessary things we hear. It is a call to use our ears not just to hear, but to discern and perceive goodness.

Curly Hair

Hanuman is also described as having curly hair, further adding to the depiction of his enchanting appearance. Though Hanuman is usually portrayed as strong, firm, and courageous, the mention of his curly hair emphasizes his tenderness and the warmth of his compassion.

In the *Mahishasura Mardini Stotram*, composed by Adi Shankaracharya, the divine mother is depicted in her ferocious form, annihilating the demon Mahishasura. Interestingly, every verse of the hymn ends with the line:

> jaya jaya he mahiṣāsura mardini ramya kapardini śaila sute

> *Victory to the Divine Mother, the slayer of the demon Mahisha, the one with tender curly hair, daughter of the mountain.*

Each verse describes the Divine Mother as having tender, curly hair, a poetic detail that softens her fierce form and reminds us that, at her core, she is the universal mother, with compassion as her default nature.

In the previous chapter, we discussed the encounter between Lord Hanuman and Bhima. According to some versions of the story, after helping Bhima overcome his pride in his physical strength, Hanuman gave him a few strands of his hair, advising him to use them wisely in moments of great need. There are at least two instances where Hanuman's hair came to the rescue.

The first instance occurred during the Mahabharata war. As the Kaurava army began losing its mighty warriors one by one, they decided to perform a special yajna (fire ceremony) to weaken the Pandavas through mystical means. When Bhima learned of this plan, he instructed one of their spies to disguise himself as a Kaurava soldier and secretly place a strand of Hanuman's hair among the items prepared for the ritual offerings. During the ceremony, as the offerings were made, the Pandavas indeed began to weaken — until Hanuman's hair was inadvertently offered into the fire. The result was not only a restoration of the Pandavas' strength but an immense surge in their power. The following day, the Kauravas were shocked to see the Pandavas stronger than ever, and to witness them annihilate one of the Kauravas' prime warriors, delivering a devastating blow to their army.

Just a mere strand of Hanuman's hair transformed a harmful attack on the Pandavas into a source of strength. When one is filled with positivity and purity, even the smallest contribution can create a profound impact on others. This is the inspiration we should draw from Hanuman.

The second incident involves a sage named Purushamriga. As the name implies, Purushamriga had a peculiar form — a human head with the body of a lion (some versions say a deer). In the Mahabharata, after the Pandavas win the war, Yudhisthira is to be crowned king and must perform the rajasuya yagna, a grand fire ceremony traditionally held at coronation. As part of the ritual, all neighboring kings, allies, sages, and dignitaries are invited. Sage Narada suggests that Bhima invite Sage Purushamriga to serve as a guard for the ceremony. Narada warns Bhima that the sage is known for his "manovega" — extraordinary speed and intellect — and that he would not agree without imposing a nearly impossible challenge.

As expected, when Bhima extends the invitation, Purushamriga accepts on one condition. He is an ardent devotee of Shiva and dislikes being interrupted while chanting the Lord's name. Moreover, with his lion-like body and voracious appetite, he could devour anything that comes close. Therefore, as they travel together, Bhima must stay well ahead of him at all times and never get close to him. But given Purushamriga's incredible speed, this seems impossible. Bhima accepts the challenge and rushes ahead with all his might, but each time, the sage quickly catches up. At this moment, Bhima remembers Hanuman's advice to use a strand of his hair in moments of crisis. Since Hanuman was an incarnation of Lord Shiva, Bhima is sure that he will come to the rescue.

Each time the sage catches up, Bhima throws a strand of Hanuman's hair towards him. Miraculously, countless Shiva lingas (the symbolic form of Lord Shiva) appear wherever the strand of hair lands. Being deeply devoted, Purushamriga stops to elaborately worship each one of these lingas, allowing Bhima to regain his lead. In this way, Bhima successfully escorts Purushamriga to the kingdom. It is believed that Lord Krishna granted Sage Purushamriga the boon of standing as guardian to his beloved deity, Lord Shiva, at the renowned Chidambaram Temple in South India. To this day, the form of the Sage can be seen at the temple entrance.

What do we learn from these stories? First, it reflects the spiritual significance of Hanuman's devotion. Hanuman's very existence was so divine that even an insignificant strand of his hair could produce numerous Shiva lingas. This just stresses the point that on the path of devotion, our dedication should be such that every pore, or strand of hair, should be surcharged with our Deity/Guru. That is to say, even the smallest part of our being should be filled with divinity. How can we fill ourselves with divinity? As devotees, our attitude should be such that we see the Divine in everything. Even the most insignificant thing should remind us of our beloved deity. When we perceive the Divine in all things, we ourselves will be filled with divinity and others will perceive the Divine in us.

The *Ishavasya Upanishad* begins with the profound statement:

īśā vāsyam idaṃ sarvaṃ yat kiñca jagatyāṃ jagat

All this is enveloped by the Divine, whatsoever moves in this creation.

Hanuman exemplifies the state where the path of devotion (seeing and experiencing only the Divine in everything) and the path of knowledge (realizing the oneness with the Supreme) converge, underscoring how both approaches complement each other.

The story of the sage chasing Bhima highlights the importance of commitment to one's spiritual practices. Despite being in the middle of a challenge, Purushamriga did not forget to worship the Shiva lingas that appeared before him. This is a reminder for all of us: even in the midst of life's challenges, whether at work, with family, or with friends, we should not neglect our spiritual practices. The sage set a perfect example of maintaining devotion, no matter how busy life gets.

The Holder of the Vajrayudha

Hanuman is considered the bearer of one of the most powerful weapons, which belongs to the king of the demigods, and the king of heaven, Lord Indra. He is usually depicted holding the vajra, which translates to a precious stone such as a diamond, which is very difficult to break. Vajra also translates to lightning, signifying that it is as powerful as a lightning bolt: swift, powerful, and nearly impossible to defend against once it strikes.

It is said that once, when Devaloka (heaven, the abode of the demigods) was attacked by the asuras (demons), the devas (gods) were being overpowered. The devas went to Brahma asking for help, but Brahma explained that this particular asura had a boon that made him invincible, except by a Vajrayudha. The problem was where would they get such a weapon? Finally, Sage Dadhichi, known for the immense power of his bones due to his yogic practices, sacrificed himself to create a weapon from his bones — the Vajrayudha. He gave this weapon to the devas to use against the asura, ultimately helping them achieve victory over evil. However, not everyone could wield the Vajrayudha; it required great capability. In the end, it was decided that only Indra was strong enough to handle the weapon and defeat the asura.

Later, when Devaloka was attacked again and Indra was overpowered by another asura known as Vritrasura, the Vajrayudha slipped from his hand, leaving him helpless. No one else could handle the Vajrayudha. The only one who could lift it and slay the asura was Hanuman, who appeared as a superhero and savior. Everyone was amazed that none of the devas could handle the

Vajrayudha, but Hanuman could. As a result, Indra and the other devas granted him the boon to hold the Vajrayudha henceforth, recognizing his unexpected capability. That is how Hanuman came to be depicted holding the Vajrayudha in his hand.

Bearer of the Flag of Victory

"Dhvaja virajai" can be interpreted in two ways: one, the flag rests in Hanuman's hands; or two, Hanuman sits upon the flag. The flag symbolizes victory. Hanuman himself embodies victory and always brings triumph to those who have him on their side. As we discussed previously, whoever has Hanuman by their side will always be victorious. We talked about how Sugriva became king, how Vibhishana became king, and even how Rama became king, all with Hanuman on their side. The flag symbolizes victory, and Hanuman's presence ensures success for those who align with him.

There is a reference associating Hanuman with a flag in Mahabharata. We discussed how Bhima met Hanuman and how Hanuman taught him a lesson about overcoming ego. Similarly, Bhima's younger brother, the ace archer Arjuna, was also somewhat egoistic, in this case regard to his unparalleled archery skills. Hanuman had to teach him a lesson as well.

It is believed that Arjuna met Hanuman during his pilgrimage to Rameshwaram near the southern tip of India, where their conversation drifted to Arjuna questioning Lord Rama's prowess in archery. Arjuna boasted that he would have built a bridge with his mighty arrows, rather than relying on a monkey army to toil for it. Hanuman seemed very inquisitive and said he did not know a strong bridge could be built with arrows. He requested Arjuna to build one for him on a nearby water body. Arjuna obliged, but as soon as Hanuman touched the bridge, it collapsed completely. Arjuna then built stronger and larger bridges, but each time, Hanuman's mere touch shattered them. Hanuman told Arjuna, "I thought you would build a strong bridge. It is unable to bear my mere touch. Think of the whole monkey army and my lord walking on it." Along with the bridges, Arjuna's ego was also broken, and he was deeply humbled. Along with the lesson, Hanuman blessed Arjuna by promising to protect him during the Mahabharata war. This is why Arjuna's chariot is depicted with a flag bearing Hanuman's image, the kapi-dhwaja, symbolizing Hanuman's presence and divine protection. Hanuman sits atop the flag, signifying the victory that his presence ensures.

Folklore also says that before the Mahabharata war, Lord Krishna requested Hanuman to be present on Arjuna's chariot to protect it, as Hanuman had boons of invincibility against deadly weapons. Hanuman humbly accepted the request. How could he ignore the request by his lord in his reincarnated form? One may wonder: If Lord Krishna himself is the charioteer, why is Hanuman's protection even necessary? Of course, Lord Krishna, the Supreme Being incarnate, needed no assistance in protecting Arjuna. But this arrangement carried a deeper message for Arjuna, and for each one of us. Krishna represents the ever-present Supreme, always ready to guide and protect. But Hanuman represents the true devotee. The real question is: Is the devotee awakened within us? The Lord is always there — but to receive his grace, the presence of a sincere, devoted heart is essential. Only then is the divine equation complete.

It is believed that after the Mahabharata war ended and the Pandavas emerged victorious, Arjuna carried a sense of pride about his contribution to the victory. Noticing this, Lord Krishna instructed him to step down from the chariot and move a safe distance away. Though puzzled, Arjuna obeyed. Then, Krishna removed the kapi-dhwaja flag and stepped off the chariot himself. To Arjuna's amazement, the chariot immediately burst into flames and was reduced to ashes. Krishna turned to Arjuna and said, "Do you still think you are the reason for the victory?"

It was the presence of Krishna, the Divine, and Hanuman, the true devotee, that had protected the chariot throughout the war. Without them, it would have been destroyed much earlier. This teaches us that divine grace, when received with true devotion, is what truly protects and sustains us. That is when grace becomes active in our lives.

Another interpretation of the terms vajra and dwaja comes from the field of palmistry. In palmistry, there are various lines on your palms that represent different aspects of your life. One line, called vajra, represents how powerful one is, while another line, called dwaja, represents how far-reaching your fame will be.

Hanuman is described as "one who has both in his hands," meaning he possesses both immense strength and far-reaching fame. Thousands of years after his birth, we are still discussing and revering him, which itself demonstrates the aspect of dwaja - his enduring fame. The fact that we are still talking about Hanuman today underscores his power (vajra) and fame (dwaja), qualities he holds firmly in his grasp.

Always a Learner

The last part of the verse depicts Hanuman as the one who wears the sacred thread - kandhe munja janeyu sajai. This sacred thread is like a spiritual seatbelt that safeguards a student on their journey of seeking true knowledge. In the tradition of Sanatana Dharma, the sacred thread ceremony, typically held for boys around the age of seven, involves wearing the thread across the body from the top of the left shoulder. It's a symbol of protection and dedication to the pursuit of knowledge.

The fifth verse of the *Hanuman Chalisa* depicts Hanuman wearing this sacred thread. Although Hanuman was established in wisdom and strength, he maintained the attitude of a student throughout his life. He learned from his father, Kesari, and, as we discussed earlier, from the Sun God, Surya Deva. Later, he became a student of the sage Narada Maharshi, from whom he learned the creative arts. He also learned from Lord Rama, his ultimate master.

Moreover, Hanuman was humble enough to learn from any situation and from anyone, regardless of who they were. He learned from Jambavan, the bear who revealed his true power; Vibhishana, Ravana's brother; Sita; Lakshmana; and even Lava and Kusha, the twin sons of Rama and Sita, who were born much later. Despite being much older and wiser, Hanuman remained humble enough to learn from them.

This attitude of being ever open to learning is a vital lesson for spiritual aspirants. As Amma says, we need to have the heart of a three-year-old child — innocent and ever ready to grow. If we consider ourselves fully grown, we hinder our potential for further growth. The sacred thread that Hanuman wears symbolizes this journey and the attitude of lifelong learning.

Insights on the Path of Bhakti from verses 4 & 5:

- Constant chanting of the mantra - remembrance and imbibing the qualities of the deity/guru is an essential part of spiritual progression.

- Defining our beauty - we become good-looking by looking at the goodness in others.

- Be self-sufficient and independent.

- The primary factor determining our strength and fame is our own inner qualities. What others think and say about us is superficial.

- Ever be a beginner, humble as a student, ready to learn and grow even more.

Verses 6 and 7

Being truthful to yourself
Serve and act for the Lord/guru
Be aware of the context of the situation

śaṅkara suvana kēsarī nandana ।
tēja pratāpa mahājaga vandana ॥ 6 ॥

शंकर सुवन केसरीनंदन ।
तेज प्रताप महा जग वन्दन ॥

śaṅkara - Lord Shiva; suvana - to become (incarnate); kēsarī
nandana - son of Kesari; tēja - power/force; pratāpa - glory;
mahājaga - the entire great creation; vandana - revered;

*O partial incarnation of Lord Shiva, giver of joy to King
Kesari. Your great majesty is revered by the whole world.*

vidyāvāna guṇī ati chātura ।
rāma kāja karivē kō ātura ॥ 7 ॥

विद्यावान गुणी अति चातुर ।
राम काज करिबे को आतुर ॥

vidyāvāna - full of wisdom; guṇī - endowed with virtues/
qualities; ati chātura - very clever/smart; rāma kāja - Lord
Rama's work; karivē kō - to perform/do; ātura - very eager;

*All knowledgeable, full of virtues, and sharp-minded,
you are always eager to serve Lord Sri Rama.*

The Incarnation of Lord Shiva

The verse describes Hanuman as the incarnation of Lord Shiva, born as the son of Kesari, and one whose radiance and glory are revered throughout the vast universe. Shankara suvana, Lord Shiva, the source of auspiciousness, becomes (suvana/subana) the son of Kesari. We discussed earlier how Lord Shiva and Lord Vishnu shared a mutual desire to worship each other as devotees. This desire was fulfilled when Lord Vishnu incarnated as Lord Rama and worshiped Shiva. Lord Rama wished to build a Shiva linga for worship before going to Lanka and instructed Hanuman to fetch one from Kailasa. However, Hanuman was delayed, so Lord Rama created a Shiva linga and performed the customary worship. When Hanuman finally returned with the linga from Kailasa, he felt saddened that it wasn't used, which is why the famous Rameshwaram Shiva Temple has two Shiva lingas — one made by Rama and the other brought by Hanuman. On the other hand, Shiva, who wanted to worship Rama, incarnated as Hanuman, dedicated himself entirely to serving Lord Rama, and exemplified the ideal disciple. Although these stories do not come directly from the Ramayana, they are drawn from folklores, and various adaptations of the Ramayana, which add depth and dimension to the epic teachings.

There is another reason why Lord Shiva incarnated as Hanuman. Shiva had granted Ravana boons of unvanquishable powers due to his sincere penance. Later when the devas (demi-gods) explained to him the consequences of the boons, he promised them that he would incarnate so as to keep Ravana in check, and would become the cause of his decline if he chose the path of adharma (non-righteousness).

The story goes that Ravana, as an ardent devotee of Lord Shiva, possessed many great qualities and abilities. He undertook severe penance to seek Lord Shiva's blessings and obtain boons. The devas, fearing that Ravana might become invincible and take over the heavens, tried to dissuade Shiva from granting any boon. However Shiva, known as Bhole Nath (the innocent Lord), was moved by Ravana's intense devotion and eventually decided to grant him a boon.

There are different versions of the story of Ravana's interactions with Lord Shiva. In some versions, Ravana asked for just one boon, and in other versions, he asked for two different boons. In the first version, Ravana asks for a boon in the form of the Atma Linga, which represents Lord Shiva's soul and is believed to bestow immortality. By tactfully asking for the Atma Linga instead of immortality directly, Ravana sought to gain immense power. Though the devas wished for Shiva to deny this request, Shiva granted the Atma Linga to Ravana.

It is believed that the Atma Linga should be treated with the utmost respect and reverence and should not be set on the ground even once. It is thought that if it touches the ground, it will become stuck and immovable. Having received the Atma Linga as a boon, Ravana was heading back to Lanka. Lord Ganesha, in the guise of a small boy, tricks Ravana into placing the Atma Linga on the ground during his evening prayers, causing Ravana to lose the benefit of the boon.

In another version, the story goes that Ravana asks for two boons: the first for the Atma Linga and the second for the most enchanting Shakti (the divine energy of creation, personified by Goddess Parvati, Shiva's consort), who represents the left half of the Ardhanarishwara form. Although Ravana's requests shock Lord Shiva, he must keep his word and grant him the boons. He does so in a clever way, however, by first granting him the boon of Goddess Parvati, who agrees to accompany Ravana to Lanka. En route to Lanka, Parvati devises a plan to fulfill the second requested boon and at the same time to free herself. She creates a stunning woman out of a frog, Mandodari, whose beauty captivates Ravana; he eventually marries her instead of Mother Parvati. The woman had been cursed to be a frog due to her misdeed, and the divine mother had promised to relieve her of the curse and transform her into a beautiful woman. In this way, all the divine resolves are fulfilled in perfect harmony.

The spiritual lesson here is that while Ravana's dedication to his penance was admirable, his intentions were rooted in selfishness. This self-interest tainted his actions, turning a potentially good deed into one that led to dissapointment. The story teaches that even good actions can have negative consequences if not done with the right attitude.

Let's understand this better with an example around Amma. Many adorable little children come to Amma for darshan. Amma has this habit of seating them right next to her on the darshan chair. I have seen these children broadly fit into two categories. The first category consists of those who are entirely calm and content, either gazing at Amma or busy with the candy she gives them. They remain still in the corner of the chair, and everyone around them adores them, smiling and laughing at their cuteness. Then there's the second category of children — those who are more restless. They can't stay still; they'll stand up, take candy off the tray, push Amma, or create more space by nudging Amma to the corner of the chair. When this happens, the volunteers nearby gently lift the child and move them away from Amma. It's not the child's fault — they don't know better — but they can't stay due to their own actions.

In a certain way, Ravana was like this second category of children. Of course children act out of innocence, and Ravana acted out of ego, but still, we have in these children a useful analogy for explaining what happened to Ravana. He was granted the boon to be close to the Lord, but instead of being content, he tried to push the Lord away and take the Lord's own Shakti and Atma. This was his mistake. Just like the volunteers around Amma, who gently move the fidgety child away, Parvati and Ganesha, the divine volunteers, moved Ravana away, saying, "It is because of your own actions that we must do this. As a result, Ravana lost both the boons he was granted.

In Sanatana Dharma, it is often said there are 33 koti devatas. This can be interpreted as 330 million deities. There are numerous deities worshiped in Sanatana Dharma with the belief that they are different representations of the same one Supreme. A more accurate interpretation of 33 koti devatas is 33 exalted or supreme (koti) deities. These include eight Vasus (who serve Lord Vishnu and assist in sustaining creation), eleven Rudras (forms of Lord Shiva responsible for dissolution), twelve Adityas (sons of Aditi who manage the elements of creation), Indra (the king of the heavens), and Prajapati (the Creator).

Each of the Rudras embody a specific quality and power associated with dissolution, transformation, and liberation. As promised to the demi-gods, one Rudra, specifically the one associated with the soul or "atma," incarnated as Hanuman and became the cause of Ravana's downfall. This incarnation emphasizes that while one might deceive or satisfy others, deceiving one's own soul or conscience is impossible. Hanuman is often referred to as "Rudra Avatara," an incarnation of one of the Rudras. He is also called "Amsa Avatara," meaning a partial incarnation of Lord Shiva.

Son of Kesari, Revered by All

Hanuman was born as the son of Kesari, his biological father. We've discussed how Hanuman is also referred to as the son of Vayu, the wind god. The 11th Rudra, destined to incarnate as Hanuman, played a role in Ravana's downfall. Lord Shiva requested Vayu Deva to carry the energy of the 11th Rudra into the womb of Mother Anjana. Vayu Deva, therefore, has a significant role in Hanuman's birth, which is why he is also referred to as Hanuman's father.

We also touched earlier on the story of Dasharatha, father of Lord Rama,

who performed a yagna to beget children. The presiding deity emerged and gave him payasam (pudding) to feed his three wives. Vayu Deva then carried a small amount of the payasam and placed it in Mother Anjana's hands. After consuming it, Hanuman was born. This explains why both Kesari and Vayu Deva are both considered Hanuman's fathers. Kesari is the biological father who gave Hanuman his body, and Vayu Deva is the one who provided his energy and soul.

Shiva, incarnated as Kesari's son in form of Hanuman, is radiant and revered across the world. Hanuman is worshiped for his exemplary character as a disciple, warrior, and individual. This is a message we need to take away - we will be revered not for what we possess but for who we are. The former is ephemeral and temporary. The latter is there to stay.

It is said that one day, Lord Rama turned to Hanuman and said, "You have done so much for me, for this kingdom, and for the world. You have been my trusted companion, my savior, my servant, my messenger, and so much more. Ask me for anything." With folded hands and a humble heart, Hanuman replied, "My Lord, what could I possibly want? All I ask is to always be at your feet. That alone is more than enough for me." But Rama wasn't satisfied. He gently urged Hanuman to ask for something for himself. After a moment of thought, Hanuman said, "Then please grant me this: that I may be remembered always, in every age." Rama smiled. He was glad that Hanuman was finally asking something for himself. But he was also a bit surprised. Could Hanuman really want to be remembered for his own sake? Before Rama could say anything, Hanuman continued, "Not for fame, my Lord. Let me be remembered only as your servant and your devotee. Let my life inspire others who walk the path of love and devotion." Rama's heart was deeply moved. Even in asking for something personal, Hanuman had only asked to serve a greater purpose. Rama placed his hand on Hanuman's head and said, "So be it. In every time and every place where my name is spoken, your name will be honored too." And so it is. Even today, across the world, Hanuman is remembered — not just for his strength, but for his love and devotion. Not for his power, but for his humility. The fact that, after thousands of years, someone wrote this book, and that you are reading it now, is proof that Rama's blessing came true.

Knowledgeable, Virtuous, and Smart

The seventh verse describes Hanuman as vidyavan (knowledgeable and wise), guni (virtuous), and ati chatur (very smart and quick-witted).

We have discussed how Hanuman is known for his wisdom. Every word and action of his was filled with devotion and faith. When Lord Rama first met Hanuman, he immediately recognized his wisdom. Similarly, Vibhishana recognized it upon their first meeting, as did Mother Sita when she encountered Hanuman for the first time. Hanuman's distinct mark of wisdom was evident in his every word and action.

There is a verse from the text *Rama Raksha Stotram* that explains how Lord Rama protects his devotees. The text describes Lord Hanuman as follows:

manōjavaṃ māruta tulya vēgaṃ
jitēndriyaṃ buddhimatāṃ variṣṭam
vātātmajaṃ vānarayūtha mukhyaṃ
śrī rāma dūtaṃ śirasā namāmi

Fast as the mind, as swift as the wind, one who has won over the senses, one who is supreme amongst the wise, son of the wind god, the supreme amongst the monkeys, O messenger of Rama, I take refuge in you.

In a text about Rama in the verses, even Hanuman is praised — that is the greatness of Hanuman. A disciple being praised amidst the accolades given to the master is the greatest blessing a disciple could receive. Some of us might have experienced our names being mentioned during the daily satsangs in Amritapuri in Amma's presence, and it brings joy to hear our names alongside Amma's. Similarly, when Lord Rama is praised, Hanuman is also honored, and this association brings immense happiness and a sense of pride to the disciple.

Hanuman is described as fast as the mind — the mind is the fastest thing in the world. It can be here one moment, on the Moon the next, then on Jupiter, then travel 80 years into the past, and then back here in an instant. He is described as one whose speed parallels the wind and can travel as quickly as the wind. He is Indriya Jita, one who has mastered and completely controls the senses in different situations. One who is Vidyavan is wise and knowledgeable of the situation he is in and all the associated factors. We have also discussed how Hanuman learned the teachings of the Vedas from Surya Deva, the Sun God. Surya Deva, who as a teacher among teachers could be compared to the best of the Ivy League professors, was so impressed by Hanuman that he accepted him as a student. Hanuman quickly mastered all the teachings of the Vedas, and Surya Deva was so fond of him that he kept teaching him repeatedly to keep him around. Guni - Hanuman is full of virtues. Ati chatur - he is very smart, and quick-witted. He cannot be fooled. In the field of management and business, there's a principle: work smarter, not harder. Working smart is often more important than working hard, and Hanuman embodies this wisdom perfectly.

Many years ago, there was a simple but profound TV commercial in India for a product called Center Shock. It's a candy with a filling that is tangy and spicy. As conveyed by the product's name, the consumer gets a shock from the center of the candy. The TV commercial is hilarious but succinctly conveys the message of working smart rather than hard. Set in the 80s, a youngster enters a run-down salon, manned by an elderly man. Looking skeptically at the old barber, the youngster shows him a picture of a model with spiked hair. He seems sure that the barber is not capable of doing a contemporary hairstyle like that and chides him as he tries to go along with his business. Not to be outdone, the elderly barber proceeds to open a drawer, take out a Center Shock candy, and feed it to the young customer. The youngster is shocked by the candy and shakes violently. Lo and behold, he ends up with the hairstyle he asked for - spiked hair. Working smart, the elderly barber understands, is more important than working hard.

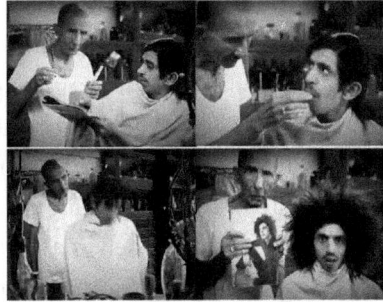

What does it mean to work smart in a spiritual context? To work smart means to understand and assess the situation as best as possible. We need to evaluate the situation we are in and determine how the principles of dharma (righteousness) apply. Sometimes, what's generally right might be wrong in a specific context. For example, patience is a virtue, but being overly patient before an exam and delaying study isn't appropriate. Dharma is contextual, so understanding the situation and acting accordingly is essential.

Working smart involves four steps:

1. Assess the situation thoroughly.

2. Determine what Dharma dictates in that particular situation.

3. Consider the bigger picture, not just the immediate scenario.

4. Act based on that understanding.

This approach ensures that you're truly working smart. For example, Hanuman, referred to as Ati Chatur, is known for his intelligence and ability to act wisely in different situations.

Let us explore a fascinating folklore tale that highlights Hanuman's remarkable presence of mind and quick-wittedness during the battle of Lanka. As Ravana began losing his best warriors, despite their seemingly unbeatable abilities, he grew increasingly frustrated. One by one, they were falling, and he couldn't understand why. Rama's army was made up mostly of simple forest-dwelling vanaras, vastly inferior in size and strength. Yet somehow, they continued to triumph. Ravana called an emergency meeting with his top advisors. One of his strategists offered a striking insight: "It is not physical strength that drives them — it is their love for Rama. That devotion multiplies their power. If we wish to defeat them, we must break their spirit." The advisor proposed a psychological attack. Hundreds of Ravana's soldiers would disguise themselves as vanaras and secretly join Rama's army. At the right moment, Ravana would fire a special weapon toward Rama that would create a massive flash of light, making it appear as though Rama had been engulfed in flames and fatally wounded. At that instant, the disguised soldiers would scatter in panic, shouting "Mare Ram! Mare Ram!" meaning "Rama is dead!" The sudden shock and confusion, the advisors believed, would paralyze Rama's army with fear, giving Ravana the perfect opportunity to strike. Though unorthodox, the plan was approved.

The next day, everything unfolded as planned. Ravana shot the weapon, and a blinding flash surrounded Rama. Immediately, the disguised soldiers ran in all directions, screaming "Mare Ram! Mare Ram!" Chaos spread like wildfire. Rama's army, unsure of what had happened, began to panic. But Hanuman, ever alert and close to Rama, quickly saw through the illusion. Rama was perfectly fine; the weapon had caused no harm. Hanuman realized the chant of "Mare Ram" was disorienting the vanaras and draining their spirit. He had only seconds to act. Amid the confusion, Hanuman leapt to a high point and began shouting at the top of his voice: "Mere Ram! Mere Ram!" meaning "My Rama! My Rama!" He timed his cries perfectly to align with the disguised soldiers's cries of "Mare ram!" The difference was just a syllable but the effect was profound. The vanaras, hearing Hanuman's voice, began to echo the chant. The fearful cry of "Mare Ram" was soon replaced by the devotional roar of "Mere Ram." The sound spread like wildfire, igniting the hearts of Rama's army once more. The power of Rama's name, especially when chanted by Hanuman with love and strength, was irresistible. Even the disguised rakshasas unknowingly began chanting

"Mere Ram." So overwhelming was the collective energy that they forgot their allegiance and merged with Rama's forces. The sky shook with the thunderous chant of "Mere Ram!" Ravana's approaching army, hearing it, began to waver. Before they could regroup, the energized vanaras launched a fierce counterattack, completely overpowering them. Ravana was left dumbfounded. "How did my flawless plan not just fail but double the strength of Rama's army?" he asked. What he didn't know was that his defeat came not from might, but from the quickwittedness of Hanuman; he turned fear into strength, panic into devotion, and confusion into clarity all by changing one syllable. That is why the verse refers to Hanuman as ati chatur — one who is exceptionally wise and smart.

Ever Eager to Perform Rama's Work

The next line of the verse reads: ramkaj karibe ko atur — one who is eager to carry out Lord Rama's work. This line highlights the significance of ramkaj (actions performed in service of Rama). The idea is to convert mundane activities into actions dedicated to the Divine or Guru.

By Amma's grace, I was able to spend about four months in Amritapuri after a long time, while completing this book. For most of my ashram life, I've been in one of Amma's organizations away from Amritapuri. I first asked Amma if I could join the ashram as a brahmachari when I was eleven years old. Amma said yes but she asked me to study at Amma's school in Kodungallur, about four hours from Amritapuri. Most of the ashram children studied there as the school near Amritapuri wasn't functional at the time. A year later, I again asked Amma if I could move to Amritapuri. Amma asked me to continue staying in Kodungallur. After high school, she wanted me to pursue my studies at Amma's college in Ettimadai, around six hours away. The engineering college in Amritapuri hadn't been established yet. Though I got to stay in Amritapuri for about four years after my graduation, most of that time I was still traveling back and forth to

Ettimadai for research work. Eventually, Amma sent me to North America. I've asked Amma a few times about my fate being physically away from her. Amma would simply say, "Why do you think you are away from me when you are doing what I've asked you to do? You are doing Amma's work."

I was blessed to be in Amritapuri for six months during the pandemic in 2020, but my visit to Amritapuri in 2025, for about four months, was especially meaningful. I got to serve as the primary harmonium player during Amma's bhajans, translate for Amma when guests came to meet her, and assist during Amma's darshan. Who would want to leave all this and return to North America? To be honest, I was dreading the day Amma would bring up the topic of going back. And then, that day arrived. Amma asked, "Aren't you doing satsang programs in North America?" I replied, "Not in the last four months." She said, "You need to return and get back to your responsibilities there." I tried to give Amma reasons to stay. "But I need to be here to play harmonium for Amma," I said. Amma smiled and replied, "That's okay. One of the other brahmacharis can manage the harmonium while you are away. And you can come back if a tour happens." Then she added, "Your responsibilities there are more important. It's like playing the harmonium too. You need to keep everyone in the ashrams and satsangs there in tune and rhythm. So, you are still playing harmonium for Amma."

For each one of us missing Amma's physical presence, Amma reminds us that if we keep Amma and Amma's thoughts in mind, our day-to-day activities will become meaningful. Like ramkaj, bringing Amma's presence into everything we do will make it Amma's work.

During one of Amma's talks on her 2018 tour, she shared an example of a doctor who was particularly short-tempered and not always pleasant to his patients. Once, he was so impatient that it almost led to the patient's death. He felt so bad that he mentioned it to Amma. Amma gave him a simple but effective solution. Amma asked him to deal with the patients with the firm belief that they were sent by Amma. His attitude towards the patients changed. The change in him made things so much easier for him and his patients. This shift in perspective transformed his mundane work into meaningful service.

Similarly, we can practice sadhana (spiritual practice) in whatever mundane activity we are involved in. For example, when driving, we can practice traffic sadhana. We might disregard traffic rules, the stop sign, or conveniently treat the red or the yellow traffic light as a green signal. But imagine driving with Amma in the car. The presence of Amma would make one more careful and respectful of the traffic rules (we wouldn't want to get pulled over by the police with Amma in the car!) In this way, imagining that we are driving with Amma transforms the act of driving into a spiritual practice. Bringing Amma, Rama, or our beloved deity into the equation for whatever deed we perform, any seemingly mundane deed can become a meaningful spiritual practice.

Amma herself exemplified this approach as a child. Due to the ill health of Amma's biological mother, Amma had to drop out of school in the 5th grade. She had to take care of household chores like cooking food for all, doing dishes, washing clothes, cleaning the house, taking care of the family cattle, and much more. It was too much for any individual to manage all these responsibilities on their own, and we are talking about a nine-year-old girl doing all these activities. But Amma could attend to all these activities with joy. How? Because she imagined that she was washing Lord Krishna's clothes, cooking for Krishna, cleaning the house for Krishna's arrival, and attending to Krishna's cows. Amma teaches us by example that this mindset can make even the most strenuous and mundane tasks blissful rather than burdensome. Hanuman also exemplifies this attitude. He was always dedicated to serving Rama, embodying the transformation of selfish and mundane deeds into ramkaj.

Insights on the Path of Bhakti from verses 6 & 7:

- Selfish motives can turn even our best efforts into unfavorable outcomes.

- Be truthful to yourself - deceiving the conscience is meaningless and unfruitful.

- Act per what the guru and scriptures teach us.

- Dedicate your actions to the guru/lord. Even mundane actions become meaningful then.

- Work smarter, not harder - assess the context of the situation with wisdom before taking action, considering the bigger picture.

Verse 8

Ever in remembrance of the Lord
Imbibe the Lord within
Live as an example

prabhu charitra sunibē kō rasiyā | प्रभु चरित्र सुनिबे को रसिया।
rāmalakhana sītā mana basiyā ‖ 8 ‖   राम लखन सीता मन बसिया ॥

prabhu - lord; charitra - story/history; sunibē kō - to hear;
rasiyā - one who enjoys; rāma - Lord Rama; lakhana - Brother
Lakshmana; sītā - Mother Sita; mana - mind; basiyā - reside.

You enjoy listening to Lord Rama's stories and divine plays;
Lord Rama, Lakshman, and Sita reside in your heart.

Reveling in the stories of Rama

Lord Hanuman is described as - prabhu charitra sunibeko rasiya -
one who is always interested in hearing the tales of Lord Rama and is
constantly immersed in remembering him. Hanuman is enthralled by
discussing and listening to stories about Lord Rama. It is believed even
today that when you discuss *Ramayana*, Lord Hanuman is present there.

There is a popular verse in praise of Lord Hanuman, underlining
his dedication towards Lord Rama:

yatra yatra raghunātha kīrtanam, tatra tatra kṛta mastakānjalim
bhāshpavāri paripūrṇa lochanam mārutim namata
rākshasāntakam

Wherever there is praise of Lord Rama sung, in every such occasion, with his head bowed in respect and humility and eyes brimming with tears of joy, is Sri Hanuman - the annihilator of demons (negativities); we bow down to him.

I'm sure many of us can relate to this. When we gather together, even in a non-satsang setting, and someone starts a story about Amma, it often triggers a chain reaction. The stories continue, and we lose track of time, captivated by the beauty and inspiration of these tales. I've experienced this many times. After a long day, I might decide to rest early, but it's hard to stop once an Amma story starts. One story leads to another, and before you know it, hours have passed. I constantly receive requests for Amma stories from satsang attendees and even feedback during scriptural discussions that I share as many Amma stories as possible. It emphasizes how these stories resonate deeply with all and create a positive impact.

In this regard, there is a beautiful folklore tale about an instance during the battle in Lanka when Hanuman came to the rescue of Rama and Lakshmana. Sage Narada, deeply impressed and pleased by Hanuman's heroics, showered him with praise, recounting all the details of the rescue. He then said to Hanuman, "Ask me for a boon." Hanuman humbly responded, "Could you please repeat the incident again?" Narada joyfully narrated the entire sequence of how Hanuman had rescued Rama and Lakshmana. At the end, he again offered, "Ask me for a boon." Hanuman once more asked, "Could you please repeat the incident?" Narada smiled and recounted it again. But after several repetitions, he grew puzzled. "Why do you keep asking me to retell the story?" he asked. "Why not just ask for a boon?" Hanuman bowed and said, "That is the only boon I seek - to hear the stories of Rama again and again. Listening to Rama's glories, Rama katha, is all I desire. Though it may appear as if I rescued Rama and Lakshmana, I know clearly that it was all his divine play. I was only an instrument in his hands. What greater blessing could there be than to keep hearing the divine stories of my Lord?"

Hanuman is the perfect example of someone who ever revels in the remembrance of Lord Rama — not just mechanically, but with deep devotion and joy. When we say, "Hanuman is constantly immersed in remembrance of Lord Rama," it doesn't just mean Hanuman is thinking about Rama but that he is imbibing Rama's qualities within, so that he can think, speak, and act like Rama. He is not merely listening to Rama's stories but exercising Rama's virtues in every moment of his life. That's why Hanuman himself is so inspiring.

When we talk about Amma or share Amma stories for hours, it becomes even more meaningful when the discussions lead to something tangible. Simply recounting the experiences is nice. But, if we draw inspiration from Amma stories and strive to imbibe the qualities of Amma that we discuss, the discussion becomes even more purposeful. If we don't aim to grow spiritually from these stories, then we haven't gotten the full benefit of these conversations. True spiritual growth happens when these stories touch our hearts and inspire us to put their lessons into action. Following in the footsteps of the deity or Guru we revere is true worship. Hanuman set this example as Lord Rama's perfect devotee, and today, he is worshipped alongside Rama. Similarly, if we are devoted to Amma, and we strive to embody Amma's qualities, each of us can ourselves become an inspiring example for others. In this context, it is worth remembering Amma's insight that whether we know it or not, we are all a role model for at least one other person. Someone else is looking up to us and following our example. Keeping in this in mind, let us allow Amma to inspire us to become the best possible role model.

The Lord Dwells in Your Heart, and You Dwell in the Lord's Heart

The second part of the eighth verse says that Lord Rama, Sita, and Lakshmana all dwell within Hanuman's heart. This aligns with his prayer, in which he asked for nothing but the constant remembrance of Rama.

Perhaps one of the most iconic stories of Hanuman, relevant to this verse, highlights his unwavering devotion and dedication to Lord Rama. While this incident isn't found in the major versions of the *Ramayana*, it is widely known and deeply inspiring to many. After the war in Lanka, a grand coronation ceremony was held in Ayodhya, where Lord Rama and Mother Sita were declared king and queen. Vibhishana, now crowned king of Lanka, presented Lord Rama with an exquisitely precious necklace. Rama graciously accepted it and requested Vibhishana to offer it to Mother Sita. Sita, in turn, said that such a valuable gift should be given to someone truly special. Everyone grew curious — who would be honored with such a gesture? She then called Hanuman to step forward.

At the time, the people of Ayodhya were unfamiliar with Hanuman's contributions — there was no live news coverage of the war back then. Lord Rama began praising Hanuman, recounting his courage, loyalty, and the crucial role he played throughout the war. Moved by his greatness, Sita handed the necklace to Hanuman. This was one of the greatest honors one could receive. But what Hanuman did next puzzled everyone. He respectfully accepted the necklace, sat in a corner, and began examining each bead. Then, one by one, he started biting into the beads and breaking them open. These were precious stones, gifts fit for royalty, and yet Hanuman was crushing them and discarding them. His behavior shocked many, and some even began to ridicule him, thinking he was being disrespectful.

Lord Rama, understanding the people's confusion, allowed Hanuman to explain himself. Rama asked, "Hanuman, why are you breaking apart such a priceless necklace?" Hanuman replied, "Everyone here seems to think this necklace is so valuable. I assumed it must contain Rama within it — so I searched. But I couldn't find Rama. I thought maybe Rama was hidden inside each bead, so I broke them open. But he wasn't there either. If Rama isn't in it, I don't see why it's considered so precious." Vibhishana, surprised, asked, "Then why do you carry and take care of your own body? Is Rama present in that too?" Hanuman responded, "Yes, Rama resides within me." "Then prove it," Vibhishana said. To everyone's astonishment, Hanuman calmly tore open his chest and there, within, shining with divine brilliance, were the images of Rama and Sita, seated in his heart.

Hanuman has often been depicted with his chest open, revealing Rama and Sita within. The image is not just symbolic; it expresses the depth of his devotion. His heart was their temple, and they lived within him always.

Beyond this incident, Hanuman always exhibited Rama within him through his conduct and qualities. When we say the Lord resides in us, it's not that if we take an X-ray or MRI scan, we will see the Lord in the image. The qualities, virtues, and character of the Lord should reside in every bit of us — in our thoughts, words, and actions. We should become a walking shrine of those divine qualities. Others should feel the Lord's presence through our conduct.

"Ram lakhan sita man basiya" could also be interpreted as "one who dwells in Rama, Lakshmana, and Sita's heart." Devotion is not just about keeping the Lord within oneself; Hanuman shows that true devotion can be so profound that it captures the Lord's attention, leading to the devotee dwelling in the Lord's mind.

In her New Year's talk in 2023, Amma mentioned an incident involving one of her devotees from the U.S. She spoke about how a child threw up during darshan. One of Amma's children immediately removed his shirt to clean the place without hesitation, not caring that his shirt might be ruined. Amma was deeply moved by his attitude, presence of mind, and selfless act. Although this happened years ago, Amma still remembers it. This is an example of how a devotee can dwell in the heart of the guru or the Lord. Our actions should be such that they capture the attention of our guru.

The above example shows how our actions should resonate with the Guru or the Lord. It's not just about making space for the Lord to dwell in our hearts; our actions should be such that they draw the Lord's attention to us. Amma gives the analogy of grace as a river that keeps flowing, and our actions should be like digging a pit near the river, naturally drawing the water into it. As aspirants on the path of devotion, our actions should be such that they make us deserving of the Guru's grace, literally pulling the grace towards us.

Insights on the Path of Bhakti from verse 8:
- Rather than just glorifying the lord/guru through stories, draw inspiration, imbibe those qualities, and live as an example. That is true worship.

Verses 9 and 10

Adapt to any given situation
Exercise strength, not arrogance
Humility is the sign of a devotee

sūkṣma rūpadhari siyahi dikhāvā ǀ	सूक्ष्म रूप धरि सियहिं दिखावा।
vikaṭa rūpadhari laṅka jarāvā ǁ 9 ǁ	विकट रूप धरि लंक जरावा॥

sūkṣma - subtle; rūpa - form; dhari - having assumed;
siyahi - to Mother Sita; dikhāvā - to show; vikaṭa -
enormous; rūpa - form; dhari - having assumed; laṅka
- the kingdom of Lanka; jarāvā - burned, set on fire.

You assumed the smallest of the forms as you visited Mother Sita.
Then, assuming a gigantic form, you burnt down the capital of Lanka.

bhīma rūpadhari asura saṃhārē ǀ	भीम रूप धरि असुर संहारे।
rāmachandra kē kāja saṃvārē ǁ 10 ǁ	रामचंद्र के काज संवारे॥

bhīma - strong and big; rūpa - form; dhari - having
assumed; asura - demon; saṃhārē - vanquish; rāmachandra
kē - Lord Rama's; kāja - work; saṃvārē - carry out.

Assuming the all-powerful form, you slayed the demons. Your
efforts facilitated and helped achieve Lord Rama's task.

Hanuman is described here as the one who assumes the subtlest of
forms, the largest of forms, and the most ferocious of forms to perform

Lord Rama's work and fulfill Lord Rama's objectives. In reflecting on these verses, then, we discuss Hanuman's incredible ability to assume various forms.

In Indian scriptures, there is a reference to the ashta siddhis, which are eight supernatural abilities. They are:

1. anima: the ability to become as small as possible

2. mahima: the ability to become as large as possible

3. garima: the ability to become heavy

4. lagima: the ability to become light

5. prapti: the ability to attain or reach anything desired

6. prakamya: the ability to fulfill desires

7. ishitva: the ability to control things and natural forces

8. vashitva: the ability to influence others

One of the later verses describes Lord Hanuman as being endowed with and bestower of the eight siddhis and the nine nidhis (precious treasures). Hanuman is renowned for possessing these eight siddhis, making him a figure of immense power and spiritual significance.

As much as these abilities may sound supernatural and mystical, they are practical things that we often engage in. For example, consider anima (becoming the smallest of the small); in the field of nanotechnology we're trying to achieve with smaller particles what we typically do with large ones — mimicking the abilities of big things on a subatomic level. Similarly, with semiconductors, we are constantly striving to miniaturize big circuits into infinitesimal ones. At times we need to become the smallest of the small to achieve the biggest of objectives.

Spiritually, anima (becoming the smallest of the small) and lagima (becoming as light as possible) signify minimizing our ego — making it as small and light as possible. This is a crucial aspect of spiritual growth. However, making our ego small and light doesn't mean we should give in or back down in situations that require us to face challenges. Mahima (becoming the biggest of the big) and garima (becoming dense and strong) remind us that we must assert ourselves when necessary. We need to exercise authority and fulfill our dharma with strength and determination.

For instance, a soldier on the battlefield must embody mahima and garima by believing in their strength and ability to face the enemy. Similarly, in certain situations, we need to be assertive and strong. Thus, we should be able to let go of the ego completely when necessary and exercise it under the framework of dharma when required. A company's CEO doesn't need to boast about his power and authority. However, during a meeting, the CEO should act like a CEO and practice his authority — that's his dharma. It would be wrong to act weak and powerless. Therefore, we need mahima, garima, lagima, and anima in our lives, and we must apply them appropriately based on the situation.

When we talk about prapti, the ability to have access everywhere, we can think of remarkable feats like reaching Mars, the Moon, and even the outer parts of the solar system. However, the most important and challenging feat is reaching other people's hearts. In the first verse, we discussed Hanuman as a kingmaker, emphasizing how he rules everyone's heart rather than just a kingdom. His greatness lies in his access to people's hearts.

Gaining access to someone's heart is the most challenging task, as it involves dislodging their ego and taking space in their heart. Our actions should motivate, cultivate love, and garner admiration, allowing us to connect with their hearts. We must consistently behave in ways that enable this connection. Let's not dismiss it by convincing ourselves that it's unattainable. We have done this with our dear ones - our parents, siblings, best friends, partners, and spouses. They have trust in us such that they are ready to compromise on their ego (likes, dislikes, notions, etc.) to give us priority in their hearts.

In Chapter 6 of the *Bhagavad Gita*, the fifth verse begins with "uddharet ātmanātmānaṁ" - *elevate yourself through the means of your own self.* We need to respect and be mindful of every factor of the situations that we find ourselves in. But the most critical factor is our own self. Ruling our minds and senses equates to being the true ruler of the moment. When we achieve this, external disturbances no longer affect us, thus granting us the qualities of ishitva (lordship) and vashitva (control).

Hanuman embodied these eight siddhis. He could become as big and ferocious as needed while being the subtlest and humblest when required. Hanuman exemplified the balance of these ashta siddhis (eight abilities), and we should also strive to imbibe these qualities in our daily lives as much as possible.

Continuing with a story from the *Ramayana*, Hanuman journeyed from the southern tip of India to Lanka by flying over the Indian Ocean. This journey was not easy. The decision to send Hanuman instead of another capable monkey, Angada, was because Hanuman possessed physical strength and the mental fortitude to overcome obstacles that could capture the mind. During his journey, a mountain-like figure suddenly appeared before Hanuman enticing him to rest. It seemed like a good opportunity for respite, but Hanuman sensed it might be a trap and chose to continue, passing the first test.

Next, Surasa, in the form of a demoness, appeared and tried to stop him. She was enormous, and when Hanuman attempted to pass, she blocked his way. Surasa declared that she had a boon allowing her to eat anything she desired. If she wanted to eat Hanuman, he would have to enter her mouth. Hanuman was in a dilemma — who would find and rescue Mother Sita if he entered her mouth? But Hanuman, strong and clever, responded, "Let me first find Mother Sita, and then I'll return to enter your mouth." Surasa refused and demanded he enter her mouth immediately. Realizing he had to outsmart her, Hanuman asked her to open her mouth wide enough to fit his large body. As she did so, Hanuman expanded his form, growing larger and larger. Surasa matched his size by opening her mouth even more expansively.

When her mouth was fully open, Hanuman used his anima siddhi to shrink instantly to a tiny size, entered her mouth, and exited before she could close it. He triumphantly declared, "I fulfilled my promise and entered your mouth. But you couldn't close it in time so now I'm free to go." Surasa, returning to her normal form, acknowledged that she had been sent by the devas to test him. Hanuman had passed the test, demonstrating his clever use of mahima and anima to overcome the challenge.

Hanuman successfully entered Lanka and found Mother Sita. To navigate the palace, he sometimes had to become extremely small to slip through gaps between doors; and at other times, he took on a massive form to break through obstacles. These episodes from the *Ramayana* illustrate Hanuman's ability to adapt his size according to the situation. When he reached the Ashoka Vatika, where Mother Sita was held, he became as small and subtle as possible out of respect. He wanted Mother Sita to view him as a son, so he approached her in a humble form.

Later, when he was captured and his tail was set on fire, he assumed a fierce, massive form to spread flames across Lanka and turn the kingdom into a burning inferno. Many episodes in the *Ramayana* highlight how Hanuman could take on a ferocious form, bhimarupa, to confront demons and uphold dharma.

Why does Hanuman take on all these forms? The most important point is that he does not use these siddhis for himself. He uses them for ramachandra ke kaj — in service of Rama, with the firm belief that whatever Rama seeks to achieve is for upholding dharma. Hanuman's actions were not driven by personal gain or selfish motives; they were acts of selflessness to uphold dharma. This emphasizes that the ashta siddhis should not satisfy selfish desires but support righteousness.

Insights on the Path of Bhakti from verses 9 & 10:

- Face every situation with full might but with the understanding that what finally fetches victory is humility.

- Our strength should empower us, not make us arrogant.

- Adapt to any situation; be prepared to display humility or toughness as the circumstances require.

Verses 11, 12 and 13

Become deserving of the lord/guru's praise
Strive for the divine embrace (non-duality)

lāya sañjīvana lakhana jiyāyē । लाय सजीवन लखन जियाये ।
śrī raghuvīra haraṣi uralāyē ॥ 11 ॥ श्रीरघुबीर हरषि उर लाये ॥

lāya - having brought; sañjīvana - the life-saving Sanjivani
herb; lakhana - Lakshmana; jiyāyē - brought to life; śrī
raghuvīra - the revered hero of the Raghu dynasty (Lord
Rama); haraṣi - with joy; ura - chest/heart; lāyē - brought;

*You brought the whole mountain peak containing
Sanjeevini (medicinal herbs to bring back to life) to save
Lakshmana's life. Lord Rama embraced you in joy.*

raghupati kīnhī bahuta baḍāyī । रघुपति कीन्ही बहुत बड़ाई ।
tuma mama priya bharata sama bhāyī ॥12॥ तुम मम प्रिय भरतहि सम भाई ॥

raghupati - the lord of Raghu Dynasty (Lord Rama); kīnhī
- did; bahuta - a lot, very much; baḍāyī - praise; tuma
- yourself; mama - my; priya - dear; bharata - Bharata
(Rama's brother); sama - similar, equal; bhāyī - brother;

*Lord Rama had high praises for you. He exclaimed,
"You are dear to me like my brother Bharata."*

sahasa vadana tumharō yaśagāvai | सहस बदन तुम्हरो जस गावैं।
asa kahi śrīpati kaṇṭha lagāvai ॥ 13 ॥   अस कहि श्रीपति कंठ लगावैं॥

sahasa - thousand, numerous; vadana - faces/mouths; tumharō
- your; yaśa - glory; gāvai - sing; asa - likewise; kahi - having
said; śrīpati - husband of the Goddess of auspiciousness (Lord
Rama); kaṇṭha - throat/neck; lagāvai - place against (embrace);

Lord Rama embraced you, saying, "May the thousand-
headed serpent Adishesha sing of your glory."

These verses revolve around an incident recorded in *Ramayana*.
During the war, Lord Rama's brother, Lakshmana, is gravely injured
and rendered unconscious. On the advice of Lord Rama, Hanuman
swiftly springs into action and goes all the way north to the Himalayas
to fetch a particularly precious, life-saving herb which finally revives
Lakshmana. Lord Rama embraces Hanuman in joy, praising him and
saying "You are dear to me like my brother Bharata."

Let us begin our exploration of these verses then by recounting
this incident in detail. The war between Lord Rama's monkey
army and Ravana's demon army was raging. One by one, Ravana
brought in his strongest allies, eventually sending his son, Indrajit, into
the battle. Indrajit was extremely capable, as conveyed by his name,
"one who conquered Indra, the king of the gods." He had defeated Indra
and possessed powerful boons, including one that allowed him to
camouflage himself with clouds and to create other illusions during
battle.

On the first day that Indrajit entered the war, he used a powerful weapon
called the naga-pasha astra, which bound Lord Rama and Lakshmana
with venomous snakes, rendering them helpless. Fortunately, Garuda,
the celestial eagle and Lord Vishnu's mount, came to their rescue,
freeing them from the snakes. Thinking he had won, Indrajit was
surprised to find them free the next day. He engaged Lakshmana in
battle again, using his illusionary powers to unsettle him. During the

duel, Indrajit struck Lakshmana in the chest with a powerful weapon blessed by Lord Brahma, causing Lakshmana to fall unconscious along with many other warriors. The weapon's curse dictated that the victim would die by sunrise. This brought fear among the monkey army and deflated their morale.

Some versions of the *Ramayana* describe how Jambavan, the bear, first checked to see whether Hanuman was safe. He was questioned by Angada and Sugriva as to why he was concerned about Hanuman alone when so many others had been gravely injured by Indrajit. Jambavan replied, "I am definitely concerned about all my dear fellow warriors. But only if Hanuman is conscious can they all be saved." He requested Hanuman to fetch Sushena, a physician who could save Lakshmana and the other warriors. In some versions of the story, Hanuman uprooted Sushena's entire house and brought it to the battlefield in his haste and love for Lakshmana and the other warriors. Sushena examined Lakshmana and declared that only a unique herb, mrita sanjivani, could save him. However, the herb was located in the Himalayas far to the north, and it had to be retrieved before sunrise to save Lakshmana's life. Hanuman, the only one capable of such a feat, set off on his mission, guided by Jambavan on how to find and identify the herb. Hanuman's journey was critical in ensuring that Lakshmana could be revived in time.

Four herbs needed to be brought. The first was mrita sanjivani, which, as mentioned, can revive someone critically injured or on the brink of death. The second was shalya karini, which helps heal wounds inflicted by deadly weapons. The third, suvarna karini, heals the skin from any wound, and the fourth, sandhani, heals broken or fractured bones. Sushena requested all four herbs, and Jambavan provided Hanuman with precise directions on where to find them. Hanuman quickly sprang into action, flying north, crossing the Indian Ocean, and passing through southern and central India. Along the way, he had to face many challenges and obstacles set by Ravana and his allies, but he successfully overcame them in order to return before sunrise.

Upon reaching Mount Dronagiri, where the herbs were located, Hanuman saw that it contained various herbs and became concerned about identifying the correct ones in time. Knowing he was on a time-sensitive mission and could not afford to make a mistake, Hanuman decided to uproot the entire mountain and carry it back in order to ensure he would have the right herbs. He carried the mountain back to Lanka, where Lakshmana lay unconscious. Some accounts say that even Surya Deva, the Sun God, assisted Hanuman in his mission by rising a little late that day. Hanuman returned to Lanka in time, saving Lakshmana's life. The herbs were also used to revive the other members of the monkey army, bringing them all back to life.

Lord Rama was so overjoyed and grateful to Hanuman that he embraced him in a moment of pure joy. The *Ramayana* describes how Lord Rama, overwhelmed with happiness, hugged Hanuman and praised him for his selfless deed. Hanuman's efforts to save Lakshmana and the other monkey warriors was not driven by personal gain, but by deep faith and selflessness.

Praise from the Lord

Rama tells Hanuman that he is as precious to him as his own brother Bharata. He hugs Hanuman tightly and says, "May you be praised by everyone for your deeds and for who you are." These verses of the *Hanuman Chalisa* convey Rama's deep appreciation and love for Hanuman, highlighting the significance of Hanuman's actions.

Being praised by the guru or the Lord is one of the greatest blessings because a guru often hesitates to praise a disciple. The reason is that praise can inflate the disciple's ego, the biggest hurdle on the spiritual path. Therefore, if a disciple is not ready or does not have control over their ego, the guru is cautious in offering praise.

There is a story that Amma often shares about a person who was searching for a guru. When he finally found a revered guru, he asked to be accepted as a disciple. The guru responded, "I can't accept you just like that. I need to know who you are, what you know, and what you don't know. Only then can I accept you as my disciple. So, do one thing: write down everything you know and bring it to me." The man took a year to write a series of books, as he had learned so much. He returned to the guru with the books, expecting to be accepted. The guru quickly skimmed through them, appearing unimpressed. He said, "This is all very wordy gibberish. Can you make it more precise?" Disheartened, the man took another three years to condense the content into a single book. When he returned, the guru skimmed through it again and said, "Too wordy, too disorganized. Make it into a five-page abstract." Now even more disheartened, the man took ten more years to reduce the content to five pages. He brought it back, but the guru, still unimpressed, asked for a one-page summary. The man spent years condensing it further, and when he finally returned, he handed the guru a blank page. The guru smilved and said, "Now you are ready to become my disciple." The guru always observes how boastful or egoistic we are and works to counteract that. When

Rama praises Hanuman, it shows that Hanuman has his ego under control.

Speaking of ego, I recall an experience during the Europe tour a few years ago. Swamiji usually leads the first session of bhajans during Devi Bhava, but he wasn't there for the London program. After a couple of bhajan sessions, Amma told me that she felt a little tired and dissatisfied and asked me to go and sing for an hour. I felt so proud that Amma asked me to sing so that she could feel rejuvenated. My ego was definitely swelling as I went to sing, and the session went quite well, adding to my ego. There were several groups scheduled to sing. Because I was squeezed in for an hour, all the other groups had their time reduced and were pushed down the list. Some members of the bhajan groups, who were initially upset about their time being cut, came up to us afterward and said that our bhajan session went so well that they thought their sessions being shortened was worth it. My ego swelled even more. A brahmachari standing next to Amma came up to me and said, "Amma kept praising you while you were singing, saying how content she feels now after hearing you." My ego was now fully inflated, almost ready to burst. Later, I went to stand near Amma for translation. I expected Amma to turn to me and say, "Wow, you had such an awesome session, I'm feeling much better." Instead, Amma looked at me and remarked, "I have such a severe headache, and this guy kept singing more and more songs, making my headache even worse." A guru does not unnecessarily praise a disciple. The guru's main role is not to inflate our ego, but to chip away at it. Though we don't always realize it, the ego is ultimately the cause of all our suffering.

In this context, however, Lord Rama goes beyond those norms, not just praising Hanuman but doing so effusively. This shows how prepared Hanuman is. Rama recognizes Hanuman's control over his ego, which is why Rama praises him without hesitation. The takeaway here is that as a spiritual aspirant, we should make ourselves deserving of the Guru's praises. That happens when we genuinely let go of our ego - our likes/dislikes, expectations, notions and pride.

Equating to Brother Bharata

Lord Rama tells Hanuman "You are so special that you are like my brother Bharata," underscoring how much he values Hanuman's selfless contribution. The question may arise: why did Rama not compare Hanuman to Lakshmana, who was always by Rama's side and served him? Rama, being a purnavatara (complete incarnation) of Lord Vishnu, was beyond likes and dislikes and loved all his brothers equally. However, Bharata was physically away from Rama, ruling Ayodhya having placed Rama's sandals on the throne and refusing to take the throne himself. This act of sacrifice and devotion while being physically away, made Rama remember Bharata often, so he spontaneously compared his feelings for Hanuman to his feelings toward Bharata rather than those for Lakshmana.

In Amritapuri, the swamis and brahmacharis sometimes joke that it's a blessing to be away from Amma. While in Amritapuri, they sometimes find it challenging to get access to Amma. However, those away from the ashram are often remembered, called, or spoken about by Amma, giving them more frequent interactions with her. A similar thing happened during the inaugurations of Amrita Hospital in Faridabad (on the outskirts of Delhi, India) in August 2022. Since I had traveled internationally, I decided not to go near Amma, thinking it was safer given the risk of COVID-19 infection then. A couple of times, when Amma was passing by, she called me over and asked why I hadn't come closer. I explained that I wanted to keep her safe, and she just said I was being crazy. I only had two brief encounters with Amma during those days. But then, a few days later, I contracted dengue fever and was quarantined. Once Amma found out, she called me twice a day for the next five or six days, checking in on how I was doing. Sometimes the calls came at 3 AM, other times at 1 PM, but she didn't let even half a day pass by without calling me. This was in the midst of all the important things Amma had to do managing the inauguration of India's largest private hospital by the Prime Minister of India. Selfishly, I thought to myself, "It's almost good that I got dengue!" Otherwise, I would have only seen Amma briefly here and there. But because of the fever, Amma called me regularly, and I got to speak to her more often than I would have otherwise.

It's not that Amma, in remembering those who are away from her, is bound by attachment or likes and dislikes; it's just that when you're away, she wants to make sure you're okay and reaches out more often. Similar may be the reason Rama remembered Bharata instead of Lakshmana when he praised Hanuman.

Then Rama says, "Let innumerable mouths sing your praise." This reminds me of the way Amma sees only goodness in each one of us. And although Amma herself is beyond the need for praise, it's evident that she becomes happy when she hears one of her children being praised for an inspiring or selfless action. Amma often mentions that our conduct should be such that it inspires others and deserves praise. When Lord Rama says, "Let a thousand mouths sing your praises," it means that Hanuman became deserving of that praise through his qualities, and Rama was issuing a blessing that he may ever remain so.

As spiritual aspirants, the takeaway here is that our words, thoughts, and actions should be filled with patience, understanding, acceptance, awareness, humility, love, compassion, and other such virtues. When we embody these qualities, people will naturally praise us — not for our wealth, talents, or achievements, but for our character. Such praise doesn't lead to ego but instead reinforces our good qualities.

Rama embracing Hanuman is highlighted here because it was not common for Rama to embrace someone. It was a unique blessing for Hanuman. Thus, the few times Rama embraced someone, including Hanuman, are noted for their importance. Having reached the ultimate spiritual state, Hanuman received Rama's embrace multiple times for his good deeds.

We are blessed to have a guru like Amma, who embraces us whether we do good deeds or not. It's important not to take Amma's embrace for granted but to recognize its significance. We should live up to Amma's message and not let her embrace be in vain. When Amma is asked how she can embrace so many people joyfully, despite the physical toll it takes on her, she explains that she sees herself in everyone and everyone in herself. This feeling of oneness eliminates Amma's identification with any pain she experiences in the process of embracing others hour after hour, day after day. Amma's embrace itself symbolizes this oneness, the acceptance of everyone without distinction, and the unconditional love that Amma embodies. It represents becoming one with the Divine, where there is no duality, only unity.

So while Amma doesn't demand anything of us, as spiritual aspirants we should strive to purify our thoughts, words and actions such that we make ourselves deserving of praise from our Guru or Lord, and elevate ourselves such that we become established in a divine embrace, one with the Guru or Supreme.

Here are a couple of fun facts related to the geography mentioned in the story of Hanuman carrying the mountain. As the story goes, Hanuman traveled to the Himalayas in North India, uprooted a large part of the Dronagiri mountain, and brought it to Sri Lanka. This event occurred thousands of years ago, yet we can find signs of this incident in modern geography.

In the Himalayan range in the state of Uttarakhand, there is a location where people pay their respects to Hanuman. This is believed to be where Hanuman obtained the sanjivani herb. The geographical layout of the region features a trough, which appears to have been created by a significant landslide, possibly corresponding to Hanuman's uprooting of the mountain.

On the Sri Lankan side, in the southern district of Galle, there is a coastal town with a mountain called Rumassala. This mountain is peculiar regarding its vegetation, soil, stones, and even its fauna, which are different from those in the surrounding region. This anomaly suggests that this mountain may have been transported from a foreign land. The renowned English science fiction writer Arthur C. Clarke noted that the magnetic properties of this mountain are inconsistent

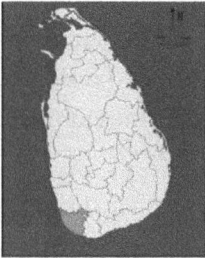

Galle District - Sri Lanka

Rumassala Mountain Unwantuna Town

Hanuman Shrine Rumassala Mountain

with the surrounding area, similar to the effects of a meteor strike. This further supports the belief that a part of Dronagiri fell there with great force.

These fun facts help us wrap our heads around the idea of Hanuman bringing a mountain from one country to another without being stopped at customs! Additionally, at Rumassala, there is a shrine dedicated to Hanuman

where people pay their respects. This shrine adds to the historical and spiritual significance of the location.

Another similar spot is Maruthuva Malai near Kanyakumari on the southern tip of India. This rugged mountain overflows with medicinal plants and is a vital source of Ayurvedic curative herbs. It is believed that Maruthuva Malai is a section of the Dronagiri mountain that dropped at that spot when Lord Hanuman flew over while carrying the mountain to Lanka. In April 1984, Amma visited this mountain with the earliest ashram residents. Amma's visit to the place is recorded in Awaken Children, volume 4, page 51.

Insights on the Path of Bhakti from verses 11, 12 &13:

- Be prepared for the guru to point out our ego often and seldom praise us.
- However, our thoughts, speech, and actions should be such that they deserve the guru's praise.
- Strive for the divine embrace, becoming one with the Lord and established in the state of non-duality.

Verses 14 and 15

Humility is the way
Grace - making every factor conducive
Be established in one's own Self

sanakādika brahmādi munīśā ।   सनकादिक ब्रह्मादि मुनीशा।
nārada śārada sahita ahīśā ॥ 14 ॥   नारद सारद सहित अहीसा॥

sanakādika - Sanaka and the divine brothers; brahmādi - the Trinity, Brahma, Vishnu, and Shiva; munīśā - the best of the sages; nārada - Sage Narada; śārada - Goddess of knowledge; sahita - including; ahīśā - Adishesha, the serpentine demi-God;

Sanaka and other Sages, Lord Brahma and other Gods, Narada, Devi Saraswati and Seshnag (the king of the serpents)…

jama kubēra digapāla jahāṃ tē ।   जम कुबेर दिगपाल जहां ते।
kavi kōvida kahi sakē kahāṃ tē ॥ 15 ॥   कवि कोविद कहि सके कहाँ ते॥

jama - Yama, the lord of Dharma and death; kubēra - kubera, the lord of wealth; digapāla - the presiding deities of each direction; jahāṃ tē - from wherever; kavi - poet; kōvida - the learned one; kahi sakē - about to speak or express; kahāṃ tē - where from;

…Yama, Kubera, Dig-paalakas (protectors of each of the directions), poets, and singers; they all fall short of praising you to the fullest of your greatness.

These two verses list several names of those who have showered limitless praises on Hanuman. Let's first explore the personalities mentioned, and then delve into their spiritual significance.

Sanaka and Others

The verses begin with the term "Sanaka and others," which refers to the four sages known as the Kumara brothers: Sanaka, Sanandana, Sanatana, and Sanat Kumara. These brothers are embodiments of wisdom and knowledge, having taken a vow of celibacy and remaining eternally youthful.

According to tradition, the Kumara brothers were born from the mind of Lord Brahma, representing pure knowledge. Unlike other creations intended to propagate further, they chose to dedicate themselves entirely to preserving and spreading the ultimate knowledge found in the Vedas. They are said to have received their wisdom from Dakshinamurthy, a form of Lord Shiva, who imparted this knowledge in complete silence. Despite their unparalleled wisdom, even these exalted sages acknowledge that their praises of Hanuman are insufficient. The term sanakadhika emphasizes that even the greatest knowers of truth cannot fully encapsulate Hanuman's divine glory.

Brahma and others

The next term is brahmadi, which refers to Brahma and others. Brahma the creator is part of the Trinity alongside Vishnu the preserver and Shiva the destroyer. These three fundamental aspects of existence — Generation, Organization, and Dissolution — verily define God, the force behind the three fundamental principles of creation. Even these highest deities, the Trinity, find themselves unable to adequately praise Hanuman; they fall short of words to capture his glory.

Munisa

Following this, the term munisa refers to the sages and seers of ancient times. To be precise, it refers to the term isa - the best amongst the sages and seers. These highly evolved souls, some of whom were celibate while others were householders, were intensely focused on the pursuit of ultimate truth alone. Their appreciation was reserved for only the highest truth, yet even they find themselves lacking the words to fully praise Hanuman.

Narada

Next is Narada, also referred to as Brahmarishi. A brahmarishi is a sage or seer who has attained the supreme level of spiritual enlightenment. Narada is considered one of the highest among all sages, and the *Puranas* describe him as someone who could easily walk into the abodes of Lord Shiva, Vishnu, and Brahma, and converse with them. This accessibility reflects his spiritual purity, allowing him to connect with the Divine without any barriers.

Narada is known as the epitome of devotion, particularly for his deep bhakti. He authored the *Narada Bhakti Sutra*, a text that reveals the secrets of devotion. Narada is typically depicted holding a veena, a grand musical instrument called Mahati, which symbolizes his mastery of all 64 forms of art. He also carries a kartal, a small wooden percussion instrument used to create rhythm during the chanting of divine names, representing his constant remembrance of the Divine. Despite his immense knowledge and devotion, even Narada finds himself falling short of words to fully praise Hanuman.

Sharada

The next name mentioned is Sharada or Goddess Saraswati, the embodiment of knowledge. Saraswati represents the entirety of knowledge in creation. Even she falls short of having enough words to praise Hanuman. The image below highlights the significance of the form of Mother Saraswati. She embodies the all-encompassing, ultimate knowledge. Tulasidasi says that even this entirety of knowledge

Rosary Beads
Constant, steadfast effort
Shraddha – One pointedness

Vedas (Scriptures)
Represents ultimate knowledge – Supreme Truth
We should behold the TRUTH
in every action, every moment.

Peacock
Peacock represents beauty
Inner beauty – maturity out of wisdom
Peacock shows off its beauty only in specific situation

Veena (Musical instrument)
Given highest of regards amongst musical instruments
Tune our mind, like the strings on Veena

Lotus Seat
Divine resides in a completely blossomed heart
Understand and accept everyone

Swan
Represents Viveka and Vairagya
Right discernment and dispassion
Swan (mythological) has the ability
to separate the water from the milk

White Color
White represents purity
White reflects every color frequency
Love and serve others with knowledge you gain

cannot fully express Hanuman's greatness.

Ahisa (Adishesha)

Then comes Adisesha, also referred to as Shesha or Sheshanaga and sometimes as Ananta. Adisesha is the serpent with numerous heads, the king or lord of all serpents, as well as the ruler of all creatures that reside beneath the Earth's surface (patala loka). He is typically

depicted as supporting Lord Vishnu, who is shown lying on Adisesha in Yoganidra, the ultimate state of bliss or detachment. Adisesha symbolizes the foundation of existence, carrying the weight of the universe. With his thousand hooded faces, Adisesha can bring out a thousand expressions at once. Even that volume is not sufficient to fully describe the glory of Hanuman.

Jama (Yama)

Then comes Yama, also known as Kala. Yama is the lord of death, and Kala in Sanskrit translates to time. Yama is not a cruel god; instead, he embodies time itself. Everything in creation is a function of time: birth, growth, decay, and eventually death. Yama represents this inevitable passage of time, which is why he is called Kala. Yama is punctual and unwavering in his duties. When

the time arrives, there are no exceptions; his role is to ensure that all things reach their destined end right on time. This precision of Yama is typically recalled humorously by elders in Indian families. As a child, I remember hearing that the lord of rain and thunder, Lord Indra, may be late or elusive as weather forecasts are often consistently inconsistent. However, Yama is not like this. He is always on schedule, reflecting the certainty and inevitability of time. He is usually referred to as Dharma-Deva - the deity of dharma. He acts per dharma with no leniency whatsoever. And this very lord of dharma finds Hanuman supremely praiseworthy.

Kubera

Kubera is the next deity mentioned here. Kubera is the lord of material wealth and prosperity and is also referred to as the lord of the yakshas, the semi-divine beings. He represents material prosperity and abundance. Kubera is often depicted alongside Goddess Lakshmi, the goddess of prosperity, and Lord Ganesha, the remover of obstacles. Together, they symbolize the flourishing of wealth, where obstacles are overcome, and prosperity thrives.

Digpala

Next, we have the Digpalas, or guardians and protectors of the directions. There are eight primary directions: North, South, East, West, Northeast, Southeast, Northwest, and Southwest, each guarded or presided over by a deity.

- Kubera, the lord of materialistic wealth and prosperity, guards the North.
- Yama, the lord of time and death, is the guardian of the South.
- Indra, the lord of the sky/weather, and king of the demigods, guards the East.
- Varuna, the lord of water (oceans, rain, etc.), guards the West.
- Ishana, a form of Lord Shiva (Rudra), guards the Northeast.
- Agni, the lord of fire, guards the Southeast.
- Vayu, the lord of wind, guards the Northwest.
- Nirriti, the lord of disintegration, guards the Southwest.

In puja and homa rituals, these directions are acknowledged and defined through specific mudras or hand gestures. The Digpalas are also depicted as being in constant praise of Hanuman, yet even they fall short in expressing his full glory.

Kavi and Kovid

Poets, scholars, and musicians all fall short of expressing the greatness of Hanuman through the medium of their talent and expertise.

Spiritual Significance of the Praises

Looking at it from a spiritual perspective, these deities and demigods don't need to praise anyone. Praise often serves a purpose, whether to gain favor or express admiration, but these divine beings are beyond such needs. However, Hanuman's greatness is such that even these beings do their best to fully praise him, and even then find themselves at a loss for words. And it isn't just about literal praise, but rather grace. Their grace naturally and unconditionally flows toward Hanuman. By making himself praiseworthy even by the gods, he himself becomes the embodiment of grace. When all the various factors in a given situation fall into place and are conducive to success, we can attribute this to divine grace. Hanuman shows us that a true devotee will have the grace manifested in all the possible factors. He was bestowed with the grace of ultimate knowledge (Sanaka and others); the ability to create, sustain and dissolve (Brahma and others); having complete control of a given situation right from its inception, sustenance, and cessation; arts, abilities, and devotion (Narada); penance and perseverance (Munisa); wisdom (Sharada); control over the lower tendencies, negativities, downward forces (Ahisa); time (Yama); auspiciousness and prosperity (Kubera); space, place (Digpal); expression and performance (Kavi); maturity and context (Kovid). Every factor becomes of service to a true devotee and flows into place in the form of grace.

Amma always says, "May divine grace protect you," and "May you have divine grace in any endeavor you undertake." One way of understanding that is all factors associated with a situation or task falling into place smoothly. When everything aligns perfectly, we say we have grace. Conversely, when one or more factors do not align, we experience a lack of grace. In essence, grace is the harmonious and favorable unfolding of circumstances, enabling success and well-being in our efforts.

When we wish someone a "safe journey" or say "happy journey," what we are really offering is a prayer for grace. This means we're hoping that all the factors associated with the journey fall into place smoothly. For example, if a person needs to catch a flight, their Uber driver should be alert and attentive; the car needs to be in good condition; drivers of every other vehicle on the road should drive safely and not cause an accident; the airport should be functioning normally without delays, the security personnel should be fully staffed and well coordinated; every seemingly insignificant screw/rivet on the airplane should be in place; the pilots and cabin crew should be healthy and punctual; the air traffic control unit should not be overwhelmed; and the weather should be conducive, just to name a few factors. All these elements, many of which are beyond our control, must align perfectly for a journey to be truly safe and uneventful. This alignment of circumstances is what we refer to as grace. When all these elements fall into place, we experience a smooth journey free of disruptions.

Similarly, when deities are depicted as praising Hanuman, it's symbolic of all these various factors (represented by the deities) coming together in harmony to ensure the smooth execution of a task or endeavor. These factors cannot help but favor Hanuman because he was constantly engaged in Lord Rama's work and executed his tasks with a selfless attitude.

In essence, the ability to manage all variables effectively makes one the master of that situation. Most people in India must be aware of Rajinikanth, a famous South Indian actor known for his larger-than-life roles. In his movies, he defies the laws of physics and reality. People humorously comment that there is nothing impossible for Rajinikanth.

There are a series of humorous Rajinikanth jokes that highlight his supposed superhuman abilities. For example, "Rajinikanth doesn't need a watch because he decides what time it is"; "Rajinikanth never ages because time can't keep up with him"; "Rajinikanth doesn't do push-ups, he rather pushes the earth down"; or "We cry when we cut onions, but when Rajinikanth cuts onions, the onions cry." These jokes, though exaggerated and humorous, metaphorically reflect the idea of total control over a situation.

In a spiritual context, a realized master like Amma is a real life superhero who has excellent command and control naturally.

Despite the challenges faced, everything around them appears to fall into place harmoniously, symbolizing their mastery over life's situations. This mastery isn't about defying natural laws but about aligning circumstances through a deep connection with the divine or universal consciousness. If we read Amma's biography, we come across numerous episodes that highlight the immense challenges she has faced — challenges that most of us could hardly imagine. Despite these difficulties, none of them held her back; instead, they became stepping stones for her growth. Amma exemplifies how one can turn obstacles into opportunities and positively impact the lives of millions. Her ability to maintain control over her circumstances stems from her inner strength and mindset, not from external conditions.

As Amma teaches, it's not the external situation that needs changing but our own attitude and mindset. Mahatmas like Amma remain unshaken by external factors because they rely solely on their inner Self. In simple terms, their happiness, enthusiasm, and drive to act aren't dependent on the people or circumstances around them. They draw their energy, motivation, and joy entirely from within themselves. Because they rely solely on their inner Self, external factors don't disturb them. As a result, the conditions around them naturally align to become favorable.

Let us revisit the 5th verse from the 6th chapter of the *Bhagavad Gita*, the first part of which was discussed earlier:

uddhared ātmanātmānaṁ nātmānam avasādayet
ātmaiva hyātmano bandhur ātmaiva ripur-ātmanaḥ

*Uplift yourself through the power of your own self; let not
your self fall to an abominable state; your own self is your best
companion, and your own self is your worst adversary.*

There is a popular story of the Mushika Stri, the mouse woman. Once a bird caught a mouse and was about to eat it. However, the mouse was clever enough to wiggle out of the bird's grasp and fell as the bird was flying. By chance, the mouse landed in the hands of a sage praying with his hands open. The sage transformed the mouse into a beautiful girl whom he accepted as his daughter.

As the girl grew up and reached marriageable age, the sage sought a perfect match for her. He asked his daughter whom she wished to marry, and she replied that she wanted to marry the mightiest being they could see — namely, the Sun. The sage approached the Sun God, asking if he would marry his daughter. The Sun replied that he would be delighted but added that he wasn't the mightiest. The Sun explained that his light could be dimmed by a cloud, so the Lord of the Clouds must be mightier. They then approached the Cloud God, who admitted he was not the strongest, as the Wind could easily push him around. The Wind God was then approached. But, he also claimed that he wasn't the mightiest, for he was powerless against a mighty mountain that could block his path. The Lord of the Mountains was next to be approached, but he revealed that a tiny mouse was mightier than him, as it could dig holes in him, and he could do nothing about it. In the end, the girl had to transform back into a mouse and marry a mouse, recognizing that she was meant to be who she truly was.

This story illustrates that no matter where we go, we ultimately have to return to our true Self. Because mahatmas (realized souls) are rooted in their own true nature, all the factors around them automatically fall into place. Even if circumstances don't align perfectly, these factors do not affect them, and thus everything becomes conducive to their purpose.

Hanuman represents one who has mastered control over his ego, which is so often the root of many problems. Through his humility, devotion, understanding, and patience, Hanuman subdued his ego. Because of this, all factors, whether positive or negative, seem favorable to him. Thus, these two verses convey that even powerful entities are left in awe, unable to fully praise him, as Hanuman's transcendence of ego makes him unaffected by external factors.

Insights on the Path of Bhakti from verses 14 and 15:

- Praise and ridicule may come our way. Let them be the means to make us even more humble.
- Humility makes us receptive to grace.
- Grace, in a given situation, is simply the seamless alignment of all factors to achieve the desired outcome.
- Our self is the most significant factor - be established in the Self!

Verses 16 and 17

Good company
Proximity of a Mahatma

tuma upakāra sugrīvahi kīnhā ।   तुम उपकार सुग्रीवहिं कीन्हा ।
rāma milāya rājapada dīnhā ॥ 16 ॥   राम मिलाय राज पद दीन्हा ॥

tuma - you; upakāra - help; sugrīva - Sugriva, a character in *Ramayana* who eventually becomes king of Monkey kingdom - kishkinda; hi - verily; kīnhā - did, performed; rāma - Lord Rama; milāya - allying with; rājapada - state of kinghood; dīnhā - gave;

You helped Sugriva (the king of the monkey kingdom Kishkinda). You made him friends with Rama which gave him his kingship back.

tumharō mantra vibhīṣaṇa mānā ।   तुम्हरो मंत्र विभीषन माना ।
laṅkēśvara bhayē saba jaga jānā ॥ 17 ॥   लंकेश्वर भये सब जग जाना ॥

tumharō - your; mantra - words of wisdom; vibhīṣaṇa - Vibhishana, Ravana's younger brother; mānā - heeded; laṅkēśvara - Lord of Lanka; bhayē - established as; saba - all, whole; jaga - world; jānā - came to know;

Vibhishana humbly heeded your advice. The whole world knows of the fact that he became the king of Lanka because of your advice.

Both these verses are about the importance of good company, and Lord Hanuman is the perfect example. When Sugriva and Vibhishana associated with Hanuman, they were both elevated to an exalted state, materially and spiritually. Materially, Hanuman's support and intent helped them become kings. Spiritually, through Hanuman's guidance and company, they found refuge in Lord Rama, leading to lives that were more meaningful and selfless. This illustrates the profound impact of being in the company of a perfect being like Hanuman.

I recall a memorable moment with Amma in the mid 90s when I was much younger. The children at the ashram had a chance to be around Amma, and I got to ask Amma about something she often mentioned. Amma would tell us to avoid bad company, but at the same time, she also emphasized looking for the goodness in others. I asked Amma, "If we're supposed to see only the goodness in others, how does the concept of bad company fit in? How can both go hand in hand - avoiding bad company while seeing the good?"

Amma's response was enlightening. She explained that when she says to avoid bad company, it doesn't mean we should hate a particular individual. Rather, it means that every person may have some negativity, some shortcomings, or something that is not right or dharmic. Amma would never say to hate the person for that; instead, she advises us to avoid the adharma, the negative actions. The emphasis is on avoiding the bad actions, not the person. At the same time, Amma encouraged us to look for the goodness in people and respect them for that goodness, because everyone has some positive qualities.

Amma often gives the example of a broken clock. Even a broken clock, which may seem completely useless, shows the correct time twice a day. So even something seemingly flawed has its moments of usefulness. Similarly, if we look at a person the right way, we can find the goodness in them. Therefore, when Amma says to avoid bad company, she means we should avoid the negative qualities in people, not dismiss them entirely from our lives.

I recall an experience much later during my undergraduate studies at Amma's University. One semester was dedicated to doing an internship in a software company in Chennai, a major city in South India. Staying at the Chennai ashram was impractical due to the daily commute. I had an option to stay with some of my classmates in a small rented apartment close to the office. However, my roommates had habits like drinking and smoking, which I was neither accustomed to nor comfortable with. I faced a dilemma: should I reject them and move out, or should I follow Amma's advice to look for the goodness in others while avoiding their negative actions?

I decided to practice what Amma had taught me. When they engaged in meaningful activities, I participated with them, and when they indulged in activities I didn't agree with, I simply avoided them. Initially, they teased me, but over time they began to respect my choices, and a good rapport developed between us despite our differences. They saw that though I avoided them when they engaged in certain deeds, I never disliked them. Our friendship grew to the point that, in our final year of college, we initiated a project to help underprivileged students in nearby government schools. We provided career training and information about opportunities available after high school, which greatly benefited the students. I often reflect on this experience, realizing that if I had rejected them outright, labeling them as "bad," we might not have been able to achieve this small but meaningful project. This taught me the value of Amma's advice about seeing the goodness in others while avoiding their negative actions. It's a lesson that has produced positive outcomes in my life.

When taking the company of Hanuman, no such considerations come into play, as he is an embodiment of goodness in all its many forms. His company can take you a long way forward in both material and spiritual progress, leading to profound transformation. This is exemplified by Sugriva and Vibhishana, whose lives changed dramatically through their association with Hanuman. The positive influence of his presence and guidance is a testament to the transformative power of good company.

Sugriva

Sugriva was the brother of Vali (or Bali), who was the king of Kishkinda. Vali was immensely powerful and nearly invincible, even causing Ravana to flee from a confrontation. However, Vali was also extremely egoistic and boastful, leading to a less-than-righteous life. One day, Vali engaged in a duel with a demon named Mayavi, who lured him into a cave. Before entering, Vali instructed his brother Sugriva to wait outside for 14 days, boasting that he would return victorious within that time. If not, Sugriva should consider him dead. Inside the cave, Mayavi created illusions of Vali's suffering, making it seem as though Vali was in grave danger. Sugriva, seeing trickles of blood and hearing what seemed like Vali's cries, assumed the worst when Vali did not return after 14 days. Believing his brother was dead, Sugriva took on the responsibility of ruling Kishkinda as the new king.

However, Vali did eventually emerge from the cave victorious but enraged to find Sugriva on the throne. Without listening to Sugriva's explanation, Vali accused him of treachery and tried to kill him. Moreover, he wrongfully took away his wife, Ruma, from him. Sugriva, no match for Vali's strength, fled and sought refuge on Mount Rishyamukha, where Vali could not follow due to a curse from the sage Matanga. Although Sugriva was safe, he lived in constant fear, with low self-esteem, lacking in both courage and confidence. During this time, Hanuman, who was one of Sugriva's ministers and his wisest advisor, played a crucial role in supporting him.

It was at this juncture that Lord Rama and Lakshmana came into Sugriva's life. As we discussed earlier, Rama and Lakshmana were searching for Sita when they arrived in Kishkinda. Sugriva, upon hearing from his aides about two skilled and capable warriors entering the region, immediately feared they were assassins sent by Vali and considered fleeing. In his panic, Sugriva was unable to think clearly.

Hanuman intervened, trying to dissuade Sugriva from acting prematurely or in haste, and to give him mental strength. His words were filled with courage and reassurance. Hanuman then climbs Rishyamuka Parvata to observe Rama and Lakshmana as they approach. Upon seeing them, he quickly realizes they don't seem to have any harmful intent, sensing instead a divine aura about them. Hanuman shares this observation with Sugriva, but Sugriva, paralyzed by fear, refuses to believe it. He sends Hanuman to investigate further, instructing him to disguise himself as a hermit.

Hanuman's eloquence, clarity, and calm demeanor immediately reveal his true nature to Rama, who recognizes that Hanuman is no ordinary hermit. Hanuman, in turn, realizes that Rama is not there to harm them but to help. When Rama asks Hanuman to reveal his true identity, Hanuman explains Sugriva's desperate situation. Hanuman then brings Rama to Sugriva and convinces him that Rama is there to help, not harm. Rama instructs Sugriva to challenge Vali to a duel and assures him that he will handle the situation. Despite his initial fear, Sugriva confronts Vali; as they fight, Rama, hiding behind a tree, shoots Vali, bringing an end to his tyranny.

Naturally, a question arises: why did Rama shoot at Vali while hiding behind a tree? This action seems questionable and may initially appear unethical. However, after shooting Vali, Rama did not flee. Instead, he emerged from his hiding place and approached Vali with humility and respect. The term used in the *Ramayana*, particularly in the Kishkinda Kanda, is "with respect," emphasizing Rama's demeanor as he approached Vali without any attitude of confrontation. When we make a mistake or perform an act that contradicts dharma, our natural instinct is often to escape the situation. I remember as a child in India, we would play cricket on the streets; if someone hit the ball hard and high, accidentally breaking a window, everyone would immediately scatter to avoid blame. This is a common reaction, but Rama's response was different. He remained committed to his actions because he knew they were based on dharma.

As Rama approached him, the injured Vali addressed Rama with seemingly respectful yet sarcastic words. He praised Rama as righteous, self-controlled, and dedicated to dharma, but these were veiled accusations, implying that Rama's actions were anything but dharmic. Vali's wife, Tara, had warned him about Rama, but Vali had believed that Rama would not do anything unethical. Now, he accused Rama of siding with dharma.

Rama listened patiently while Vali finished his rant. When Vali was done, Rama began by asking Vali who was questioning dharma. Rama pointed out that Vali had consistently disregarded moral principles, the prosperity of his subjects, and social conventions. Vali lived according to his whims and desires without any consideration for others. Rama reminded Vali that he was in no position to ask or comment about dharma.

In his rant, Vali had put forward three main questions: (i) Who gave Rama the authority to punish Vali? (ii) Why didn't Rama seek Vali's help and strike an alliance with him to find Sita? Wasn't it wrong not to strike an alliance with the ruling king but his enemy? and (iii) Why did Rama attack him when Vali had not threatened him in any way? Rama addressed these questions systematically.

First, Rama clarified that he was acting as the representative and member of the royal family of the Ikshvaku dynasty, which had jurisdiction over the Kishkinda kingdom. This gave him the authority to punish wrongdoers. He explained that Vali's actions, particularly his treatment of his younger brother Sugriva and the forced marriage of Sugriva's wife, Ruma, were adharmic. According to the scriptures, a younger brother should be treated like a son, and his wife like a daughter-in-law. Vali's actions violated these principles, so Rama had to intervene.

Concerning Vali's assertion that he had not threatened Rama and that it was wrong for Rama to attack him from behind a tree, Rama clarified that, as a king, Vali's actions involved more than personal issues; they had public consequences due to his royal status. A king is always a public figure, and his actions affect his subjects. Therefore, Rama had a responsibility to act in the interest of the people. Moreover, Rama reminded Vali that being a kshatriya (warrior), Rama had the right to hunt an animal from hiding. Animals aren't typically hunted face to face. Vali being a monkey, Rama hadn't engaged in misconduct by attacking him from behind a tree. Moreover, Vali had received a boon from Brahma that allowed him to absorb half of the power of anyone who confronted him. To uphold dharma, Rama had to strategize accordingly and there was nothing wrong in strategizing according to the opponent's strength. Additionally, as an incarnation of Vishnu, Rama could have confronted Vali directly, but that would have violated Brahma's boon, rendering it meaningless. Therefore, Rama respected the boon and acted within its constraints.

Lastly, Rama addressed why he had not sought Vali's help finding Sita instead of Sugriva. Rama explained that, though he knew Vali was a better option, he had to stand by dharma, not by personal gain. Although Vali might have been a stronger ally in the search for Sita, Rama supported Sugriva because it was the right thing to do.

Ultimately, Vali recognized his mistakes, apologized to Rama, and received a boon absolving him of his misdeeds.

After defeating Vali, Rama crowned Sugriva the king of Kishkinda. Sugriva, who had lived in fear and ignorance, was transformed under Hanuman's guidance. Hanuman's influence led Sugriva to dedicate his life to Rama, focusing on finding Sita and upholding dharma. As a result, Sugriva was elevated spiritually and materially, becoming the king of Kishkinda.

Vibhishana

Let us consider now the case of Vibhishina, whose situation could be well explained as, "right person, wrong place." He was born in the asura clan, the clan of demons, and was Ravana's brother. He had to walk a tightrope all the time because he was torn between his loyalty to his asura clan and his kingdom, while also aspiring to be spiritually oriented and devoted to dharma. Asuras, or rakshasas, are typically egoistic, and their dominant qualities are based on ego, leading them to engage in actions that may not always be dharmic. Vibhishana, being part of that clan, felt a sense of loyalty but also struggled with his own desire to follow the path of dharma.

When Hanuman went to Lanka in search of Sita, he visited various rooms, chambers, and quarters around the palace, encountering only the negative vibrations of the asuras. Everyone was self-centered, except in one chamber - the quarters of Vibhishana. There, Hanuman sensed a positive energy and the sound of the divine resonating. He was naturally drawn to Vibhishana's quarters and realized that he had found a misfit in the asura clan — a righteous soul in the wrong environment. In their discussion, Hanuman offered Vibhishana guidance that would profoundly alter his life. Hanuman told Vibhishana that he had to choose between his personal dharma, which tied him to his brother and kingdom, and the greater dharma, which served the greater good of creation and society. This advice planted a seed of change in Vibhishana.

Later, during a court session, when Ravana was justifying the abduction of Sita, Vibhishana objected, pointing out that Ravana's actions were wrong. Ravana, enraged, banished Vibhishana from the kingdom. Maybe it was meant to be. This act marked the beginning of Ravana's downfall. Ravana dismissed the good company he had in his younger brother.

Vibhishana then went to Rama, who welcomed him despite initial objections from others. Rama saw Vibhishana's noble intent and interestingly referred to him as "Lankesha" - meaning the Lord of Lanka, during their very first meeting.

When Rama defeated Ravana, Vibhishana was crowned as the rightful king of Lanka. There was a moment when Lakshmana questioned why Rama did not take the throne himself, but Rama responded, as recorded as a verse in *Ramayana*:

> api swarṇamayī lankā na me lakshmaṇa rōchate
> janani janma bhumiścha svargāt api garīyasī

> *Moreover, O Lakshmana, though bedecked with gold,*
> *the golden Lanka does not interest me; the mother, the*
> *land of birth is far superior to even the heavens.*

Rama crowns Vibhishana, demonstrating his lack of attachment to power. Rama could have easily claimed the throne of Lanka himself, and no one would have questioned it, as it was within the norms. However, he chose to make Vibhishana the king and then returned to Ayodhya. For Vibhishana, everything began when he met Hanuman, the right and good company he needed. Hanuman guided him towards the path of righteousness. Afterward, Vibhishana fought on Rama's side against the adharma of Ravana and became the righteous king of Lanka, living a life fully aligned with dharma. Hanuman's company brought this transformation in his life.

Insights on the Path of Bhakti from verses 16 & 17:

- Good company is critical for spiritual and materialistic growth.
- The company of a realized being (mahatma) takes us to an exalted state.

Verse 18

Yearn to learn
Persevere for the Source
Let the ego be consumed by grace

juga sahasra yōjana para bhānū | जुग सहस्र योजन पर भानू।
līlyō tāhi madhura phala jānū ॥ 18 ॥   लील्यो ताहि मधुर फल जानू॥

juga - a very long period of time; sahasra - thousand,
innumerable; yōjana - measurement of distance; para
- at; bhānū - the Sun; līlyō - take, consume; tāhi - that;
madhura - sweet; phala - fruit; jānū - thought;

*You flew towards the Sun, which is thousands of Yojanas (precise
measurement of distance) away, mistaking it for a sweet fruit.*

This verse is based on the incident wherein Hanuman, as a child,
leaps up into the sky to reach out to the all-effulgent sun, far, far
away, in order to consume it, mistaking it for a fruit. This may seem
metaphorical, but there is a lot to reflect on here.

The sun, Bhanu, is described as being a great distance away. Yuga
translates to a defined long period, and sahasra means thousand, as
seen in *Lalita Sahasranama* (1000 names of the divine mother) and
Vishnu Sahasranama (1000 names of Lord Vishnu). The first part of the
verse, "yuga sahasra yojana," can be interpreted in two ways. First, in a
generalized sense: "yuga" implies a long period of time, and "yojana"

is a measurement of distance, suggesting that the sun is exceptionally far away. This phrase conveys the vast distance and time it would take to get to the sun.

The second interpretation delves deeper into the specifics, where "yuga sahasra yojana" is broken down into components, each conveying a specific aspect of time and distance. Some people argue that this detailed interpretation can be unnecessary or misleading, so it's essential to consider both the generalized and specific interpretations. In any case, let us look into the details of this calculation, which involves three terms: yuga, sahasra, and yojana.

Yuga refers to a long period of time, and the entire period of creation is divided into four Yugas: Satya Yuga (the golden age of righteousness), Treta Yuga, Dvapara Yuga, and Kali Yuga (the dark age where righteousness is in decline). These Yugas are sequential, moving from the golden age to the dark age.

Amma often emphasizes the importance of righteousness in each Yuga and shares a particular story to illustrate this. The story is about a person who dies and reaches Yamaloka (the abode of Yama, the Lord of Death and Dharma), where Chitragupta, Yama's assistant, sits in his office. Everyone who arrives must first go into Chitragupta's office, where he evaluates their good and bad deeds to decide their fate. Inside, the person notices three peculiar clocks. The first clock has only the hour hand, the second has only the minute hand, and the third one has just the second hand. When he inquires about the clock, Chitragupta responds that the three clocks show the number of sins committed by human beings. The first clock represents Satya Yuga and the hand moves very slowly because sins were seldom committed in this period. The next clock represents Treta Yuga. Here the hand begins progressing faster, showing there were more misdeeds committed in this period. The third clock with the second hand shows that in Dwapara Yuga, sins became even more frequent. So the person asks him, "what about the dark age of Kali Yuga?" Chitragupta responds, "It's so hot in this office, I'm using that clock as the ceiling fan." Misdeeds in Kali Yuga are so rampant that the clock moves as fast as a ceiling fan.

The *Manusmriti*, a text written over 2,000 years ago, discusses the calculation of time for each Yuga. It begins with Satya Yuga and notes that each subsequent yuga is shorter in duration and calculated with respect to the previous yuga. From the series of verses in the *Manusmriti* that talk about the specific calculation of the time period of the yugas, we are focusing on only the last verse which is more relevant to our discussion of the calculation of the Sun's distance from us:

yadetat parisaṅkhyātamādāveva chatur-yugam |
etad dvādaśasāhasraṃ devānāṃ yugam ucyate

This is how the length of the four time periods (yuga) is calculated; twelve thousand such time cycles are the deva's (demi-god's) yuga.

With the preceding verses explaining the calculation of the time period of each yuga, the above verse concludes that the term "yuga" for the heavenly/celestial beings is 12,000 times that. Thus, we will be associating the number 12,000 for the term "yuga" so as to calculate the Sun's distance.

Sahasra translates to 1,000, and a single yojana is roughly 7.5 to 8 miles. Thus, yuga sahasra yojana, as mentioned in verse 18, can be interpreted as:

Yuga sahasra yojana
12,000 x 1,000 x 7.5 to 8
≈ 90 to 96 million miles

The verse yuga sahasra yojana para bhanu can then be translated as, "the sun is situated at 90 to 96 million miles."

Today, the Sun is commonly understood to be about 93 million miles from the Earth.

Tulasidas mentions this calculation in the *Hanuman Chalisa* way back in the 16th century; a somewhat accurate calculation doesn't appear in the annals of Western scientific history until 100 years later, and even then, it's less accurate than the one found in the *Chalisa*. It's also worth noting that because the Earth's orbit around the sun is an ellipse rather than a circle, the exact distance isn't constant, which may account for the range of distances provided by the *Chalisa*. The clarity of the ancient sages and seers of Sanatana Dharma is truly baffling.

One Who Gobbled the Sun

The Sun is up there, quite a distance away, and what did Hanuman do? He sprang into the sky to gobble it up, thinking it was a sweet, delicious fruit. It is said that when Hanuman was a baby, he had all the traits of a monkey, full of energy and incredibly difficult to control. Hanuman had a huge appetite and needed to be fed constantly. His mother, Anjana, was overwhelmed trying to keep him satisfied. She gave him every kind of food from fruits to cooked meals and more, but he was still not content. He kept demanding more, throwing tantrums until she was helpless. Finally, she told Hanuman that she was going out to get more fruits for him. Unable to control his hunger, Hanuman kept calling for his mother. When he didn't get a response for a long time, he decided to go out looking for her. As he stepped outside, he saw a beautiful, round, bright "fruit" in the sky. Mistaking it for the fruit his mother had gone to fetch, he leapt into the sky, reaching for the Sun, and tried to gobble it up.

The story continues with other events when the gods, particularly Lord Indra, intervened to stop Hanuman, fearing that consuming the Sun would create an imbalance in creation. We will explore that part of the story later, during one of the subsequent verses.

When we look at this story from a spiritual perspective, Hanuman's great appetite can be seen as an immense desire to learn and perceive as much as he could. He absorbed knowledge from his parents and those around him, but was never satisfied — he always sought more. He wanted to learn everything, even beyond what was offered by the greatest masters, including those well versed in the Vedas. With his insatiable hunger for knowledge, he went directly for the Sun, symbolizing the pursuit of supreme knowledge.

The Sun, as Hanuman's guru, represents the source of all knowledge. Everything we perceive, we see because it is illuminated by light from the Sun. But what about the source of that light? The Sun represents the origin of knowledge, and Hanuman wasn't content until he reached for this ultimate source. Spiritually, this episode of Hanuman lunging toward and gobbling the Sun symbolizes his desire to internalize and fully understand the supreme truth. Hanuman's act of "gobbling the Sun" represents the internalization of the ultimate knowledge that the Sun embodies.

There is an old bhajan that Amma composed and sings regularly:

amme bhagavatī kāli māte
ninne nyān innu piḍicchu tinnum

O Mother, Supreme Goddess, Mother Kali;
I would catch hold of you and devour you.

onnukil enne nī tinniḍeṇam
allenkil innu nyān ninne tinnum

Either you eat me, or I will eat you today.

The bhajan has a depth that only someone like Amma could dare to express in a song. The song has profound meaning. "Today, I'm going to devour you, I'm going to eat you," seems like a daring statement to make to the Divine Mother. In 2023, during one of the evening bhajan sessions in Amritapuri, Amma sang this bhajan. After the bhajan, Amma asked everyone, "What would it mean to devour the

Divine Mother?" Eventually, Amma explained the significance of "eating" the Divine Mother as a way of internalizing her, becoming the very embodiment of her qualities. It means wanting the nature of the Divine Mother to become our nature. And, in the second line, we are asking the Divine Mother, in the ferocious form of Kali, to either devour our ego or else bless our efforts to internalize her, by imbibing her virtues.

This line, "Either you eat me, or I will eat you," also suggests the two paths of spiritual growth: bhakti yoga and jnana yoga. When I say, "I devour you," it represents jnana yoga — the path of knowledge — where I try to understand and internalize what the divine "you" represents. "You eat me" refers to bhakti yoga, where divine grace consumes my ego, helping me transcend it through humility and surrender. Both paths lead to transcending the ego and reaching a state of perfection.

When we hear about Hanuman flying into the sky and gobbling the Sun, we understand that he internalized divine qualities and the ultimate knowledge — the very light of wisdom that Surya Deva, the Sun God, represents. Hanuman didn't settle for anything less; he sought the ultimate truth and lunged for it. As spiritual aspirants, we need to draw inspiration from Hanuman's relentless pursuit of wisdom.

Insights on the Path of Bhakti from verse 18:
- Whatever our goals, always aspire for the ultimate knowledge of the Supreme.
- "Seek, learn, and grow," should always be our attitude.
- Strive to be deserving of divine grace, allowing it to flow into us and consume the ego completely.

Verse 19

Ever chant the divine name
Recognize your strengths
Be determined, but not obsessed

prabhu mudrikā mēli mukha māhī ।   प्रभु मुद्रिका मेलि मुख माहीं।
jaladhi lāṅghi gayē acharaja nāhī ॥ 19 ॥ ज लधि लांघि गये अचरज नाहीं॥

prabhu - Lord; mudrikā - symbol (the ring); mēli - took;
mukha - mouth; māhī - in; jaladhi - ocean; lāṅghi -
leaped; gayē - went; acharaja - surprise; nāhī -not;

*Carrying in your mouth Lord Rama's ring for Mother
Sita, you jumped and flew over the ocean to Lanka. It
is no surprise that you could achieve this feat.*

We have discussed how Lord Rama, along with Lakshmana and the
monkey army (vanara sena), headed south in search of Sita, based on
information about Ravana abducting her and taking her to Lanka. They
eventually reached a southern point in India, where they faced the
challenge of crossing the ocean to reach Lanka. Hanuman was chosen
to undertake this task. Lord Rama gave him his precious golden ring
with Rama's name inscribed on it, intended as a token to show Sita
upon finding her. We also discussed how Hanuman, after placing the
ring in his mouth, was said to have acquired a golden hue.

Hanuman knew he would encounter many obstacles on his journey across the ocean, so he had to secure the ring carefully. He considered various options: wearing it, which he found disrespectful; holding it in his hand, which seemed insecure; and tying it in his clothes, which also posed the risk of losing it. Finally, Hanuman decided to carry the ring in his mouth. Although this might seem a humble and innocent choice, Hanuman's reasoning was profound. He believed that Lord Rama's name, inscribed on the ring, should always be on his tongue, as his tongue should constantly chant Lord Rama's name. Therefore, keeping the ring in his mouth was the most respectful and secure choice. This shows not only Hanuman's innocence but also his wisdom. The first part of the verse highlights how Hanuman carried Lord Rama's ring in his mouth during his journey.

The second part says that Hanuman flew across the ocean, and that this comes as no surprise because of his immense capability. We've discussed this before, particularly in the context of when the search for someone to cross the ocean began. There was Angada, the monkey prince, who was the son of King Vali. Angada, like his father, was physically strong, while Hanuman was not only physically able but also mentally strong. This combination was crucial because crossing the ocean involved many challenges, including the enticing allure of Lanka, which could trap one in illusion (maya).

Even Hanuman had to be reminded of his abilities, as Jambavan sat with him and told him that he had the strength to cross the ocean with ease. This reminder of his own true nature was the first step in Hanuman's journey.

Mainaka

As Hanuman began his journey across the ocean, he encountered

numerous obstacles that only someone with both physical and mental strength could overcome. We'll discuss three of these main obstacles, starting with the first one: the Mainaka mountain.

The Mainaka mountain presented itself as an obstacle when Hanuman took a leap from the southern coast of India towards Lanka. As Hanuman flew at great speed, the Mainaka mountain rose from the ocean. Initially, it seemed like the mountain was creating a hurdle, but in reality, Mainaka had good intentions. He was devoted to Lord Rama and wanted to help Hanuman by offering him a place to rest. Mainaka respectfully said, "I am your friend. Come and rest on me. I know you have been flying for a long time." However, Hanuman, determined and focused on his mission to find Mother Sita and deliver Lord Rama's ring, declined the offer. He was resolved to reach his destination without delay. Despite his determination, Hanuman didn't want to disrespect Mainaka's kind gesture. He thought, "How can I ignore him when he's trying to help me?" So, instead of resting, Hanuman decided to step on the mountain to show his respect and then take an even bigger leap. This allowed Mainaka to assist Hanuman without compromising his mission.

This episode teaches two important lessons: first, Hanuman's unwavering determination to achieve his goal without getting sidetracked by comfort, and second, his ability to balance his focus on the goal with respect for others' good intentions. Hanuman's actions show that while remaining dedicated to our goals is crucial, it's equally important not to become so obsessed that we lose sight of other important factors.

Hanuman's encounter with Mainaka demonstrates the importance of balancing determination with practicality and respect. Allow me to share a relevant personal experience. I decided to give up chai and coffee in 2003 because I found that I had been overindulging. However, in certain situations, like during Amma's tour, while making chai for the swamis or Amma, I would mentally debate whether I should taste a sip to make sure the drink was prepared as required. I realized that I needed to taste it to ensure I was doing it right. If I had refused to taste it because of my strict principle, I would have missed the practical point of preparing it well. Giving up chai and coffee may have been a good decision. But being over-obsessed with it would defeat the purpose of being practical, which is an important aspect of spirituality.

Surasa

The second obstacle Hanuman faced was Surasa. We have discussed this encounter in detail in the chapter dealing with verses 9 and 10. Just to recap, Surasa was a demoness with a boon that anything she set her eyes on had to enter her mouth and be consumed. When Surasa saw Hanuman, she declared that she would consume him, insisting he had no choice but to enter her mouth. Respecting her boon and ability, Hanuman grew bigger and bigger, forcing Surasa to open her mouth wider and wider to accommodate him. Thereafter, Hanuman transformed himself into a very tiny form. He entered and exited Surasa's now humongous mouth before it could shut, thus doing his dharma but still outwitting her. Surasa then revealed to Hanuman that she was there to test his abilities at the request of the demi-gods, and was thoroughly satisfied with his physical abilities along with his quick-witted wisdom.

Simhika

The third obstacle Hanuman encountered in his journey across the ocean was that of Simhika, a demoness who could pull down or eclipse anything by sucking in its shadow. After dealing with Surasa, Hanuman flew towards Lanka with great speed, but suddenly felt a barrier pulling him downward. He realized it was Simhika using her power to capture his shadow and drag him down. Having been consumed by Simhika, Hanuman knew there was no compromising with her. He used all his might to tear through her body, emerging victorious and continuing on his mission.

This encounter symbolizes how negative tendencies and emotions can drag us down, pulling us into confusion and indecision. Hanuman teaches us that the only way to overcome these negativities is to confront them head-on with strength and determination, without compromise.

After overcoming all these hurdles, Lord Hanuman successfully crosses the Indian Ocean and reaches Lanka. In Lanka, Hanuman encounters Lankini, a demoness who guards the borders of the kingdom — essentially serving as its immigration officer. She questions him about the purpose of his visit. Hanuman explains that he has come to explore the much-talked-about beauty of Lanka. Unsatisfied with his response, Lankini attacks him. Ever respectful toward women, Hanuman first responds gently, then uses minimal force to overpower her. Lankini realizes she is not confronting an ordinary being and recalls a curse that had turned her into a demoness. She had been told that a monkey would one day be the instrument of her liberation. Accepting this, she allows Hanuman to enter the kingdom. Hanuman's ocean crossing and the major hurdles he faced and overcame provides a blueprint for how to achieve success and overcome obstacles in pursuit of our goals.

1. Identify and understand your strengths: The first and most crucial step is recognizing your potential and limitations. Being fully aware of what you are capable of, and what you are not, is essential before embarking on any journey.

2. Stay determined and focused, but at the same time flexible: Like Hanuman, who resisted the temptation to rest on Mainaka mountain, we must remain steadfast in our focus. However, we should also avoid becoming overly obsessed with our goal to the point of ignoring everything else. Balance is key.

3. Employ humility alongside strength: As shown in the encounter with Surasa, sometimes humility, rather than sheer force, can help us overcome obstacles. It's not just about fighting through challenges but also about knowing when to be humble.

4. Face negativities head-on without compromise: When it comes to dealing with negative tendencies or obstacles, like Simhika, there should be no compromise. We must confront and overcome them with determination and strength.

This approach, illustrated by Hanuman's journey, is a profound and comprehensive recipe for achieving our goals. Verse 19 of the *Hanuman Chalisa* conveys this message.

Insights on the Path of Bhakti from verse 19:

- Chanting the name of the Divine helps us stay focused and present in all that we do.
- Recognize the strengths we have.
- Be determined to reach the goal but do not be obsessed with it. Flexibility is critical.
- Have the attitude of no compromise when it comes to our inner negativities and negative tendencies.

Verses 20 and 21

Making the impossible possible
Becoming deserving of grace

durgama kāja jagata kē jētē ।
sugama anugraha tumharē tētē ॥ 20 ॥

दुर्गम काज जगत के जेते।
सुगम अनुग्रह तुम्हरे तेते॥

durgama - difficult; kāja - task; jagata - world; kē - of;
jētē - however many; sugama - easy; anugraha - blessing/
grace; tumharē - your; tētē - if there (exists);

*Even the impossible tasks in the world become
possible because of your grace.*

rāma duārē tuma rakhavārē ।
hōta na ājñā binu paisārē ॥ 21 ॥

राम दुआरे तुम रखवारे।
होत न आज्ञा बिनु पैसारे॥

rāma - Lord Rama; duārē - at the door; tuma - you;
rakhavārē - guardian; hōta - happen; na - not; ājñā -
permission; binu - without; paisārē - enter/access;

*You are the doorkeeper of Lord Rama's royal court.
No one can enter it without your consent.*

The two verses here discuss divine grace. The 20th verse refers to durgama, dur - a negative prefix, and gama - proceedings, meaning that which is difficult to accomplish. The verse refers to the challenging tasks in the world, those which are hard to complete. Every endeavor we venture into has hurdles and complications in some form or the other. We then find the term gama with a positive prefix - su. This indicates that with divine grace, durgama becomes sugama, meaning the most challenging tasks become easy to manage. Grace simplifies even the most impossible tasks, making them attainable. The 21st verse speaks of Lord Rama's door, the access to his abode, with Hanuman being its guardian. It says that without Hanuman's permission, we cannot enter the abode of Lord Rama. Hanuman embodies the attitude and qualities we need as spiritual aspirants. That is the key to attaining grace. It makes everything possible for us, including access to the ultimate state that the Supreme is established in.

We have discussed difficult situations in *Ramayana* and how Lord Hanuman often came to the rescue during such challenging moments. Hanuman saves the day when Sugriva mistakes Lord Rama and Lakshmana for assassins sent by his cruel brother, Vali. Fearful, Sugriva is ready to flee, but Hanuman intervenes, suggesting they assess the situation first. Upon meeting Lord Rama, Hanuman senses divinity in him and persuades Sugriva to seek his help. Thus, Hanuman helps Sugriva defeat Vali and become king. Later when the entire monkey army, along with Rama and Lakshmana, reached the southern shores and realized Lanka was on the other side of the ocean, Hanuman once again came to the rescue. When Ravana's son Indrajit struck down Lakshmana, Hanuman again came to the rescue, retrieving the entire Dronagiri mountain with its medicinal herbs to save Lakshmana and the other wounded members of the monkey army. These are just a very few instances of Hanuman's role as a rescuer when things got difficult.

Let us discuss another interesting incident from the *Ramayana*. Ravana had earned a boon from Lord Brahma after performing rigorous penance, in which he had offered parts of his own body, including his ten heads, as sacrifices. It's said that when Ravana was about to sacrifice his tenth head, Brahma appeared and was pleased with his penance. Brahma restored Ravana's form and granted him a boon. Ravana, like many asuras, asked for immortality, as he didn't want to die. But Brahma denied him immortality, saying that was something no one could grant. So, Ravana asked for a boon that would be a work-around to attain immortality. He prayed that no demi-god, celestial being, demon, or beast should be able to kill him. In effect, he wanted invincibility. However, Ravana underestimated humans, considering them inferior, and thus didn't ask for protection against them.

Considering the loophole, Lord Vishnu incarnated as Lord Rama in human form to defeat Ravana. But even with this advantage, killing Ravana proved difficult. Every time Rama shot an arrow, Ravana's wounds would heal instantly due to his boon. Seeing Ravana recover each time — rendering Rama's efforts seemingly in vain — struck fear in the hearts of the monkey army, the demi-gods in the heavens, and the sages and seers, as described in the *Ramcharitmanas*.

A Thai adaptation of the *Ramayana* describes the moment when everyone is struck with fear, witnessing Rama's tireless efforts appear to be in vain. Seeing that no one is taking action, Hanuman thinks, "I need to do something." He wonders who might know of any possible weakness Ravana may have. It occurs to him to ask Vibhishana, Ravana's brother, who had defected to Rama's side to uphold dharma. Hanuman urges Vibhishana to think hard about what makes Ravana seemingly invincible. That's when Vibhishana remembers a boon Ravana had received. The *Ramcharitmanas* states that Vibhishana tells Rama that Ravana has a reservoir of the nectar of immortality in his

navel. As long as it remains intact, Ravana cannot be killed.

Upon learning this, Rama takes up a powerful weapon (some versions say he took the Brahmastra, a deadly weapon blessed by Lord Brahma) and prepares to strike Ravana's navel. Other versions say that Rama aimed multiple arrows at both Ravana's navel and heart. The *Ramcharitmanas* describes the scene vividly: fire blazed in all ten directions, animals howled deafeningly, lightning flashed, thunder roared from the sky, powerful winds blew, and the earth shook as Ravana fell to the ground, finally annihilated.

As per several traditions in Sanatana Dharma, the human body is believed to have seven energy centers (chakras), with the manipura chakra located at the level of the navel. There are seed mantras (usually comprised of a single syllable) associated with each chakra. Interestingly, the mantra for the navel chakra is ram. It was here in the navel chakra that Rama finally struck Ravana to put an end to his tyranny. One of the aspects that manipura chakra is usually associated with is "gut feeling," the intrinsic thoughts that guide us between right and wrong. Let us be open to divine grace to strike us right here, in order to help guide us on the right path.

When the going gets tough, how do we seek grace? Hanuman, the embodiment of bhakti, can be invoked within us to receive grace. Hanuman comes to the rescue whenever tasks become durgama - difficult to complete or endure. When he saw Rama struggling to emerge victorious against Ravana, he did not sit back in fear. Instead, he stepped forward to find a solution, even though he knew that Rama, despite his unparalleled abilities, was going through this for a divine reason. The spiritual insight here is that when challenges arise, we need the embodiment of devotion to awaken within us. Qualities like dedication, hope, positive thoughts, fighting spirit, and perseverance must rise.

When life presents a situation to us, it is our mind that deems it difficult or easy based on various notions we have formed. A situation considered difficult by one person may be regarded as fun by someone else. For example, a person may consider it a life threatening situation when asked to swim across an olympic-size swimming pool. Whereas, for someone else, it would be a joyful and fun activity. So to deal with the so-called difficult situation, the mind has to be adequately conditioned. When we are empowered with the virtues discussed above, difficult tasks effortlessly become easy and fun to accomplish, as our mindset and attitude changes. The Hanuman within us turns durgama into sugama, making the impossible possible. These qualities of devotion are what truly enable us to overcome obstacles with ease.

A natural question may arise. Is that really possible? Of course, we aren't Hanuman. How can we be like that? As a matter of fact, we are definitely capable of that. We often overlook the fact that when we harness our positive traits, we can transform things beautifully. We have the ability to practice this at every moment.

Let us consider this example. Have we seen superheroes who perform extraordinary deeds in real life? I guess our answer is "no." But consider this. I recall a very beautiful and profound video I once saw. It's an online interview conducted by an organization featuring many individuals. The video is funny at first when the interviewer, with a serious demeanor, presents the job description and what it would demand from the candidate if selected. The title of the position is Director of Operations. However, the interviewer explains, the responsibilities go far beyond that. The requirements are quite extensive. Constantly being on your feet, exerting yourself, and maintaining high stamina are necessary. The interviewees are genuinely taken aback, displaying surprised expressions. One of them asks, "For how many hours?" The response is about 135 hours a week, which may increase during crises, leading to a schedule of 24 hours a day and 7 days a week. The interviewees are flabbergasted. Another inquires about breaks. "No breaks available," responds the interviewer. "Is that even legal?" asks another interviewee. The interviewer assures them that it is entirely legal. "What about lunch breaks?" The response: "You may have lunch if the associate allows you to take a break for lunch, and only after the associate has finished eating." The reactions from the interviewees include comments like, "I think that is pretty intense," and "No, that's crazy." The interviewer continues to add more requirements. "This job demands extreme negotiation and interpersonal skills; we need someone who might have degrees in medicine, finance, and culinary arts; the associate requires constant attention and may need you to be with them throughout the night; you may literally have to give up your life; there are no vacations — in fact, during Christmas, Thanksgiving, New Year's, and holidays, the workload increases; there's almost no time to sleep; all of this needs to be done with a happy disposition." The insane list keeps going on, leaving the interviewees completely confused. One of them calls it "cruel and a sick twisted joke." And then comes the final blow: the interviewer states there will be no salary offered for this position. At this point, the video becomes profound and very touching. The interviewer says, "What if I tell you that many people, millions, have taken up this job — and they are called mothers?" Every interviewee unequivocally agrees, and some are even moved to tears. Every time I play this video during my talks, I notice at least a few people tearing up while watching it.

But the point here is that mothers, who are just normal human beings, act as superheroes who take up responsibilities that are inarguably impossible. It is a durgama responsibility they are taking up. But dare to tell a mom how she is crazy to be a mother, taking up this responsibility, and I'll have to next meet you in a hospital — any mother would take offense at this advice. They make the supposedly durgama into sugama. They will even tell you that this seemingly insane responsibility is a pleasure and blessing. Why is that? Precisely because the virtues and goodness in them take the upper hand. When dedication or devotion toward a cause comes into play, the impossible becomes possible.

Amma says that the very concept of motherhood is unparalleled in this world. Mothers are given the highest regard of all relationships. Sanatana Dharma lists the mother and father before the Guru and God for worship. That is the respect and recognition accorded to a mother. The mother's feeling of "mine" towards her child makes her devotion and dedication possible. What if one goes beyond that and practices the same for everyone? That is the example that great masters set and inspire us greatly with. Look at Amma's example. She dedicates her life to others at every single moment. You can see Amma spend anywhere from 10 to 15 to even 22 hours sitting in one place, embracing people, and listening to their problems. She forgoes even the basic things like food, rest, and nature's call to do this. Amma has been doing this for almost 50 years, literally every day of her life. It is unheard of, unprecedented, and unparalleled. What makes the durgama into sugama for Amma is that she has the broadest concept of "mine", which encompasses everyone and everything; all of creation. She sees all as her own, and thus is willing to undertake any sacrifice for the sake of others. That is the beauty of it. It would be undisputable to say that if someone has toiled tirelessly, more than anyone else, to build a massive network of spiritual and humanitarian activities worldwide, it is Amma.

During Amma's programs, we all become little Hanumans, accomplishing things we wouldn't otherwise attempt. Some people are like Hanuman carrying the Sanjivani mountain, tackling huge tasks with ease. People who never step into a kitchen might spend hours there, washing massive pots. Others, typically uncomfortable with social interactions, might become "May I help you" volunteers, line coordinators, or crowd control volunteers. What was once durgama (difficult) becomes sugama (easy) through devotion and dedication towards Amma. Amma teaches us that neither God nor Guru requires our devotion. Instead, our devotion is reflected through our positive attitude towards others.

When you ask Amma, "Aren't you suffering doing this?" Amma responds, "No, in love, in oneness, there is no effort, no suffering." Hugging over 40 million people in her lifetime seems impossible, yet for Amma, it is sugama (effortless). It's all about her attitude, which transforms the impossible into the possible. When Amma is asked another question, "But how are you able to do all this?" she often says, "It's just kripa (grace) that is making it happen." Amma frequently uses the phrase, "Let grace protect you; may divine grace guide you." As a reminder, when we talk about grace, we are in fact referring to three factors:

1. Adhyatmika: This refers to the self - our mindset, mood, strengths, and weaknesses. It encompasses the personal factors that influence how a situation unfolds.

2. Adhibhautika: Pertaining to our physical surroundings - the people, things, and conditions around us. While we don't have full control over these factors, we can still make some effort to bring them under partial control.

3. Adhidaivika: These factors are beyond our control and are often called "divine" factors. These include unexpected events or influences we cannot predict or manage.

Grace is when all these factors align favorably. For example, when taking an exam, the adhyatmika factors can be managed by preparing ourselves mentally for the exam, planning and executing things per the plan. Adhibhautika factors may also play a role, like a party happening in the neighbor's house when we are preparing for the exam. Or we lose power the night before the exam. Or the exam hall is too cold or hot, the pen we are using runs out of ink, the person sitting next to us keeps sneezing or coughing, creating distractions, etc. Though these factors may be beyond our control, we can do something about them and manage them with the right attitude. We can request the air conditioner or heater to be set to the right temperature, borrow a new pen from a friend, or be seated in a different place where there is less distraction. Though not entirely under our control, we can handle the situation by working around it. But adhidaivika factors are beyond our control altogether. Having prepared for the exam well and answered as planned, what if the evaluator had a fight with their spouse just before taking a look at our answers? It is highly likely we won't be scoring well. Grace is when all these factors fall into place and become favorable to us. One of the ways to make the factors favorable for us is through bhakti. The qualities and virtues associated with bhakti need to be strengthened within us.

Access to the Ultimate Goal with Grace

The 21st verse says, "You are the guardian of Lord Rama's abode, his doorkeeper, and to gain access, I need your permission." Essentially, to reach the divine abode or the ultimate goal, we need the grace that bhakti provides, and Hanuman represents this devotion. Only through bhakti can we access that door to Lord Rama's grace.

In the *Holy Bible* there's a similar verse: "I am the gate. Whoever enters through me will be saved," from the Gospel of John 10:9 (New Testament). It speaks about gaining access to divine grace through the right path, just as Hanuman guides one to Rama.

Another verse in the *Holy Bible* says: "Enter through the narrow gate. For wide is the gate and broad is the road that leads to destruction, and many enter through it. But small is the gate and narrow the road that leads to life, and only a few find it," from Matthew 7:13-14 (New Testament). To pass through this narrow gate, we need humility. A big ego won't fit; we must become small, which is precisely what bhakti teaches us.

It's like the story of a particular mahatma. A man approaches him and says, "I want to become your disciple. Can you please accept me?" The mahatma responds, "What qualifications do you have to become my disciple?" The man takes this as an opportunity to list his achievements: "I have mastered scriptures, studied under sages, given talks..." He goes on and on. The mahatma finally says, "I will accept you as my disciple if you can follow me into my small hut." The man agrees, but as the mahatma enters the hut, he walks straight into the low door frame, banging his head. The disciple is shocked but tries to help him. Again, the mahatma tries to walk in without bending and gets his eyes poked by the thatched roof. A brick even falls on his head, and he's left bleeding. The disciple, confused and concerned, says, "Sir, you need to bend down to enter the hut." The mahatma replies, "That is my teaching to you. If you want to enter, you must become small. For all the boasting you've done, you will only suffer if you keep your ego inflated. You will bang your head, poke your eyes, and hurt yourself. Learn from these experiences and deflate your ego. Only when you humble yourself can you enter this door and become my disciple."

This is essentially the understanding conveyed by the 21st verse. Hanuman is guarding the door, and only with his permission can we pass through. What does "his permission" mean? It means we must become like him - humble and small, with a deflated ego. Only then will we have his grace to enter, and when we enter, we receive divine grace, which ensures everything falls into place.

In fact, traditional homes in India, even those from the recent past, were designed with small doors and high steps. I remember my own grandparents' home as part of an agraharam (a row of houses belonging to the Brahmin families), which had low ceilings and high thresholds, making it necessary to bend down to enter. If you walked in with ego, you would hit your head on the strong wooden frame. I've experienced this myself, running around as a child, smashing my head against the top of the door frame. The idea behind these low doors is symbolic: No matter how great the house is, or how much I have achieved outside, I need to humble myself to enter. Anyone wishing to enter must bow down. The door constantly reminds us to let go of our ego.

This is not just an Indian tradition. Many Asian traditions, and even some ancient European ones, require a bow as a sign of humility. For example, on Japan's Shinkansen (bullet train), the ticket checkers bow every time they enter or exit a car, regardless of whether passengers notice or appreciate it. Even though they have the authority to remove anyone from the train, they still bow. It's an inspiring tradition, maintaining humility in a high-tech, futuristic setting.

The 20th verse discussed how to make complex tasks easy. For that, we need bhakti and all the qualities associated with it. Hanuman, the embodiment of those qualities, grants us access to the ultimate abode when we develop those qualities, as conveyed in the 21st verse.

Insights on the Path of Bhakti from verses 20 & 21:

- Bhakti helps obtain grace, making even impossible deeds easily possible

- Grace can be threefold - our own grace, grace of the surroundings (things and people), and grace of the factors beyond.

- To practice bhakti is to practice all possible good qualities in every moment (dedication, selflessness, understanding, acceptance, broad-mindedness, patience, etc.)

- Bhakti facilitates us to the ultimate abode, the highest state of oneness.

Verses 22, 23 and 24

Faith and surrender (the ego)
Self-confidence
Bhakti is for the brave

saba sukha lahai tumhārī śaraṇā ।   सब सुख लहै तुम्हारी सरना।
tuma rakṣaka kāhū kō ḍara nā ॥ 22 ॥   तुम रक्षक काहू को डरना॥

saba - all; sukha - well and happy; lahai - feel/experience;
tumhārī - your; śaraṇā - feet (refuge); tuma - you; rakṣaka
- protector/savior; kāhū kō - why; ḍaranā - fear;

*One who takes refuge in you will always experience happiness
beside them. When you are there to protect us, why fear?*

āpana tēja samhārō āpai ।   आपन तेज सम्हारो आपै।
tīnōṃ lōka hāṅka tē kāmpai ॥ 23 ॥   तीनों लोक हांक तें कांपै॥

āpana - yours; tēja - power/force; samhārō - can match
(fight); āpai - you; tīnōṃ - all the three; lōka - world;
hāṅka tē kāmpai - tremble in the mighty roar;

*Only you can match your might. All three worlds
would tremble in front of your power and force.*

bhūta piśācha nikaṭa nahi āvai ।   भूत पिसाच निकट नहिं आवै।
mahavīra jaba nāma sunāvai ॥ 24 ॥   महावीर जब नाम सुनावै॥

bhūta piśācha - evil forces; nikaṭa - near; nahi - not;
āvai - come; mahavīra - the great and courageous one
(Hanuman); jaba - when; nāma - name; sunāvai - heard;

*Evil forces can't even come to the vicinity when and where the
chanting of your name can be heard, O supremely courageous one!!*

These three verses underscore the might of Hanuman to help us firm up our faith in him, develop an attitude of self-confidence and courage, and kindle the strength within us to face every situation in life. The 22nd verse states that once we take refuge in Lord Hanuman, we have nothing to fear due to his protection and care. By letting go of our ego, unnecessary likes and dislikes, expectations, and so on, our chances of happiness increase. We have fewer conditions to meet to feel joy. In this state, there is no room for worry or fear. The next verse reassures us that we are taking refuge in him who is unparalleled. Only Hanuman matches his own might. The 24th verse adds that his mere name renders evil and negative forces powerless. Our security is ensured by none other than Mahavir, the supremely courageous one. This verse urges us to stay strong and positive.

All three verses remind us that the path of devotion is for the brave. Surrendering one's ego cannot be done by one who is too fixated on self-centered thoughts. We need to firm up our faith not just in the Divine but in our own self. We must understand that our faith is our strength when we speak of divine protection. It's not about blindly believing nothing will go wrong by invoking Hanuman's name. Rather, it is the faith that even if something goes wrong, we are in safe hands and are capable of getting through it.

Surrender - Taking Refuge

The first verse talks about sharana — taking refuge at your holy feet. The idea is, "When I take refuge in you, I feel happiness and bliss." However, there is often a misconception that surrender or refuge means giving up or giving in. True refuge or surrender does not involve abandoning the fighting spirit or the courage to face situations. It is not about passively handing everything over to the Divine. Instead, it means doing your best, entirely investing in your actions, and, once the action is complete, accepting the outcome — whatever it may be. We then acknowledge that everything is in the Divine's hands. This is the true essence of surrender: giving your best effort and then cultivating the attitude of acceptance, recognizing that the result is beyond your control.

Let's look into Amma's words in this regard from *Awaken Children* Vol 2, page 40:

"If you find it difficult, then you should pray before doing the work, 'O my beloved Lord, I am going to do this work; please give me enough mental strength to do this as a worship of You. Help me to do this work with the right attitude. This is Yours, not mine. I am doing it with Your power, not mine.' Then do the work sincerely, with concentration, and as best as you can without thinking of its fruit. Try to derive happiness from the spirit in which you are doing the work. When it is over, again pray, 'O Lord, thank you for Your blessings and guidance. I now surrender both the action and its fruit at Your Feet.' When this is practiced daily and constantly, it will become spontaneous.

Once the work is done, having put in as much effort as you can, with an attitude of surrender, then there is no need to worry about the fruit. Fruit is something which will manifest in the future. Worrying about the past or future is meaningless. The former is no more; it has no validity. Even if you go on brooding about things that went wrong in the past, they will not be corrected. The future is also not in your hands. It is controlled by the Supreme. A true devotee who has surrendered everything to the Supreme will not worry about the past or future. For him, whatever happens is God's will. He accepts everything as His prasad."

So, what do we hear from Amma? There is absolutely no discount on the effort we must put in. We definitely need to give it our best. While putting in the effort, we should maintain an attitude of non-doership and humility. Once the action is completed, develop the attitude of acceptance. All this together is what constitutes surrender. Thus we can clearly see that surrender is not about giving in or giving up.

A very popular verse from the *Bhagavad Gita*, Chapter 2, Verse 47 says:

karmaṇy-evādhikāras te mā phaleṣhu kadāchana
mā karma-phala-hetur bhūr mā te saṅgo 'stvakarmaṇi

You have the authority over your actions, but not the fruits of the actions. Be not motivated by the fruits of the actions (considering yourself to be the cause of the result) and do not resort to inaction.

Our authority lies in how we perform the action. We have complete control over the method, the attitude, and the approach. However, the *Gita* reminds us here, we never have complete control over the outcome. Perform actions with this understanding and avoid expecting a specific result. Recognize that many factors influence the outcome, not just our efforts, and that we alone are not the cause of the result. At the same time, do not fall into inaction either. These four principles together define true surrender: effort, humility, recognition of external factors, and persistence.

So, let's summarize what surrender is in two key points:

- Surrender involves taking responsibility - developing enthusiasm, love, and the right attitude while performing our duties and actions. Do the action with the attitude of non-doership, letting go of the pride and self-centered attitude. This is the initial aspect of surrender: putting in effort and intention.

- Once the action is completed, develop an attitude of acceptance. The outcome may not always align with our expectations, but surrender means accepting it as it comes. This balance between effort and acceptance defines true surrender.

We discussed in the last chapter the three factors that play a critical role in any given situation that we are in: a) adhyatmikam - factors about ourselves such as our thoughts, attitude, memory, notions, ability to process thoughts, mood, anxieties, etc. b) adhi-bhautikam - the factors pertaining to the physical realm of things and people around us; though we don't have complete control over them, we still can partially control them or work around them. c) adhi-daivikam - the factors that are totally beyond our control. True surrender involves having a good understanding of and acknowledging these factors in a given situation and acting accordingly.

Who is one of the best examples of this? Lord Hanuman. He never remained uncommitted or inactive. Whenever a situation demanded it, he always sprang into action, never saying, "I don't want to do this." Second, he never failed to do his part with complete enthusiasm, giving his one hundred percent with love. Whether in the search for Mother Sita, attending to Lord Rama or the monkey army's needs, or carrying the entire Dronagiri mountain, Hanuman always demonstrated his dedication. Lastly, Hanuman always acted with humility, never driven by ego, perfectly exemplifying surrender through his commitment to Lord Rama.

When we have a guru like Amma in our lives, practicing surrender becomes easier; this doesn't mean giving up and letting Amma handle everything, but rather doing our part as best we can while anchoring our thoughts and confidence in Amma. This enables us to maintain an equipoised attitude, a state wherein our expectations don't drag us to extreme emotions.

A good example of this concept happened during the 2024 FIFA World Cup in Qatar. After many games, France and Argentina reached the finals. Three types of people watched the game: those supporting France, those supporting Argentina, and those who didn't mind who won but just wanted to enjoy the game.

For the first two groups, their happiness swung up and down with the score. When Argentina scored, their fans were happy, while the French supporters were disappointed, and vice versa. This back-and-forth kept emotions high throughout the game. However, the third group, those without expectations for a specific outcome, simply enjoyed the experience, whether Messi or Mbappé scored. They weren't emotionally invested in one team winning, so they enjoyed the entire game. This shows the value of letting go of expectations and accepting whatever comes, just like those in the third group who found joy in every moment. True surrender is not about giving up but about going beyond the ego and expectations. When that happens, we are always blissful.

So, when the verse says, "Take refuge in Hanuman," it doesn't just mean rushing to Hanuman and holding his feet alone. True refuge means imbibing his qualities — humility, strength, and surrender. When we do that, we experience nothing but joy and happiness.

You are the Protector; Why Fear?

The second part of the 22nd verse says, "When you are there as my protector, where is there room for fear? What should I fear?" Once we surrender, relief naturally follows.

As Amma often explains, once we board a train or airplane, there is no point in carrying our luggage on our head or shoulders. We should simply place it under the seat or in the overhead bin and enjoy the journey. Similarly, once we surrender, we let go of our burdens with the attitude of detachment, and there is no more room for fear and pain thereafter.

I recently watched a talk by a devotee of Lord Hanuman. He was comparing Rama's might against Ravana's. In this comparison, the speaker emphasized how Ravana had the upper hand in many ways. He had a powerful army, formidable boons from Lord Shiva, and the battle was taking place in Lanka, his stronghold. Meanwhile, Rama, despite being the incarnation of Lord Vishnu, was in his human form and abiding by human limitations. Rama had only a band of monkeys by his side, without established weapons or fortifications. Yet, Rama had a significant advantage - Hanuman. Despite Ravana's tactical, military, and strategic superiority, the key factor that swung the war in Rama's favor was Hanuman. Hanuman's unwavering devotion and ability to take action at crucial moments made all the difference.

There were once several passengers traveling on a bus through the countryside. The rundown bus was severely overcrowded with passengers, luggage, and even a few animals. The condition of the bus was so poor that if someone sneezed too hard, it might have fallen apart. To make matters worse, the bus driver was erratic in his driving. He didn't care about potholes. He would accelerate recklessly, then slam on the brakes only when he was right behind the vehicle ahead, often while honking loudly. Sometimes, the brakes wouldn't work, causing every passenger to gasp in fear. The bus driver frequently drove on the wrong side of the road to overtake slower vehicles, even with oncoming traffic. Just as a head-on collision seemed inevitable, he would swerve back into his lane. People screamed and panicked. Once, he went downhill on a steep road with a sharp turn approaching. Despite the weak brakes, he showed no signs of slowing down. Right at the edge of a cliff, he somehow steered the bus safely back onto the road. Some passengers fainted from the terrifying experience. One of the passengers, who was panicking like everyone else, noticed a small girl sitting next to him completely unaffected by the chaos. She was calmly working on her crayon drawing. Surprised, he asked, "Aren't you scared by the crazy driver?" Without looking up, still focused on her drawing, she replied, "Don't worry. That's my daddy. My mom told him to be home before 6 p.m. He knows he'll be in trouble if he's late. He'll take me home safely."

When we have faith, fear is automatically dispelled. Faith gives us hope, encouragement, and the strength to face any situation with the right attitude. That's why the 22nd verse says: "Tum rakshak kahu ko darna?" When you are my protector, what — and why — should I fear?

Keeping Away the Evil Forces and Negativities

The 24th verse continues along the same lines, saying that "When I call out your name, evil forces — ghosts and such — won't even come near me." I can really relate to this. I mentioned earlier the fear I had of darkness and being alone. When I was little, a few friends would often share ghost stories. Those stories had a lasting impression on me, making me very uncomfortable in the dark. I've shared how staying alone in Amma's DC ashram was initially a considerable challenge for me. In 2011, there was an earthquake measuring about 5.9 or 6.0 on the Richter scale in Washington DC; the combination of expecting aftershocks and the fear of darkness in the night was unsettling and rather rattling. Back then, when I felt fear, I would chant the *Hanuman Chalisa* or Amma's mantras. In fact, I didn't just chant; I would scream the *Hanuman Chalisa* or one of Amma's bhajans, hoping that my scream would scare away any ghosts! It seems naive now, but in those moments, I felt helpless and did whatever I could.

In hindsight, it makes sense. Calling out to Hanuman by chanting the *Chalisa*, or to Amma through bhajans or mantras, brought me a sense of courage. I hoped Hanuman or Amma wouldn't actually appear in front of me because that would have scared me even more! But the act of chanting gave me strength. Why? It's difficult to explain, but chanting brought me courage. Definitely the unnecessary fears were being replaced with positive divine thoughts to a good extent. Afterward, I felt a sense of "Bring it on!"— until the fear crept back, and I would chant again. The power of chanting or remembering the Divine awakens the qualities of strength that Hanuman and Amma represent.

When these qualities are temporarily awakened within us, fear dissipates. If we could keep those qualities constantly awakened, we would always be fearless, just like the state of an enlightened mahatma. No negative forces or negativities can come near us when we invoke Hanuman within.

An important question to address here is where are the negative forces actually coming from? They are actually from within us. Our own negativities manifest as what seems like negative forces. So, when we say Hanuman is our protector and savior and there is no need to fear, it means that fearlessness comes from within us when the qualities of Hanuman or Amma are invoked. When we understand the true source of fearlessness, then Hanuman or Amma appearing in physical form to protect us from external negative forces becomes unnecessary.

He Alone is Equal to His Might

What does it mean when the 23rd verse says that "Only you can match your own might?" Hanuman represents the ultimate state; once someone reaches that state of realization, the ultimate state of existence, they are only affected by their own self. External factors, people, and situations don't bother them. Though we are speaking of Hanuman's might in a literal sense, the spiritual implication is deeper. A person who has reached the ultimate state is unaffected by the world and dictates their own path.

Recently, we had a session with members of Amma's international youth movement, AYUDH, where we discussed self-confidence. One point we touched upon was that you are what you are, and you aren't what you think others think you are. To simplify it - you are what you are, not what others think of you.

We are easily influenced by what we think others are thinking about us, but it is often just our imagination. As much as I might be concerned about what others think of me, they are more concerned about how I perceive them. For others, we are not the priority. Once in a while, they may tease or advise us, but most people are obsessed with their own self-image, not ours. So, if we think someone is constantly judging us, it's worth remembering that it's likely just our imagination.

Hanuman represents that state of being wholly established in the Self. Other things, people, concepts, situations, and ideologies are all secondary. They don't affect him. For a realized being (mahatma), what matches their might is only themselves and nothing else. In the discussion of verses 14 and 15, we looked at the verse from *Bhagavad Gita*, Chapter 5, that conveys that we are our own best accomplice, and we are also our own worst foe or nemesis. External factors may act as triggers, but ultimately we are the cause for our rise or fall.

One of the Indian newspapers in the early 1990s described Amma as a very successful and impactful individual. They mentioned how she overcame four types of barriers: gender, financial, language, and educational. Despite the circumstances of being born female in rural India in the 1950s, growing up in a poor family, speaking only Malayalam, and being a fifth-grade dropout, Amma has made a tremendously positive impact worldwide. She faced ridicule and blame from her own family, neighboring villagers, and others, but none of this ever stopped her. This ties directly into the same point: Amma dictates terms for herself. A realized Master is like that. It doesn't matter if people offer praise or ridicule; it doesn't affect them. Amma often says, "One who garlands you today may throw stones at you tomorrow, and one who throws stones today may garland you tomorrow." A true mahatma, a truly realized master, remains unaffected by either treatment. They are established in their own Self. That's why, if anyone can defeat you, it is your own self, not others.

Three Worlds Tremble in Your Mighty Roar

The second part of the 23rd verse conveys how the three worlds tremble at Lord Hanuman's mighty roar. We have already discussed the three worlds in the context of verse 1. The three forms of the world are entirely under the control of a being who has realized their True Self. Nothing other than the Self affects such a being. Rather, the world seems to follow the command of such a being.

I'm reminded of a minor incident from a recent program. A couple of years ago, a toddler got hold of a tiger mask. When he wore the mask, he thought he was a tiger and began to roar. Of course, it wasn't frightening at all — it was pretty cute! But every time he roared, people around him pretended to be scared. If someone wasn't reacting, he would go right up to them and roar until they pretended to tremble. The toddler's attitude was, "I'm a tiger, and I'll make you tremble," even though it was just a game. Imagine having that same attitude but with the knowledge of who we actually are. When this verse talks about understanding that "I have control over how I feel," it means that with the right mindset, we can align with creation as if it is responding to our will. It's not ego but wisdom that creates a positive impact.

When we create a positive impact, we may find that the people and situations around us automatically seem to start acting in alignment with our will. I remember another example from my college days. One of my classmates was very studious and intelligent. He wasn't particularly great at making friends though. There was another individual with several friends he could count on to complete any task. The former would often complain about how no one supported him at all. While the latter wasn't particularly studious and talented, he always created a positive impact and feelings in his friends. His love and service toward his friends naturally created a feeling of loyalty in them toward him as well.

Similarly, Lord Hanuman or a mahatma like Amma positively impact those associated with them. Though they have no intention of ruling over others, their own love and service to others, and all the positive changes they have engendered in others' external situations and inner attitudes, naturally builds a loyal and devoted following without any particular effort on their part.

Insights on the Path of Bhakti from verses 22, 23 & 24:

- Verse 22
  - Surrender to the guru/Divine
  - That doesn't mean we give up or give in.
  - Do all actions giving our very best and with the right attitude. Then develop the attitude of acceptance, acknowledging that many factors are beyond our control.
  - Remove self-centered thoughts from the equation.
- Verse 23
  - Be self-confident
  - Only we have the power to decide how we want to feel.
  - Others (people and things) can be triggers, but the decision on how to think and feel is on us.
- Verse 24
  - Devotion and surrender are for the brave. There is no room for fear.
  - Faith and trust dispel fear.

Verses 25 and 26

Cure for the worst ailment - ego
Thoughts, words, and actions through shraddha

nāsai rōga harai saba pīrā ।   नासै रोग हरै सब पीरा।
japata nirantara hanumata vīrā ॥ 25 ॥   जपत निरंतर हनुमत बीरा॥

nāsai - put and end to; rōga - disease/ailment; harai - remove;
saba - all; pīrā - sufferings; japata - chant; nirantara -
relentlessly; hanumata - Lord Hanuman; vīrā - courageous;

Diseases will be cured, and pain and suffering will be healed
when a devotee constantly repeats the brave Hanuman's name.

saṅkaṭa sē hanumāna chuḍāvai ।   संकट तें हनुमान छुड़ावै।
mana krama vachana dhyāna jō lāvai ॥26 ॥   मन क्रम वचन ध्यान जो लावै॥

saṅkaṭa - problem and sorrow; sē - from; hanumāna -
Lord Hanuman; chhuḍāvai - relieve, free us; mana - mind
(thoughts); krama - actions; vachana - words; dhyāna
- meditation/control; jō - one who; lāvai - brings;

Hanuman will rescue those who meditate upon him through their
thoughts, actions, and words from troubles and tribulations.

The five-face depiction of Hanuman

The 25th verse conveys that Hanuman is the one who destroys or cures
diseases and nullifies all forms of suffering. It highlights Hanuman

as vira, emphasizing his courage and readiness to face challenges. The verse suggests that those who call out to Hanuman or remember him gain the strength to overcome their difficulties and diseases. The 26th verse speaks of adverse situations and how Hanuman helps one overcome them — not by escaping, but by facing them. It emphasizes the importance of aligning one's thoughts, speech, and actions with meditation, enabling one to overcome challenges with Hanuman's guidance.

Let's delve into the spiritual aspect of this concept. There is an interesting form of Lord Hanuman called Panchamukhi Hanuman, which we'll discuss in more detail later. For now, let's briefly touch on this form.

Panchamukhi Hanuman refers to the five-faced Hanuman — pancha meaning five, and mukhi meaning faced. The five faces have various interpretations, and one such interpretation is that they represent the five pranas, or vital forces, within our body - prana, apana, udana, vyana, and samana. These vital forces are essential for the involuntary functions of our body that happen without conscious control, such as the beating of the heart, the functioning of the lungs, the filtration by the kidneys, and so forth. These functions are powered by these pranas, enabling the body to operate smoothly.

1. Prana – Governs the region between the mouth and the chest, assisting in functions like respiration, sensory perception, and the initiation of digestion.

2. Apana – Covers the navel and below, responsible for the reproductive and excretory systems.

3. Vyana – The pervasive force throughout the body, supporting the circulatory and nervous systems.

4. Udana – Governs the area from the throat upwards, including the brain, speech, sensory processing, and thought.

5. Samana – Located between the chest and navel, related to the digestive system, metabolism, and assimilation of nutrients.

For the body to function normally, all five pranas need to be in balance. Any disruption or imbalance in these forces can manifest as physical or mental ailments. The Panchamukhi form of Hanuman symbolizes the balancing of these five vital forces, contributing to the prevention or healing of diseases. Similarly, Panchamukhi Ganesha also represents these forces, embodying the energy that maintains harmony in the body. Hanuman is described as one who "nase roga" or eradicates diseases. This verse signifies how a divine power, or grace, keeps the body functioning by balancing these vital forces within us. We are literally at the mercy of this force for even the basic functioning of the body.

Physical ailments are one part of the picture, but the most significant disease each of us has is our ego. The ego is the most challenging disease because it is difficult to prevent, diagnose, and cure. Unless we practice control over our mind and senses (shama and dama), the ego will manifest in some form.

In Indian scriptures, this is referred to as bhavaroga - roga meaning disease, and bhava referring to the vicious cycle of birth and death, where one is born, dies, and is reborn. Bhavaroga describes this cycle, which traps us in worldly existence. The leading cause for this is our ego. Actions performed egocentrically pull us deeper into this vicious cycle.

The 842nd name of the Divine Mother in *Sri Lalita Sahasranama* is:

Om bhava rogaghnyai namah

Oone who eliminates the disease of birth and death.

This name refers to her role in helping us overcome bhavaroga, the endless cycle of rebirth.

Similarly, in the *Guru Gita*, there is a verse that talks about the guru who cures bhavaroga:

yōgīndra mīḍyam bhavarōga vaidyam
śrīmadgurum nityamaham namāmi

*One who is supreme amongst those in the highest state of union
with the Supreme, one who is the physician that cures the
disease of the vicious cycle of birth and death, I bow down to
the Sadguru, the spiritual preceptor, the enlightened Master.*

Some regional versions of the *Ramayana* refer to Panchamukhi Hanuman or the five-faced form of Hanuman. Additionally, some tantric texts describe this form of Hanuman. This form of Hanuman can be interpreted as embodying the qualities needed to conquer the ego and guide us in our spiritual journey.

The *Krittivasi Ramayana*, written in Bengali, contains a reference to Panchamukhi Hanuman coming to the rescue of Rama and Lakshmana from the demon Mahiravana. As with many traditional epics, there are multiple versions of this story involving various characters. Here, we'll explore just the main parts of the story, focusing on the spiritual message it conveys.

Mahiravana (sometimes called Ahiravana), a brother of Ravana, enters the conflict between Lord Rama's monkey army and Ravana's forces. As Ravana's demons begin to fall one by one, he finally calls upon Mahiravana, who is said to be the lord of the netherworld (Patala Loka). Mahiravana was a worshipper of Maya Devi (the goddess of illusion) and possessed the power to mesmerize anyone. He reveals his plan to Ravana: Abduct Rama and Lakshmana, take them to the netherworld, and sacrifice them to the Divine Mother. Vibhishana becomes aware of this plan and warns everyone. Rama and Lakshmana are placed under constant guard. One evening, while Rama and Lakshmana are asleep and Hanuman is guarding their tent, Mahiravana approaches in the disguise of Vibhishana and is allowed inside. Using his powers,

Mahiravana casts a spell over the entire army, putting everyone into a deep sleep. He then abducts Rama and Lakshmana, taking them to the netherworld to use in his sacrificial ritual. As the others scramble for a solution, Hanuman — always enthusiastic and committed to action — immediately sets off for the netherworld to confront Mahiravana. However, Mahiravana has a boon that protects him: He cannot be killed unless five lamps burning in five different directions are extinguished simultaneously with a single blow. Understanding this, Hanuman assumes the form of Panchamukhi Hanuman, a five-faced form representing different divine aspects. With this form, he is able to extinguish all five lamps at once, thereby nullifying Mahiravana's protection. Hanuman then defeats Mahiravana and rescues Lord Rama and Lakshmana.

The five faces of Panchamukhi Hanuman each have symbolic significance:

1. Hanuman (Monkey Face): Represents the control of the restless, wandering mind — an essential aspect for overcoming ego.

2. Varaha (Boar Face): An incarnation of Lord Vishnu, symbolizing courage and strength. The boar is known for its fierce resolve, attacking even predators if challenged, and embodying a "never give up" spirit.

3. Garuda (Eagle Face): Another form related to Lord Vishnu, Garuda is the enemy of snakes and symbolically represents the ability to overcome negativity, illusions, and poisonous thoughts.

4. Narasimha (Lion Face): Yet another incarnation of Vishnu, Narasimha's fierce, unyielding nature signifies that when confronting negativity or ego,

there is no room for compromise. We must face our inner demons head-on and decisively.

5. Hayagriva (Horse Face): The epitome of wisdom and knowledge, Hayagriva reminds us of the need for discernment, understanding, and enlightenment to overcome ego and ignorance.

Through Panchamukhi Hanuman, we see the five qualities needed to overcome the "disease" of ego: control of the mind, courage, determination to face challenges without compromise, the will to overcome negativity, and wisdom. Lord Hanuman exemplifies these qualities, and the five faces underscore what we may not always perceive from his typical form.

Panchamukhi Hanuman serves as an inspirational symbol, showing us the path toward inner mastery and the dissolution of ego.

In the life of a mahatma like Amma, adverse situations and suffering are not uncommon. A realized master who has overcome the ego has the ability to step aside and just be a witness. While suffering may appear outwardly, they are mentally unaffected.

Having physically taxed herself for the last 50 years through her ceaseless efforts to embrace everyone who comes to her, we can ask the question - is Amma suffering? The answer could be yes, but, no. People go to her saying, "Amma, I have thyroid issues, high blood pressure, diabetes, and back pain," or some other problem. Amma often sympathetically responds, "I have those issues too." Amma faces many of these health issues herself, but does she suffer? Certainly not. When giving darshan, she appears entirely unburdened by these ailments.

Additionally, Amma's many charitable projects could also be seen as burdensome. Her institutions and projects pose their own challenges. The university, with its students, has its unique problems; the housing projects have theirs. The many villages that Amma has adopted across India each have legal, social, and governmental matters to address. Each ashram resident's illness or problem could be considered a burden on Amma. Astoundingly, instead of feeling overwhelmed and anxious like many of us might, she instead took the opportunity to call each person in Amritapuri who fell ill with Covid-19 to check in on them during the pandemic. Viewed from the outside, these situations could easily be perceived as causing suffering or stress. Yet, Amma does not allow them to weigh her down or affect her mental state. A person who has control over their mind and ego has the ability to dictate their own terms, choosing whether a situation will become a burden or remain neutral.

When we think about problems or difficulties, some people commonly consult Vedic astrology (Jyotish). People often rush to an astrologer to find out what's causing their troubles. In astrology, nine planets or planetary deities are considered influential. Among these, we have the Sun (Surya Deva) and his offspring, Shani, the lord of Saturn. While the Sun represents brilliance, Shani, or Saturn, is often associated with darkness and lack of brilliance. Shani tends to have a negative reputation; people often react with dread when they hear they have Shani in their chart, fearing a challenging period ahead.

But here's the real question: Is Shani the problem, or does the issue lie elsewhere? Spiritually speaking, Shani is not the problem. Shani is simply fulfilling his role and duty. Surya Deva has two sons: Yama, who administers justice after death, and Shani, who delivers justice during our lives. Shani's job is not to cause harm but to reflect back to us the consequences of our actions.

This reminds me of my elementary school Hindi teacher, Rose Ma'am. Rose Ma'am was strict, and back in the 80s in India, it was common for teachers to administer corporal punishment. If you didn't do your homework, Rose Ma'am would twist your ears and make you stand outside the classroom. This would earn you the ironic title of an "outstanding student" because you were literally standing outside! She wasn't popular with many of the students, who complained about her strictness. Especially during lunchtime, they would say things like, "She's so bad; she's such a problem." However, one very studious classmate, always in the teachers' good graces, often told others, "Do you really think she's the problem? I never have issues with her because I always do my homework. You're getting punished because you don't do yours. Rose Ma'am isn't the problem; you are the problem for not doing your part."

Similarly, Shani is like Rose Ma'am. He simply enforces the consequences of our actions. If we "do our homework" in life, meaning we act responsibly and humbly, Shani has no reason to punish us. However, if we let our ego grow unchecked and neglect our inner work, Shani will inevitably twist our metaphorical ears and put us in time-out. The real issue isn't with Shani; it's with how we approach life. So, during a Shani phase, it's only those who are prideful and attached to their ego who need to worry. Those who have control over their ego and act with humility have nothing to fear from Shani.

As a matter of fact, a true spiritual being never really needs to worry about Shani (Saturn). Shani simply doesn't affect a true spiritual soul. Our attitude ultimately decides whether Shani will be a problem for us. In Vedic astrology, Shani is often associated with hard work and obstacles. Someone going through a Shani phase has to work harder; things don't come easily, which is why Shani is sometimes seen as troublesome. But if we think about it, hard work is actually a good thing. We often praise someone by saying they are hard-working. So, hard work can be positive if we view it that way. A genuine spiritual person typically embodies qualities that align with what Shani represents. Such a person would naturally be hardworking, modest, and content with minimal requirements. In that case, what effect can Shani have on them?

Consider this story: A man visits an astrologer and says, "Please help me. I'm going through my Shani phase, and I'm terrified of it." The astrologer replies, "Sure, let me look at your chart. Place a 1,000 rupees on the table, and I'll provide remedies." The man responds, "I don't have a 1,000 rupees." The astrologer says, "Okay, 500 will do." The man replies, "I don't have 500 either." The astrologer tries again, "Then place 250." The man declines again, saying "I don't have that much." Eventually, the astrologer asks for just 10 rupees. The man looks in his pockets and says, "I don't have 10 rupees." Finally, the astrologer says, "If you don't even have 10 rupees, what more can Shani possibly do to you?"

This story, while humorous, has a profound message. Not having 10 rupees symbolizes a lack of attachment and minimal desires. When a person is genuinely unattached, with no significant possessions or desires, Shani — or any astrological influence with a negative connotation — has no power over them. In a spiritual sense, Shani can only affect us to the extent that we are bound by material attachments. Hanuman represents that state where one goes beyond likes, dislikes, and ego. When we transcend ego, suffering or negativity has little effect on us.

There are mythological references in which Saturn (Shani) and his ally Mars (Mangala) are portrayed as enemies of the Sun (Surya). In these stories, Hanuman plays an important role — both through humble negotiation and sheer might — in reconciling them and restoring their friendship with Surya. If we examine this symbolically, it makes logical sense. Surya represents brilliance and illumination. Shani, often associated with dullness, symbolizes hard work and toil. Our lazy, inertia-prone mind tends to resist effort, making it difficult to attain brilliance — thus creating a natural conflict between Shani and Surya. When we add aggression (Mangala) to the mix, the situation becomes even messier. Aggression without direction or discipline can disrupt both effort and brilliance. So what is the solution to this stalemate? Bhakti — devotion or dedication. When we cultivate true dedication, we gain the drive to work hard (Shani) and channel aggression (Mangala) toward a noble goal. This is how we ultimately attain brilliance (Surya). This is what the story of Hanuman

— symbolizing bhakti — represents. Hanuman guided Shani (hard work) and Mangala (aggression) toward serving Surya (brilliance). It is said that, in gratitude, Shani granted Hanuman a boon, saying that those who worship Hanuman on Saturdays (shani-var), Shani's day, would be spared Shani's negative influence. Mangala (Mars) also offered a similar boon, saying that worshipers of Hanuman on mangal-var (Tuesday) would be free from Mars's disruptive effects.

Thus, Hanuman became known as the one who rescues devotees from difficulties and dispels troubles and worries. This story beautifully illustrates that with spiritual strength, we can transcend difficulties, overcome even the influence of celestial forces, and achieve inner peace.

Making Thoughts, Words, and Actions into Meditation

We need to understand this protection in a spiritual sense, because Hanuman represents a state of egolessness. Once we attain that state, we naturally overcome various problems. The 26th verse mentions that negative effects will not influence us when we devote ourselves to Hanuman. But how can we truly devote ourselves to Hanuman? By dedicating our thoughts, speech, and actions to him — bringing mindfulness (bodha) and meditation into everything we think, say, and do. This practice of integrating meditation and devotion is the best way to worship Hanuman. Though traditionally Tuesdays and Saturdays are set aside for worship, ideally, we can do this every day. However, these designated days serve as reminders, much like Mother's Day serves to remind us to honor our mothers, even though we appreciate them year-round. Similarly, Saturday and Tuesday worship encourages us to deepen our devotion. When we say that we devote ourselves to Hanuman, it means to bring mindfulness into our thoughts, words, and actions.

If we look at the lives of mahatmas, especially Amma, we see that Amma practices shraddha (this Sanskrit roughly translates to awareness, but we will explore its elements in the pages to come) in every moment. Meditation, in the sense of sitting down with our eyes closed, is just the beginning — it's the tip of the iceberg. True meditation happens when every moment of our life is carried out with shraddha; that's when life itself becomes meditation.

A satsang member once asked me, "Amma gives darshan for so long; when does she find time for archana and meditation? Does she go back to her room and do the thousand names or meditate?" I told them, "What do you think she's doing here?" Look at her darshan itself — it's the perfect example of shraddha, of meditation. When Amma embraces someone and whispers, "My dear child," or "Don't worry," that is her archana. She's probably doing ten thousand names a day, whispering into each person's ear. Simply being with others is her meditation. When Amma gives darshan, she is entirely present with each person. She listens to their problems; if they cry, she cries with them. If they laugh, she laughs with them. She offers them solutions when needed — she is entirely present. Simultaneously, if someone on her side has a question — sometimes life-changing — she answers them with the utmost shraddha. At the same time, if the person on the prasad line on her left side is careless, she will point out to them that they have not included the holy ash, an apple, or a banana in the prasad bundle. In addition to all this happening during darshan, she's completely aware of what is happening around her. Sometimes, when I stand next to her for translation and a thought crosses my mind, she turns around to give me a hint that she's aware of it. Once, while I was singing the bhajan Anjana Sridhara during darshan, I missed a stanza. It's a long song with several stanzas. Suddenly, a couple of Hershey Kisses landed on me out of the blue. When I opened my eyes, I realized they were from Amma, and she was pointing out that I missed that stanza. This is a perfect example of shraddha — complete awareness amidst all that she is involved in during darshan. Every moment of Amma's life is meditation.

When we practice shraddha in every moment, we incorporate meditation into our thoughts, words, and actions, and life itself becomes meditation. We gain the ability to choose whether or not to suffer. Whether the situation around us is adverse or favorable, we can decide how we want to respond. This choice is entirely under our control.

Let's briefly review the elements of shraddha. Shraddha can be loosely translated as awareness. Practicing awareness in what we do means engaging with complete concentration, staying focused, and avoiding distractions from things or people around us.

Practicing shraddha involves:

1. Practicing concentration and focus in whatever action we perform

2. Faith and trust in ourselves, in others involved, and in the situation and resources at hand — like trusting the bus driver, the bus itself, and our own decisions when traveling.

3. Respect for the situation, for ourselves and our abilities, and for others as they are.

4. Positive attitude: Approaching situations with a constructive and proper mindset.

5. Love for whatever we do; doing it wholeheartedly.

6. Patience and acceptance: exercising patience and accepting the outcome, whatever it may be, regardless of our efforts.

7. Awareness and consciousness: Being aware of everything happening around us, including people's attitude, backgrounds, and the implications of our actions and thoughts.

8. All these qualities enveloped in true knowledge/wisdom - with the right discernment of dharma (discrimination between what is right and what is wrong).

Combining all these qualities — concentration and focus, faith and trust, respect, a positive attitude, love, patience and acceptance, awareness and consciousness, knowledge, and wisdom — means that we are truly practicing shraddha. In this way, every thought, word, and action becomes meditation. Therefore, one who brings meditation into each action, thought, and utterance is exercising shraddha in its fullest form.

These verses point out that Hanuman helps us overcome difficulties, the disease of ego, and adverse situations. When we truly become one with Hanuman, these issues cease to be problems for us — that is the true spiritual message. However, as devotees who see ourselves as separate from Hanuman, we may believe that Hanuman is rescuing us from our challenges. When we embrace the principle of oneness with Hanuman, we embody his qualities and can rise above any situation.

Insights on the Path of Bhakti from verses 25 & 26:

- Devotion is the medicine for the most significant disease of all - our ego.
- Devotion brings bliss and helps overcome difficulties and suffering.
- Practice shraddha in every thought, word, and action that we perform.

Verses 27 and 28

True Master serves rather than commands
True devotee is dedicated to the master's noble cause
Living everyday boundlessly is immortality

saba para rāma tapasvī rājā ।   सब पर राम तपस्वी राजा।
tinakē kāja sakala tuma sājā ॥ 27 ॥   तिनके काज सकल तुम साजा।

saba - all; para - upon; rāma - Lord Rama; tapasvī
- ascetic; rājā - king; tinakē - whose; kāja - work;
sakala - all; tuma - you; sājā - facilitate;

*Ruling over all is Rama the tapasvi - the greatest of the
ascetics. Through your devotion to him, you assist in all
the tasks taken up by such an extraordinary being.*

aura manōratha jō kōyi lāvai ।   और मनोरथ जो कोई लावै।
sōyi amita jīvana phala pāvai ॥ 28 ॥   सोई अमित जीवन फल पावै॥

aura - other; manōratha - desires; jō kōyi - all those;
lāvai - bring; sōyi - that; amita - boundless; jīvana
- life; phala - fruit/result; pāvai - obtain;

*Whoever brings their many desires and wishes to you,
are showered with boundless life as fruit (of their action).*

Being the True Master

Lord Rama, to whom Hanuman is devoted, is a unique king — a personification of perfection. Known as Raja Ram, he is the king who rules over all, yet he is a tapasvi, someone who personally endures the trials his subjects face. Rather than sitting on a throne and giving orders, he rules by example, inspiring his people through his own actions and dedication. In this sense, Lord Rama is called Tapasvi Raja — a king who undergoes penance and empathizes deeply, touching the hearts of his people. His rulership is one of understanding and shared compassion, making him not only a ruler but a true role model for all.

When people ask Amma, "So many come to see you from around the world; wherever you go thousands line up for your darshan.
You seem to be the queen of this spiritual empire," she responds, "No, not the queen; rather, Amma would prefer to be a sweeper than a queen." Amma would rather be a sweeper who helps cleanse our minds. When you observe Amma sitting in her chair, with thousands waiting to see her, it becomes clear that she is the one making the greatest effort. She spends hours embracing individuals, listening to their struggles, and providing comfort, all while sacrificing her own basic needs.

That's how a true ruler should be: a genuine king or ruler has the attitude of a servant, feeling they are here to serve rather than rule over others. Only with this perspective can they truly fulfill their responsibilities in the best way possible. To serve in this way, one must have control over personal likes, dislikes, emotions, and selfish motives, remaining selfless. Only one who has overcome their ego can be a true king. That is the very example Lord Rama personified.

Bhagavad Gita Chapter 6 verse 17 goes as follows:

yuktāhāra-vihārasya yukta-cheṣhṭasya karmasu
yukta-svapnāvabodhasya yogo bhavati duḥkha-hā

For one who is controlled/temperate in eating habits and
in recreation (activities); regulated in exertion in action;
moderate in sleep (dream) and wakefulness; yoga (ultimate
union with the Truth) becomes the destroyer of pain.

When we talk about moderation in food and sleep, who could serve as a better example than Amma? In Amma's life, food and sleep aren't just secondary; they seem to be almost insignificant, as if they're simply along for the ride, barely registering amidst her efforts. Despite the intense physical and mental exertion she undergoes daily, Amma hardly sleeps or eats.

Take, for example, Amma's tours. They truly illustrate her remarkable resilience. She travels from India to Japan, a three-and-a-half-hour time difference. After arriving in the evening, she begins her programs the very next morning with no concept of jet lag. After a few days in Japan, she flies to Seattle, a location 14 hours behind India. She arrives in the afternoon and, once again, starts her programs the following day without missing a beat. Meanwhile, everyone else is visibly jet-lagged — I myself have occasionally missed evening bhajans because I overslept. Adjusting to the drastic time differences can feel impossible. But for Amma, jet lag doesn't seem to exist; she seamlessly continues her work, regardless of time zone or location. It's as if the concept itself is foreign to her because she's simply immersed in what she does, wherever she is.

And as it is "Amma's tour," Amma is presumably the ultimate authority or boss of events. But she doesn't reign from a throne or direct orders. Instead, much like Tapasvi Raja, Amma leads by example, giving herself entirely, both physically and mentally, to the service of others.

Throughout the tour, we all have seva, and while we stretch ourselves — sacrificing food, sleep, and comfort — it's incomparable to Amma's effort. Each time we enter the hall, seeing Amma giving darshan belittles any sacrifices we've made. Some of the tour staff have even shared with me that they have left the hall and gone to sleep while

Amma is giving darshan late into the night, and come back to the hall after a night's sleep only to find Amma back where she was when they left, having herself slept only two hours or less before returning for the next morning's program. Amma remains seated, embracing one person after another tirelessly. Many leaders do not set such an example, and it's rare, perhaps unprecedented, to find one who does so continuously. One can argue that one may have seva even after Amma leaves after the last program in a city. But mind you, we are done after a few hours of cleaning and restoration. Amma goes on to the next place, just to begin yet another marathon session with darshan. This happens 365 days a year. There is truly no way to compare the scale of her efforts logically to our own.

So, is Amma the "boss?" Absolutely. But why? Because she exemplifies the highest standard of service, embodying the spirit of a servant leader. Her dedication to others truly makes her a leader. In this way, she sets a leadership model through service, creating a lasting impact by showing how to serve selflessly.

Before we had the main hall built in Amritapuri, where Amma's bhajans now take place in the evening, it was just an open ground. When Amma's birthday program approached, a vast tent was erected, much like the current hall setup but temporary. Construction for the tent would start almost a month in advance, with poles, metal sheets on top, and lots of work going on.

I recall an instance in 1996 when preparations for Amma's birthday were underway. Amma came for bhajans and then took a walk around the construction site. She noticed many nails and sharp objects scattered on the ground and commented that, during the birthday celebrations, most people would be barefoot, so this was dangerous. She suggested that all the nails and sharp objects should be removed, and everyone agreed that it should be done. However, once Amma went back to her room, everyone else went back to their routines, and the task was quickly forgotten. The next day, after the bhajans, Amma again went to inspect the birthday program site and saw that the nails and sharp objects were still lying around. She was surprised, saying, "No one did anything about this? Amma will do it herself." She asked everyone to step aside, saying, "Amma mentioned it yesterday, and no one did it, so now Amma will do it herself." A few lucky ashram children, including me, were able to join Amma, and she personally helped pick up every nail and sharp object, collecting them in a bag. Just imagine the scene — someone visiting the ashram for the first time might see a woman sitting on the ground, carefully picking things up with some children. If they asked, "Who's the boss here?" and someone pointed to her, saying, "That lady sitting on the bare ground with a bunch of children, picking up nails and stones is the boss," it's hard to imagine they would even believe it right away.

The typical mold or framework we have for a ruler or boss is quite different: someone sitting on a throne or in front of an elaborate desk, commanding others. But a true ruler is someone who, like Amma, sets an example by coming down to others' level, working with them, and often working even harder than them. Because we have all seen Amma set this kind of example, you can see these same values embraced by everyone throughout Amma's organization - it has become the culture of the organization. A true king, therefore, would be a tapasvi — a perfect ascetic and hard worker — someone who sets an example through their service to others. This is why such a leader is referred to as a true Raja.

Being a True Devotee

When we devote ourselves to the spiritual master, the master sets an example of how a true devotee should be. The master exemplifies devotion by embodying it fully. As devotees, our efforts should provide the best support for the noble cause of the master in uplifting the world. The 27th verse states that Hanuman undertakes all tasks on behalf of the great tapasvi raja, Lord Rama, ultimately aiding and overseeing Rama's noble endeavors. Lord Hanuman was so dedicated to Lord Rama that he offered himself entirely to his service, setting aside his own comfort, needs, likes, dislikes, and ego. This is the true sign of devotion.

Let's look at a story that illustrates Hanuman's boundless enthusiasm for serving Lord Rama. Hanuman was so innocent and childlike in his devotion that he would constantly be by Rama's side, always engaged in seva (selfless service). Mother Sita felt that Hanuman should take a break and give them some privacy — he was always around, doing something or the other. She gently suggested to Lord Rama that he ask Hanuman to step away for a while. Rama smiled and said, "Okay, if you say so." He then summoned Hanuman and told him that he was relieved of all duties for the time being and should stay away for some time. Hanuman was clearly taken aback and disheartened, but he humbly accepted Rama's command. Sita let out a small sigh of relief.

Some time later, Lord Rama asked for some milk. Sita couldn't find any in the kitchen and began calling for a maid to fetch some. While she was looking, she heard Rama's voice again — this time requesting hot water boiled with tulasi (Indian basil) leaves, as his throat was hurting. Sita set off to find tulasi leaves, but the palace's indoor garden didn't have any. She began looking for the gardener to help when she again heard Rama's voice — urgently asking for a letter that Angada, the monkey prince, had sent. Sita searched every room for the letter, but in vain. Just as she was about to tell Rama she couldn't find it, she saw him walk out of the palace. In a way, she felt relieved — his continuous requests were definitely overwhelming for her.

That night, as they were retiring to their bedroom, Sita was about to apologize to Rama for not being able to fulfill any of his requests that morning. But before she could say a word, Rama said gently: "I'm so thankful to you. You take care of me so well. Even with Hanuman gone, everything I needed was still taken care of." Sita looked puzzled. "I have to confess," she said, "I wasn't able to complete a single task you asked for." Rama seemed surprised. "But why do you say that? I asked for milk, and it was in my room within a minute. I asked for hot tulasi water, and that too appeared quickly. Even Angada's letter arrived just in time — I was able to send a reply with the messenger leaving for Kishkindha." Sita was astonished. "But I didn't do any of that," she confessed. "Then who did?" she asked. With a smile, Rama replied, "Do you really not know who it was? Of course, it was Hanuman."

He then summoned Hanuman and asked him directly. Hanuman bowed and said: "My Lord, you told me to go away, and I followed your instructions. But when I saw Mother Sita struggling with your seva, how could I not help? I discreetly placed the items in your room, pretending she had done it. But, as per your command, I never showed my face to you." Tears welled up in Sita's eyes, seeing the depth of Hanuman's love — his die-hard dedication to Rama, his willingness to serve silently, even without any recognition.

When we say that Hanuman is involved in Lord Rama's tasks, we must ask ourselves: What are Lord Rama's tasks? Are they simply to fulfill Rama's basic needs, like water when he's thirsty, food when he's hungry, or a foot massage when he's tired? No, these are mundane tasks. The real tasks of Lord Rama are those that uphold dharma and benefit others. This is the essence of Rama's mission. So when it's said that Hanuman dedicates himself entirely to fulfilling Rama's tasks, it means that a true devotee pours heart and soul into upholding dharma, which the guru or spiritual master embodies.

Take Amma as an example. If we want to participate in Amma's work, we shouldn't think it means serving her directly by offering her a cup of coffee or massaging her feet. True service to Amma lies in actively supporting her mission to benefit the world through selfless service. Hanuman was entirely devoted to Lord Rama's mission, not picking and choosing tasks but giving himself completely to any endeavor that upheld dharma and benefited society. As spiritual aspirants, we can look to Hanuman as a model for dedication and service, following his example of unwavering commitment to fulfilling a higher purpose.

Desires of the Mind

The first part of verse 28 says, "Whoever brings a desire or prayer in their mind, Lord Hanuman helps the devotee with that desire." This aligns with verse 27, which describes Hanuman's unwavering dedication to assisting Lord Rama in all his tasks. One crucial task of Lord Rama is to listen to the prayers of devotees, and Hanuman fully supports this by attentively listening to these prayers and assisting however he can.

This offers a valuable lesson for all of us, especially when we are around Amma. Thousands come to her with their concerns — often deeply personal and painful. We should reflect on how we, too, can assist Amma in helping others with their problems. Sometimes, we focus solely on our own wants or dislikes, occasionally reacting negatively to others. Instead, we should ask ourselves: When someone brings their concerns to the guru, how can we embody the spirit of Hanuman by helping however we can? Amma often tells those doing seva around her during her darshan, especially those assisting with the darshan line, that people come to her seeking solutions for their suffering. And even we can play a small role in lightening their burden as they bring it to her. A simple smile, a few words filled with compassion, and a caring attitude can go a very long way.

Whenever I come across this verse in the *Chalisa*, I'm reminded of an incident that Amma often shares, which always brings her so much joy. It involves a humble, soft-spoken devotee from Montreal, known for his kind heart. This devotee travels with Amma on most tours, and one of his roles during Devi Bhava is to assist in distributing mantra cards. During Devi Bhava, people who request a mantra go through a briefing and then approach Amma to receive a mantra from her. This devotee's task was to hold the box of mantra cards and hand them to the individuals once Amma had given the mantra. One night in an exceptionally crowded city, the queue was especially chaotic, with nearly everyone who came for darshan asking for a mantra. Amma, who is always incredibly sharp with numbers, noticed that something was off. She was sure more people were requesting mantra cards than the number approaching her to receive a mantra. Curious, she had someone investigate. The person started tracing the sequence of how the mantra line was managed, and everything seemed to be in place. Every person joined the final line leading up to Amma. Then where did the people go missing, the person wondered? Upon further investigation, it was found that many in the line went missing from where this person stood at a short distance from Amma. It turned out that the devoted volunteer from Montreal had been preemptively handing out mantra cards himself. Observing the pattern of mantras given for specific deities, he thought he could help reduce Amma's workload, believing her neck and back must hurt from repeatedly turning to the side to whisper the mantra into the individuals' ears. So, with complete innocence, he simply handed out cards based on what he thought the mantra would be. Effectively, these people got the mantra from him rather than Amma. Amma found it amusing and rather than being upset, appreciated his innocent attempt to help. However, she ensured that everyone who missed the proper process was brought back to receive their mantra directly from Amma.

Amma often recounts this story with warmth, finding joy in his innocence. It reminds me of another instance involving a young girl who used to sit beside Amma during darshan, trying to give darshan herself, saying, "Let Amma rest; I'll do the darshan." These stories show the innocence and eagerness of devotees who, out of love, wish to take on the master's tasks in whatever way they can.

Amma often recalls these incidents because of the innocence of the devotees involved. However, in the case of children or others, their innocence often comes coupled with a bit of ignorance — as with the mantras, innocence was mixed with a lack of complete understanding. In contrast, Hanuman's innocence is paired with wisdom, not ignorance. This wisdom allows him to genuinely fulfill the desires of devotees, thereby taking some of the burden off Lord Rama.

Granting the Fruit of Boundless Life

The second part of the 28th verse says that those seeking Hanuman's blessings receive the fruits of their actions, leading to a boundless life. When we speak of a boundless life, it contrasts with the often-desired state of immortality. Immortality was the ultimate boon many asuras and seekers sought in the puranic episodes, desiring to live forever, often as granted by Shiva or Brahma. They hoped that eternal life would mean freedom from suffering or fear, yet, despite their efforts, they still faced constant battles, turmoil, and a lack of peace. In a true sense, both immortality and boundless life are the same. But just a blind desire for a long or endless life is meaningless.

The notion of a boundless life holds a deeper significance for spiritual aspirants. Rather than merely a prolonged existence, boundless life refers to a life lived fully — each day complete, joyful, and meaningful. This boundless life means experiencing unlimited growth, learning, and fulfillment. Unlike literal immortality, which promises only extended time without guarantees of happiness, boundless life is about quality over quantity, making it a far greater blessing. That is true immortality.

In this regard, I recall the story of Sage Markandeya. His parents, Sage Mrkanda and Mother Manasvini were unable to have a child. They performed penance until Lord Shiva appeared and offered them a boon to have a child, but with a choice: They could have a child who would live a long but relatively unremarkable life, or a child with a short life but filled with virtue and meaning. They chose the latter, opting for a child who would live life to its fullest. The story goes that through his devotion, Markandeya overcame Yama, the Lord of Death, who came to claim his life. First, Lord Yama's messengers failed to take him away, so Yama himself came to fetch him. Markandeya held on to the Shiva Linga, embracing it as Yama sprung his noose around Markandeya. As Yama pulled him away from the Shiva Linga, Lord Shiva emerged, rendering Yama powerless. Through his devotion to Lord Shiva, Markandeya ultimately achieved immortality, the ultimate state of boundlessness.

Rather than seeking a long, uncertain, or unremarkable life, focusing on living each day to its fullest potential is more important. That's what truly matters. The second part of the verse highlights the boon Lord Hanuman grants. Following his example, we can learn to live a more meaningful, spiritual life infused with devotion, selflessness, and purpose.

Insights on the Path of Bhakti from verses 27 & 28:

- Verse 27

  O true master does not sit on a throne, executing orders; rather they exercise penance and sacrifice in being of service to others.

  O A true master will be the ruler of hearts.

  O A true devotee is dedicated to realizing the master's cause of dharma and upliftment of others.

- Verse 28

  O Rather than just craving for long life or immortality, let us pray we live every day to its full potential.

Verses 29 and 30

Going beyond time
Upholding goodness, overcoming negativities
Becoming dear to your deity/guru

chārō yuga partāpa tumhārā ।   चारों युग परताप तुम्हारा ।
hai parisiddha jagata ujiyārā ॥ 29 ॥   है परसिद्ध जगत उजियारा ॥

chārō - all the four; yuga - epoch (long defined period of
time); partāpa - glory; tumhārā - your; hai parisiddha - is well
known; jagata - universe; ujiyārā - enlightened (awakened);

*Your splendor proliferates all the four ages (yugas);
your fame and greatness illuminate the world.*

sādhu santa kē tuma rakhavārē ।   साधु-संत के तुम रखवारे ।
asura nikandana rāma dulārē ॥ 30 ॥   असुर निकंदन राम दुलारे ॥

sādhu - one who has renounced worldly pleasures; santa - saint; kē -
of; tuma - you; rakhavārē - protector; asura - demons (negativities);
nikandana - annihilator; rāma - Lord Rama; dulārē - dear, beloved;

*You are the guardian of the sages and good-hearted ones. You
annihilate the demonic forces. You are most dear to Lord Rama.*

The 29th verse speaks of Hanuman's enduring glory across the four
yugas (epochs). It says that Hanuman's fame, or pratapa, is well-known
throughout all four yugas. His glory is described as a source of light that

enlightens and awakens the world, bringing illumination wherever it reaches. This verse emphasizes that Hanuman's influence and renown transcend time, continuously enlightening creation.

The term yuga here refers to a long period of time. In Sanskrit, time is often referred to as kala, which serves as a witness to the past, present, and future. Everything in existence can be related to or measured by time, as it influences all aspects of our lives. For example, when we say "I am 40 years old," we are providing context based on time, giving an idea of our stage or situation in life. If someone is 60, we might have certain expectations about their wisdom or physical state. If someone is five years old, we might assume something about their maturity or physical capabilities. In this way, time shapes our understanding of a person's state. Similarly, when we say, "I live here," and "you live there," the difference is often thought of in terms of distance, but distance can also be measured by time. "I am 10 minutes away from you," reflects this. Even space or size, another fundamental measure, can be understood through time. For instance, we might say that India is vast because traveling from the southern to the northern end can take several days. In this way, space can also be defined in terms of time.

Change — the very nature of creation — can be understood as a function of time. Over time, things evolve. For example, we were once close friends, but now we're not in touch. What happened? It's simply a matter of time. Back then, we worked together; perhaps we moved away or had a difference of opinion. Over time, circumstances changed. So everything in creation can be measured or understood with respect to time; everything is a function of time. Yuga serves as a measure of this, dividing an entire cycle of creation and destruction into four distinct periods, or epochs.

The term yuga also means pair or two, symbolizing duality. In the chapter discussing the first verse of the *Hanuman Chalisa*, we referred to a verse from Chapter 2 of the *Bhagavad Gita*, which explains how creation is designed to exist in dualities. Our sensory experiences are inherently dual — either pleasurable or painful. This duality is how creation sustains itself and maintains balance. Thus, yuga also points to the dual nature of existence.

The 657th name in the *Lalitha Sahasranama* goes as follows:

Om yugandharāyai namah

It means "one who holds the yugas" or "bearer of time." In Sanskrit, yugandhara also has another meaning: It signifies the yoke — the T-frame used in a bullock cart to connect and enable both bullocks to pull the cart. The yoke joins the two bulls, allowing them to work harmoniously. As yugandhara, the Divine Mother embodies the force that holds together dual experiences or dualities of time. Today, we might be happy; tomorrow, we may be sad. Situations and relationships shift — someone may be a friend today, an enemy tomorrow. Wealth may come one day and leave the next. All these dualities are under the Divine Mother's yoke as she creates and sustains them, allowing life to swing naturally between polarities. That's why she is known as yugandhara, who holds and harmonizes the dual nature of existence.

Based on this framework, time is divided into four yugas, each marked by a different balance of righteousness and unrighteousness, reflecting the dualities within creation. In the golden period, or Satya Yuga, righteousness prevails entirely. As we move forward in time, righteousness gradually diminishes. In the next age, unrighteousness begins to crop up but is still overshadowed by righteousness. In the third age, the two forces are in balance, but by the time we reach the final age, unrighteousness gains the upper hand. The yugas — Satya, Treta, Dwapara, and Kali — represent different balances of these dualities, oscillating between righteousness and its absence. They cycle repeatedly, with each cycle containing smaller cycles within. The best time is Satya Yuga, where righteousness dominates, and the worst is Kali Yuga, known as the darkest period. Each yuga offers different experiences shaped by the prevailing balance of these dualities.

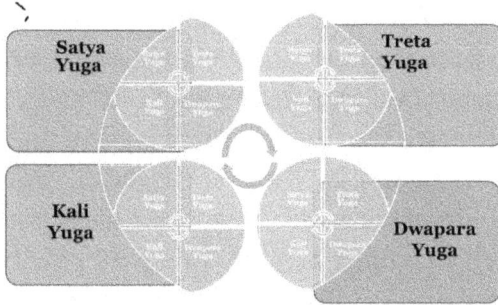

Amma beautifully explains the four yugas — Satya, Dwapara, Treta, and Kali — in a way that is easy to understand. She says that the conflict was between the asuras and devas (demons and gods) in Satya Yuga. In Treta Yuga, the conflict moved to neighboring nations, as seen in the battle between Lord Rama in India and Ravana in Lanka. Dwapara Yuga saw an internal family conflict between cousins, the Kauravas and Pandavas. Finally, in Kali Yuga, the conflict has come even closer — it now exists within each of us as a struggle between our inner goodness and negativities. The more the negativities have the upper hand, the more we face difficulties.

Glory Spanning Over the Four Yugas

The first line of the 29th verse of the *Chalisa* states, "In all four yugas, your pratapa (glory) is very well known," describing Lord Hanuman's fame as widely recognized and celebrated across all ages. He is known as chiranjeevi — immortal, one who has no end. The *Puranas* mention only a few who have been granted the boon of immortality, and Lord Hanuman stands out as one of the rare beings blessed with this gift.

There are different references to how Lord Hanuman received the boon of immortality. One version is based on what we discussed in the 18th verse, where we touched on the story of Hanuman mistaking the Sun for a fruit and attempting to eat it. Seeing this, Lord Indra, the king of the devas, felt compelled to protect the Sun. He recognized Hanuman's formidable power and used his most potent weapon, the vajra (thunderbolt) to fend him off. When it struck Hanuman, he fell unconscious and plummeted toward the Earth. Witnessing his son's helpless state, the wind god Vayu was devastated. Enraged, Vayu questioned who had dared to harm his innocent son. When no one responded, he declared he would cease functioning, withdrawing air from the world. Without air, life began to come to a standstill; people couldn't breathe, clouds stopped moving, and existence seemed to pause. Realizing the dire consequences, the devas convened to find a way to appease Vayu and defuse the situation. They apologized, and each of the devas granted Hanuman a boon. Lord Brahma blessed him with invulnerability to all weapons, no matter how powerful, and the ability to change his form and move anywhere at will. Vishwakarma, the celestial architect, granted him immunity from harm by any object, ensuring his safety. Yama, the lord of death, blessed him with ultimate health and immortality. Even Indra, who had attacked Hanuman, granted him the boon to choose the time of his death. With all these blessings combined, Hanuman essentially became immortal.

In the Uttara Kanda, the final canto of the *Ramayana*, it is said that as Lord Rama prepared to leave his physical form, he bestowed various boons on his close companions. To Hanuman, Rama spontaneously granted the boon of eternal life, saying, "You will live forever and uphold dharma, heeding my command as long as creation exists." Thus, Hanuman was blessed to be chiranjeevi (immortal), ensuring he would exist across all four yugas. His glory remains ever-respected and renowned through every era.

If we look at it spiritually, when we say chiranjeevi, it refers to someone who transcends time. In this creation, everything is a function of time — birth and death are simply points in time, and life is the period between them. A chiranjeevi is someone beyond these points, unaffected by the limitations of time because they are identified not with the physical realm but with their eternal Self. When one identifies with the eternal Self, they are no longer subject to the effects of time; they move beyond birth and death. For mahatmas like Amma, death is just another experience. Amma describes it as a comma or a period in a sentence — one sentence ends, and another begins. It's simply another event within the soul's journey.

Bhagavad Gita, Chapter 2, Verse 20 states:

na jāyate mriyate vā kadāchin nāyam bhūtvā bhavitā vā na bhūyaḥ
ajo nityaḥ śāśvato-yam purāṇo na hanyate hanyamāne śarīre

This (the Atman) is not born or dead at any time, neither 'coming into being' nor 'ceasing to exist'; it is unborn, eternal, changeless/constant, and ancient. When the body is slain, the Atman is not.

The verse refers to the Atma, or the Self, describing it as neither born nor subject to death at any time; it simply exists. It doesn't come into existence, nor does it cease to exist. This is the very essence of the Atma — it simply is. It is described as ajah (unborn), nithya (eternal), shashvat (constant or changeless), and purana (ancient, existing from the beginning). Even if the body is destroyed, the Atma remains unaffected.

For one identified with the Atma, like Lord Hanuman in his ultimate state, this is true chiranjeevitva, or eternal existence. Once fully identified with the True Self, untouched by birth and death, one transcends the limits of the physical body and becomes eternal. In this way, Hanuman, reaching the state of pure self-realization, embodies this spiritual chiranjeevi nature — an existence beyond time, unaffected by birth and death.

Enlightening the World

Lord Hanuman is chiranjeevi (immortal), with his glory spanning all four periods of time. But what's the nature of his fame? It is such that it brings light into the world — jagat ujiyārā — it enlightens and benefits creation. Fame has little value if it doesn't help others.

This reminds me of something shared by a dignitary who attended one of Amma's programs. He spoke about Amma, saying, "I've met many celebrities and VIPs who simply come and go. But when Amma comes and leaves, she leaves a positive imprint on me and the thousands she meets." This is the difference between the fame and reach of mahatmas, like Amma, and the other so-called celebrities. That's the essence of true fame — it should enlighten and uplift the world.

During Amma's 2013 Indian tour, as she arrived at the Kolkata ashram, she noticed how filthy the neighborhood was. Garbage and discarded items littered the streets leading up to the ashram. Seeing the state of the area, Amma remarked that something should be done about it.

The next day was a full-day program. As always, Amma led the meditation, gave a talk, sang bhajans, and spent hours giving darshan — meeting thousands of people, listening to their problems, offering solace, and showering them with love. It was well past 2 a.m. by the time darshan finally ended. Naturally, those who had been helping throughout the long day were eager to rest. But in a way that was so characteristic of Amma, instead of heading to her room, she reminded everyone of the filth outside and said, "Let's go and clean." Without any hesitation, she walked onto the road and began picking up trash with her own hands, gathering it into piles. Seeing Amma out there, thousands of people who just moments before had been exhausted felt a surge of energy and joined in. Within a few hours, the entire area had been transformed.

The next morning, locals woke up to a sight they could hardly believe. The streets that had

been covered in filth just the day before were now spotlessly clean, unrecognizable from their former state. It was as if the entire place had been reborn overnight. And as if nothing extraordinary had happened, Amma returned that morning for another full day of darshan—giving, giving, and giving, never pausing for a moment, never seeking rest, only pouring out endless love.

The point here is that our influence and recognition should serve a higher purpose — bringing benefit to people and society. If not, what is the value of popularity or having a following? Without taking up a purpose beyond oneself, simply becoming famous only serves one's own ego.

Whereas mahatmas like Amma use their fame solely to uplift and positively impact the world. Take Embracing the World, for instance. Inspired by Amma, her children across the globe chose not to live routine, self-centered lives but instead dedicated themselves to serving society in whatever way they could. From this simple yet profound intention, a vast network of humanitarian initiatives blossomed, organically spreading Amma's message of selfless service and love.

In the same way, just remembering Hanuman fills our hearts with positivity, awakening noble thoughts and qualities within us. This is the essence of this verse: True glory is that which illuminates the world and inspires goodness. We, too, should use whatever influence we have — no matter how big or small — to serve, uplift, and bring light to others.

Protector of Sages and Saints

Many episodes in the *Ramayana* and its variations illustrate how Lord Hanuman protected sages and hermits as they pursued noble causes. Whether through his wit or strength, Hanuman would guard them from negative forces, such as the asuras. He constantly used his abilities to serve others, especially those upholding dharma. The 30th verse of the *Chalisa* says that Hanuman protects sadhus (those who have renounced worldly pleasures and live in pursuit of truth and righteousness) and saints dedicated to positive causes. Hanuman is the protector and savior of these noble beings. He is the one who annihilates asuras, forces filled with negativity, thus earning the favor of Lord Rama. Therefore, he is ever dear to Lord Rama.

In previous chapters, we've discussed Hanuman's encounters with powerful asuras, from which he always emerged victorious. Let us take a look at some of them: In the ninth verse, we discussed Surasa, a rakshasi who tested Hanuman's might while he crossed the Indian Ocean to Lanka in search of Mother Sita. Surasa, with her wide-open mouth, tried to swallow Hanuman, who cleverly entered her mouth in a large form, then shrank and quickly escaped before she could close her mouth. During the same journey to Lanka, Simhika the demoness tried to capture Hanuman's shadow and drain his energy. She represents the force within us that can consume our positivity. Hanuman defeated her, as we discussed in the chapter on the 19th verse. Then Mahiravana, the king of the netherworlds, abducted Rama and Lakshmana to sacrifice them. Taking his Panchamukhi (five-faced) form, Hanuman put an end to Mahiravana and rescued them.

In all these situations, Hanuman stood as the protector of righteousness and dharma, safeguarding those who dedicated themselves to goodness and benefiting the world. He constantly defended the sadhus and saints, fighting against the forces of negativity. Hanuman's role is to uphold virtue and protect the righteous. The sadhus and saints he protected worked for goodness, peace, the welfare and betterment of others, thus representing the positive qualities within us. In contrast, the asuras symbolize our negativity — forces that work against the welfare of others. Hanuman is revered as the protector of goodness within each of us, constantly fighting against and overcoming our inner negativities.

Dear to Lord Rama

When we live a life of benefit to others, we become Ramadulara - Lord Rama's dear one, his favorite. Hanuman is known by various names like Shankara Suvana - the embodiment of Lord Shiva; Kesari Nandana - the son of the mighty monkey Kesari; Anjani Putra - the son of Mother Anjani, and Pavana Putra - son of the wind god. Hanuman carries many names, yet Ramadulara is particularly special.

There are instances in *Ramayana* where Lord Rama and Mother Sita treat Hanuman as their dear and favorite son. When Hanuman set out to find Mother Sita in the Ashoka Vatika, she referred to him as "son," a term that filled Hanuman with unbridled joy, as he always regarded her as his mother. Later, after Lord Rama defeated Ravana and the war concluded, Lord Rama embraced Hanuman and addressed him as "son." This acknowledgment made Hanuman feel profoundly honored and loved. Thus, Hanuman is called Ramadulara, Lord Rama's darling, a title that reflects their deep bond and affection.

Let me share an interesting folk tale that highlights how deeply dear Hanuman was to Lord Rama, all because of his pure selflessness. Long after the war, back in Ayodhya, one day, a light-hearted conversation arose between Sita and Lakshmana. What began as a playful discussion quickly turned into a friendly debate: Who is dearest to Lord Rama? Each had their own reasoning. Sita said, "I am his consort, his life partner. I share everything with him — his joys, his sorrows. Naturally, I must be the one closest to his heart." Lakshmana countered, "But I've been by his side all my life — even before you married him. I've been of service to Rama through all the ups and downs of his life." The debate grew more intense, so they decided to bring in Hanuman to help settle it. Interestingly, neither Sita nor Lakshmana even considered Hanuman as a candidate in the competition. When asked to judge, Hanuman, true to his nature, humbly folded his hands and said, "Both of you are equally dear to Rama. There's no doubt." But Sita and Lakshmana weren't satisfied.

"No," they said, "we want to know who is most dear to him." Hanuman suggested, "Why not ask Rama himself?" They quickly dismissed the idea. "He'll only give a diplomatic answer," said Sita. "He would never choose between us."

So they came up with a clever plan: They summoned the royal physician and asked him to observe Rama as he slept. One by one, Sita and Lakshmana would quietly enter his room and sit beside him. The physician would carefully monitor Rama's physical responses — his heartbeat, breathing, and movements — to see whom he reacted to more, even in his semi-conscious state.

That evening, as Rama was sleeping peacefully, the physician sat quietly beside him, ready with his instruments. First, Sita entered the room and sat gently near Rama. Almost immediately, the physician noted a slight increase in heart rate, a soft shift in his posture, and a gentle warmth in his breath. He smiled as he jotted down the details. Then came Lakshmana. As he approached, similar responses occurred — Rama stirred again, his heartbeat quickened, his body reacted subtly. The readings were complete, and now it was time to declare the result. Sita and Lakshmana sat eagerly, waiting.

The physician began, "I observed all the parameters. At first glance, your presence seemed to affect Rama in equal measure. His heartbeat rose, his body stirred, and there were clear emotional responses to both of you." "Then is it a tie?" they asked. The physician smiled. "Not quite. There was a winner. You see, I leaned in closer and placed my ear directly on Lord Rama's chest to get a clearer reading of his heartbeat." There was a pause. "What did you hear?" they asked, now completely drawn in. He replied softly, "All I heard was: 'Hanuman… Hanuman… Hanuman…'" Sita and Lakshmana turned in shock toward the corner of the room, where Hanuman stood silently, eyes lowered, hands folded, softly chanting: "Ram… Ram… Ram…" Our thoughts, words, and actions rooted in selflessness and concern for the welfare of the world help us earn a place in the guru's good books — or even to become one of the guru's favorites. Hanuman was a perfect example of this. That's why Lord Rama, even in his semi-conscious state, was naturally drawn to him.

I'm reminded of an incident Amma often shares about a young boy. During darshan, everyone was lined up to see Amma. This young boy was standing in the darshan line. A little forward in the queue sat a mother and her infant child. At one point, the baby threw up, and the mother rushed away to clean the child, leaving the mess behind. People began moving away from the spot, some complaining about the mother, some about the cleanliness in the ashram. Amma noticed the boy also disappeared briefly from the darshan line, but soon returned with a bucket and cloth. He quietly cleaned the area without being asked. Amma's attention was immediately drawn to this act of selflessness. She couldn't stop looking at him as he returned to the line. When he finally reached Amma for darshan, she couldn't help but embrace him tightly, holding him close — she didn't want to let him go. After darshan, his face stayed in Amma's mind, flashing repeatedly before her even after she returned to her room.

Amma says the Divine's — or the guru's — grace is like a river flowing perennially. If we dig a small pit beside it, water from the river will naturally flow into the pit. Similarly, our actions should be like digging that pit — creating the conditions that allow the seamless flow of grace to reach us. That's the kind of conduct we should strive for — not seeking greatness but divine grace through our selfless actions. We discussed verses 13 and 14 from Chapter 12 of the *Bhagavad Gita* in the introduction, which describe the qualities of a devotee who is dear to the Lord. Once, an ashram resident who had learned those verses approached Amma and said, with a heavy heart, that he felt dejected — he didn't see any of those qualities in himself. "Does that mean Amma doesn't like me?" he asked. Amma's response was immediate and compassionate. "It's not necessary that you already have all those qualities to be dear to the Lord. As long as you are making sincere efforts to cultivate them, you are already on my favorite list."

Likewise, the 30th verse of the *Chalisa* beautifully expresses how Hanuman strives to benefit others, uphold dharma and annihilate negativities, thus becoming Lord Rama's very dear one, Ramadulara.

Insights on the Path of Bhakti from verses 29 & 30:

- Verse 29

  ○ Everything in creation can be perceived as a function of time. The ultimate state of devotion goes beyond time.

  ○ The fame and following that such a being achieves will benefit others.

- Verse 30

  ○ Devotion is about upholding our goodness and overcoming our negativities.

  ○ Living selflessly for others' benefit makes one dear to the Lord/guru.

Verses 31 and 32

Attaining abilities and virtues
Divine name and spiritual practice - the most significant wealth

aṣṭa-siddhi nava nidhi kē dātā ।
asa vara dīna jānakī mātā ॥ 31 ॥

अष्ट सिद्धि नव निधि के दाता।
अस वर दीन जानकी माता॥

aṣṭha - eight; siddhi - supernatural abilities; nava - nine; nidhi - divine treasures; kē - of; dātā - bestower; asa - like; vara - boon; dīnha - give/grant; jānakī - Sita; mātā - mother;

You are the bestower of the eight Siddhis (supernatural powers) and nine Nidhis (divine treasures). Mother Sita granted you the boon to be so.

rāma rasāyana tumhārē pāsā ।
sadā rahō raghupati kē dāsā ॥ 32 ॥

राम रसायन तुम्हरे पासा।
सदा रहो रघुपति के दासा॥

rāma - Lord Rama; rasāyana - potion; tumhārē pāsā - in your possession; sadā - always; rahō - being; raghupati - Lord Rama; kē - of; dāsā - devoted/servant;

You have a special potion with ingredients for perfect devotion to Lord Rama. You are ever greatly devoted to Lord Rama.

The two verses we are discussing here highlight Lord Hanuman as the bestower of the ashta siddhis (eight divine powers) and nava nidhis (nine treasures), which he received as a boon from Mother Sita. They also emphasize Hanuman's possession of the nectar of Lord Rama's name and his eternal devotion to Lord Rama.

In the last chapter, we discussed how Lord Hanuman attained the state of immortality through the numerous boons he received. Connecting that discussion to the current topic of boons, we recognize Lord Hanuman as one of the most extraordinary beings across all *Puranas* and epics in the Indian tradition of Sanatana Dharma. He is perhaps unparalleled in the sheer number of boons he received, which are not merely accolades but reflections of the perfection of his character and devotion.

Boons are not simple achievements — they are earned through virtues, selflessness, and perfection in character. Lord Hanuman exemplifies this, having received 14 boons from various devas (demigods) after his famous encounter with Indra. Additionally, over the course of his life and service to Lord Rama, Hanuman earned 21 more boons, bringing the total boon count to 35.

One might say that this gives Hanuman the most substantial resume to boast about, and while that is not in Hanuman's nature to do, it is also worth nothing that these boons are not merely personal achievements. They are reflections of Hanuman's unwavering devotion, humility, and unparalleled virtues, making his life a powerful message for all of us. His life teaches us how one can become deserving of divine blessings. His achievements are not about glory for their own sake but symbolize his selfless service and perfect character.

The ashta siddhis and nava nidhis, the most significant boons Hanuman possessed, are at the same time spiritual powers and symbols of the ideal traits and qualities of spiritual aspirants. Hanuman's character is the foundation that made him not only worthy of these boons but also an eternal beacon of spiritual guidance. As we explore these siddhis and nidhis further, let us reflect on how Lord Hanuman's life and virtues can inspire us to cultivate similar qualities, making us receptive to divine blessings and spiritual growth.

Let's begin with a folklore story associated with Lord Hanuman — or, more precisely, with Ravana. As we've discussed before, Ravana was immensely capable and, most notably, deeply devoted to Lord Shiva. His devotion to Lord Shiva was unparalleled, demonstrated through extraordinary penance and numerous hymns praising Lord Shiva. However, the critical character flaw that prevented Ravana from attaining the ultimate spiritual state was his ego, which dominated every aspect of his life, including his devotion. It was this ego that earned him the label of an asura (demon). Ravana's ego extended even to his relationship with Lord Shiva. He took pride in his devotion, believing that it entitled him to anything he desired from Lord Shiva. One day, Ravana decided to demand a special boon from Lord Shiva, confident that it would be granted. He journeyed to Kailasa, Lord Shiva's celestial abode, with a grand plan in mind. Upon reaching Kailasa, Ravana encountered Nandi, Lord Shiva's devoted attendant, often depicted as a bull or ox. Nandi greeted Ravana, remarking that it had been a long time since his last visit, and inquired about the purpose of his arrival. Ravana declared his intention to seek a boon from Lord Shiva. Curious, Nandi asked what the boon was, to which Ravana replied, "I want to take Lord Shiva with me to Lanka. I will keep him there, so I can obtain anything I need from him at any time."

Nandi was taken aback by this declaration and told Ravana, "That is not what devotion is about. Devotion is not about possessing, accumulating, or self-glorification. True devotion is about surrender, humility, and selflessness. Taking Lord Shiva for your personal gain goes against the very principles of devotion." However, Ravana dismissed Nandi's advice, retorting, "Don't try to lecture me. I am a great devotee, and I know what I am doing. Lord Shiva will grant me the boon I seek." Nandi, seeing Ravana's arrogance, continued to counsel him, emphasizing that devotion should never stem from ego.

But Ravana, increasingly agitated, insulted Nandi, saying, "Who are you to advise me? You are just a bull. You are far inferior to me. In fact, you are even lower than monkeys, who are themselves less evolved than humans. How dare you, a mere beast, advise me?"

At that moment, Nandi cursed him, angered by Ravana's words. "You claim superiority over others, yet your arrogance blinds you to the truth. In Kailasa, all beings are equal — there is no superior or inferior. Your pride and ego are unbefitting of a true devotee. I curse you: a being you consider inferior will become the cause of your downfall."

This curse, rooted in Ravana's own arrogance, eventually came to fruition. Hanuman, along with the vanara sena (monkey army), played a pivotal role in Ravana's defeat. Despite Ravana's unmatched abilities, his powerful asuras, and his vast arsenal of divine weapons, none of them could withstand Hanuman's might and devotion. Hanuman systematically dismantled Ravana's plans and defenses. Ultimately, Hanuman became the very cause of Ravana's downfall, proving that true strength lies not in ego or power but in humility, devotion, and righteousness. Ravana's story serves as a powerful reminder of the dangers of arrogance and the ultimate triumph of virtue over vice.

As mentioned in the last chapter, Hanuman was so crucial to Lord Rama's victory over Ravana that he embraced him as his own son. After the victory was won, Lord Rama instructed Hanuman to go to Mother Sita and inform her of the triumph over Ravana. Hanuman, ever obedient and devoted, went to Mother Sita and delivered the joyous news. In her immense joy and jubilation, Mother Sita bestowed a remarkable blessing upon Hanuman. She declared, "May you have the boon of aishwarya (prosperity). May you be the possessor of the ashta siddhis (eight supreme abilities) and the nava nidhis (nine forms of wealth)." Thus, Hanuman received these extraordinary gifts from Mother Sita, making him the embodiment of immense spiritual power and material abundance. This is why the verse states that this boon was bestowed upon Hanuman by Janaki Mata (Mother Sita).

Ashta Siddhis - the Eight Supernatural Abilities

We discussed the ashta siddhis — anima, mahima, garima, laghima, prapti, prakamya, ishitva and vashitva — in the chapter discussing Verses 9 and 10, and the full list of the ashta siddhis along with their definitions can be found there.

As mentioned earlier, Hanuman cleverly avoided being eaten by the demoness Surasa by growing and then rapidly shrinking in size. This incident from the *Ramayana* beautifully showcases Hanuman's mastery of the abilities of anima and mahima.

From a spiritual perspective, these siddhis (perfections) hold deeper meanings. Anima and laghima — the ability to become small, light, and insignificant — represent the spiritual quality of humility. To diminish one's ego and become humble is one of the most significant spiritual achievements a seeker can strive for. However, the abilities of mahima and garima — to become larger, heavier, and assertive — are equally important when the situation demands it.

We discussed the example of a soldier on a battlefield earlier. When upholding dharma, humility alone is not enough. A soldier in battle cannot afford to say, "I am modest and humble; I do not want to hurt anyone. Hello, enemy soldier, I bow down before you." That is not the attitude one should have when protecting righteousness. In such situations, one must practice mahima and garima, displaying authority and strength and exerting all their abilities to uphold justice.

A balanced spiritual aspirant should strive to master both anima, overcoming ego, and mahima, using assertiveness and strength to serve righteousness. These qualities, when employed appropriately, make one truly virtuous.

When it comes to accessing or controlling something (ishitva and vashitva), one option is to use force. However, using force is rarely the best solution. Anything achieved by force is often temporary because it invites opposition. As Newton's third law of motion states: for every action, there is an equal and opposite reaction. Similarly, anything we acquire or control through force will eventually encounter resistance. What is acquired by force can often be taken away by force.

A celebrity or superstar might influence us greatly, but their influence typically stays at the level of our mind, not our heart. It is temporary; today's superstar might be forgotten tomorrow, replaced by someone else. Such influence is fleeting because it does not touch the deeper aspects of our being. True influence, however, enters the heart and has a lasting impact. For this, mere external charisma is not enough. What is required is humility, sincerity, and virtues that resonate deeply with others. If a superstar practices anima (humility and the ability to become small) and laghima (lightness or simplicity), they can genuinely touch hearts and create positive, lasting influence (ishivtva/vashitva).

Lord Hanuman is the perfect embodiment of this principle. His humility and virtues made him deserving of the numerous boons he received. Hanuman is known as the humblest of the humble, yet he possessed immense might and greatness. He could become the mightiest of the mighty, but he only displayed his strength when necessary — always in the service of upholding dharma (righteousness) and opposing adharma (unrighteousness).

The *Kathopanishad* states:

anoraṇīyān mahato mahīyān

*One who is smaller than the atomic particle and
one who is greater than the greatest*

It describes the Divine, the Ultimate, as having the capacity to become smaller than even the tiniest nuclear particles — smaller than the anu (atom) or paramanu (subatomic particle). At the same time, the Divine is also the greatest of all great things, concepts, or beings.

The prelude chanting (laghunyasam) of the *Sri Rudram*, the Vedic text dedicated to Lord Shiva, includes the phrase:

brahmāṇḍa vyāpta deha

One whose very being pervades the whole creation.

The essence of the Divine is its ability to be both infinitely small and seemingly insignificant, yet also infinitely vast and supremely significant.

In the *Patanjali Yoga Sutra*, the formula for attaining perfection states:

janma auṣadhi mantra tapaḥ samādhijāḥ siddhayaḥ ||4.1||

Siddhi (perfection) can be attained through the following means:

1. Birth (janma): By valuing the precious gift of life and making the right use of it.
2. Herbs (aushadhi): By consuming the right substances at the right time and in the right way to maintain control over the senses.
3. Mantra: Through constant remembrance and mastering control of the mind.
4. Tapas: Through penance, dedication, and sincere effort.
5. Samadhi: By achieving equanimity and maintaining a balanced, composed mind in all situations.

Nava Nidhis - The Nine Divine Treasures

Next, we move on to the nava nidhis, the nine treasures. These treasures are typically associated with Kubera, the demigod of wealth. Kubera was Ravana's half brother, both being sons of Sage Vishrava. Kubera is regarded as the embodiment of abundance and the lord of prosperity. According to tradition, Kubera once ruled over Lanka, but he was vanquished by Ravana and forced to flee. He eventually settled in the Himalayas, where he established the city of Alaka, or Alaka Puri, known as the city of abundance.

Kubera is often depicted carrying a bag brimming with wealth, commonly symbolized by gold coins. As the guardian of the nava nidhis (nine treasures), Kubera is revered as the custodian of immense prosperity and riches.

The nava nidhis symbolize not just material wealth but also spiritual virtues. Let's explore their meanings:

1. Padma
   - Literal Meaning: Though it literally means lotus flower, it is also interpreted as a lake filled with gems and precious mineral deposits.
   - Spiritual Aspect: Our heart should be like the lake of abundance, treasuring precious virtues that spring from love, compassion, and selflessness.

2. Mahāpadma
   - Literal Meaning: The great lotus flower that has completely blossomed, opening up all the petals
   - Spiritual Aspect: Mahāpadma signifies the heart's and mind's supreme opening to spiritual unity - advaita (non-duality), underscoring profound spiritual enlightenment.

3. Shankha
   - Literal Meaning: Naturally formed conch, created through a long process of mineral accumulation.
   - Spiritual Aspect: The conch, being closed in form, reminds us to turn our senses inward. When blown, it produces the primordial sound, AUM, symbolizing the essence of the universe and the need for introspection.

4. Makara
   - Literal Meaning: A precious black mineral, often used historically for natural decoration, such as eyeliner.
   - Spiritual Aspect: Makara, also meaning crocodile, teaches patience and precision. Just as a crocodile waits motionlessly for its prey, we are reminded to remain calm and focused, acting

with precision when the moment arises. This is also reflected in the yoga posture of makara asana, which calms the mind.

5. Kacchapa
   - Literal Meaning: Tortoise - the tortoise shell is composed of minerals, and was historically considered valuable.
   - Spiritual Aspect: When attacked, the tortoise pulls its limbs into its shell, symbolizing the need to turn inward and practice self-control during challenging times. It encourages us to delve into our inner self and maintain composure.

6. Mukundaḥ
   - Literal Meaning: A bright red mineral, such as cinnabar, which is often used to create vermilion and other precious items.
   - Spiritual Aspect: The red color represents shakti, or energy, symbolizing action, courage, and the ability to bring change.

7. Kundaḥ
   - Literal Meaning: Jasmine flowers or frankincense, both prized for their fragrance.
   - Spiritual Aspect: These treasures teach the virtue of unconditional giving. Just as jasmine spreads its fragrance to all without discrimination, we are reminded to serve and give selflessly.

8. Nilaḥ
   - Literal Meaning: Sapphire, a bluish gemstone known for its resistance to weathering and solvents.
   - Spiritual Aspect: Sapphire symbolizes steadfastness and resilience. It reminds us to remain unwavering in our attitude, especially in testing circumstances, embodying inner strength.

9. Karva
   - Literal Meaning: Earthenware or vessels created through fire-baking are considered precious for their utility and craftsmanship.

- Spiritual Aspect: Karva also means "dwarf," signifying humility. It teaches us to embrace simplicity and modesty, key virtues in spiritual growth.

The nine treasures represent not only physical wealth but also profound spiritual lessons. From humility (karva) to resilience (nila), patience (makara), and selfless giving (kunda), each treasure offers guidance for leading a balanced and spiritually enriched life. Kubera's role as the custodian of these treasures underscores the interconnectedness of material and spiritual abundance.

Amma often emphasizes the importance of cultivating inner wealth for spiritual progress, underscoring that this is the true wealth we should strive for. She remains one of the most inspiring role models for us. In this regard, it's worth reflecting on this excerpt from Amma's Keynote Address at the Parliament of the World's Religions, Barcelona, 2004:

"Our God-given abilities are a treasure meant for ourselves as well as for the entire world. This wealth should not be misused, creating a burden for us and for the world. The greatest tragedy in life is not death; the greatest tragedy takes place when our talents and capabilities are underutilized and allowed to rust while we are living. When we use the wealth obtained from nature, it diminishes; but when we use the wealth of our inner capabilities, it increases."

Lord Hanuman possesses both the eight siddhis and the nine nidhis. He received these from none other than Mother Sita (Janaki Mata). But what is the greatest treasure or wealth that Lord Hanuman possessed? This truth is beautifully expressed in the 32nd verse: The greatest wealth Hanuman possesses is the name of Lord Rama — ever-present in his mind, constantly on his lips, and eternally enshrined in his heart. His ultimate treasure is not material riches or worldly status, but his unwavering devotion; he lived his life inspired by Lord Rama, in constant remembrance of him, and dedicated to upholding the dharma that Rama embodied.

It is this unbreakable connection to the Divine that defines Hanuman. It is his greatest asset, the guiding force behind every thought, every action, and every moment of his existence. For us, too, establishing a deep connection with the Divine, our chosen deity (ishta devata), or our guru is the most incredible wealth we can ever possess. This connection, cultivated through constant remembrance and devotion, is invaluable, aiding us in countless ways and various situations throughout life.

I'm reminded of the 16th-century saint Mirabai as an extraordinary example of someone who lived a life of true and sincere devotion. Her love for Lord Krishna was so profound that she dedicated her entire existence to him. Born into a royal family, Mirabai renounced all the pleasures and comforts of royal life. She chose a life of austerity, embracing the path of a saint or hermit entirely devoted to Lord Krishna. Her devotion was so natural and heartfelt that she spontaneously composed poems and songs praising Lord Krishna and the Divine. One of her most popular devotional songs, widely sung in India and worldwide, begins with the line, "Payoji, Mane Rama Ratan Dhan Payo."

Pāyojī, maine rāma raṭana dhana pāyo

I have found the wealth of the gem of chanting the Holy Name.

vastu amolaka dī mere sadguru, kirpā kar apanāyo

My Sadguru (spiritual preceptor) has given me this priceless thing. With the guru's grace, I accept it with humility.

Janma janma kī puñjī pāī, jaga meṅ sabai khovāyo

I found the treasure of my several births; I have lost everything else in the world (I find all the other so-called achievements meaningless now)

Kharca na kute, cor na lute, dina dina baḍhata savāyo

Spending doesn't deplete this wealth, nor can a thief steal it. Day by day, it just keeps increasing.

Sat kī nāva khevaṭiyā sadguru, bhavasāgara tara āyo

On the boat of Truth, the boatman is my Sadguru.
It has helped me cross the ocean of existence.

Mīrā ke prabhu giridhara nāgara, harakha harakha jasa gāyo

Mira's lord is Krishna (the one who lifted the mountain)
and I just sing his praises in joy and bliss.

Amma often says that spiritual practice is essential in cultivating and enhancing our inner wealth. In fact, our spiritual practice is a form of true wealth in its own right. Let us reflect on this excerpt from the book Children of Immortality — Amma's birthday message from 1991:

My children, close your eyes and calm your minds. Let go of all thoughts and concentrate on the feet of your beloved deity. Don't think of your home or work or catching the bus back home. Think only about your beloved deity. Give up all talk and chant God's name. It doesn't matter how much water you pour on the branches of a tree; doing so is useless. But if you pour water at the roots, it will reach all parts of the tree. So, focus only on God's feet, for to think of anything else is as useless as pouring water on the tree branches.

If your boat is tied to the river bank, you won't be able to get across the river, no matter how hard you row. Similarly, when you pray, if your mind is tied to your family and wealth, you won't get the proper benefit of your prayers, no matter how much you pray. So, when you pray, let your mind be totally surrendered to God. My children, only this will bear fruit.

In the world of spirituality, there is no birth or death. The day the concept that we are born disappears, we have reached God's door. The realm of the Supreme Being lies beyond both life and death.

Amma has agreed to these celebrations only with the happiness of her children in mind. This is the time when your renunciation, love, and sense of equality become manifest. Furthermore, Amma gets a chance to see all of you together.

Those who have come here shouldn't go back having done nothing. Go home only after repeating a mantra and meditating for a little while. Spiritual practice is our only true wealth, and this is why Amma asks you to do archana.

As reflected in the 32nd verse of the *Chalisa*, Amma teaches that our spiritual practice and deep connection with the Supreme are our greatest treasures. Unlike material wealth, this inner wealth will never diminish — it will always support and guide us, especially in life's most challenging moments. Let us understand, recognize, and strive to cultivate this profound connection. As Hanuman shows us, it is the one true wealth that will stand by us, unwavering, through all trials and tribulations.

Insights on the Path of Bhakti from verses 31 & 32:

- Verse 31
  - Through true devotion, one can attain the eight supreme abilities and the nine wealths in the form of virtues.
- Verse 32
  - The greatest wealth for a devotee should be the divine name and spiritual practice.

Verses 33 and 34

Exhausting the karmas from several births
Attaining the ultimate state of oneness

tumharē bhajana rāmakō pāvai ।   तुम्हरे भजन राम को भावै।
janma janma kē dukha bisarāvai ॥ 33 ॥   जनम-जनम के दुख बिसरावै ॥

tumharē - your; bhajana - praises/hymns; rāma - Lord Rama;
kō - pertaining to; pāvai - obtain; janma janma - birth after
birth; kē - of; dukha - sorrow/problem; bisarāvai - annihilate;

*Singing your glory, ridding ourselves of the pain and suffering
of many lives, we can reach Lord Rama himself.*

anta kāla raghuvar pura jāyī ।   अन्त काल रघुबर पुर जाई।
jahā janma haribhakta kahāyī ॥ 34 ॥   जहाँ जन्म हरि-भक्त कहाई ॥

anta - end; kāla - time; raghuvar - Lord Rama('s) pura -
place/abode; jāyī - go/reach; jahā - where; janma - birth;
haribhakta - devotee of the Lord (Hari); kahāyī - called;

*He who sings your glory at the end of the life attains Lord Rama's
abode. For all births, he or she will be devoted to Lord Rama.*

The 33rd verse highlights the power of calling out to Lord Hanuman
with devotion (bhajan). It conveys that engaging in such devotion
to Lord Hanuman leads one to attain the ultimate state that Lord
Rama represents. By singing his praises, the sorrows and burdens

accumulated over many births, including the karmic bonds that tie us to the cycle of rebirth, are dissipated and resolved. The 34th verse expands on this idea by focusing on the ultimate moment of life — death. It states that at the time of death, one who remembers Lord Rama, the head of the Raghu dynasty, attains the dwelling or the abode of Lord Rama - the ultimate spiritual state. This implies reaching the ultimate state of union with the Divine.

For those who are reborn, the verse says, their birth will be such that they will be a Hari Bhakta - a devotee of Lord Vishnu. This implies they would have a meaningful life with virtues like humility, love, compassion, and the like. This devotion will guide them further along their spiritual journey, making them deserving of ascending to the higher states of spiritual evolution. The verse beautifully underscores the importance of making the last moment of life meaningful, filled with the remembrance of the Divine, thus ensuring a spiritually enriched next birth or ultimate liberation.

The 33rd verse emphasizes that singing Lord Hanuman's praises and being devoted to him helps one attain Lord Rama. This attainment can be interpreted in two meaningful ways:

1. Attaining Joy and Pleasantness: "Rama" signifies joy and pleasantness. Devotion to Lord Hanuman leads one to a state of true happiness, where life becomes pleasant, harmonious, and filled with long-lasting or even everlasting joy.

2. Attaining the Ultimate State: The verse can also be understood as reaching Lord Rama, the embodiment of the ultimate spiritual state. Lord Rama represents the supreme realization of Oneness - the ultimate truth of existence.

Thus, the verse conveys that the path of devotion to Lord Hanuman is not merely an act of worship but a transformative journey. It can lead to lasting happiness, inner peace, or even to the highest spiritual realization, wherein the devotee experiences Oneness with the ultimate divine reality. In this conveyance, the verse reiterates the point made earlier - that the path of bhakti is not inferior to any other. Bhakti is equally capable of leading one to the ultimate state of liberation and self-realization.

From a spiritual aspirant's perspective, Lord Hanuman is the perfect example of a true devotee. He teaches us how to embody humility and surrender while fully utilizing our abilities in service to the Divine. Despite his immense powers and achievements, Hanuman remained humble and unassuming, always attributing his successes to the grace of the Divine.

When a spiritual aspirant sings Lord Hanuman's glories, they strive to cultivate these qualities - humility and selflessness, the absence of ego and pride. These are the hallmarks of a true devotee and form the foundation for spiritual growth. Lord Hanuman exemplifies how one can possess unparalleled abilities and still remain grounded, selfless, and ever-devoted to the Divine. We can aspire to embody these ideals through devotion and progress on our spiritual journey.

One of the outstanding contributions attributed to Lord Hanuman is the *Hanumad Ramayana*, a version of the *Ramayana* composed by Lord Hanuman himself. While not widely known, the *Hanumad Ramayana* is considered Hanuman's first-hand account of the events surrounding Lord Rama's life. As someone directly present during all critical moments of the *Ramayana*, Hanuman's recounting carried a unique authenticity and depth. Lord Hanuman, known for his profound arts abilities and poetic prowess, is said to have created a work of unparalleled beauty and sophistication. Many traditions suggest that the *Hanumad Ramayana* is superior in composition to any other *Ramayana*. However, two versions of what happened to this remarkable work reflect Hanuman's humility and detachment.

According to one account, after completing his *Ramayana*, Hanuman etched it onto rocks in the Himalayas or carved it onto stone tablets.

Around the same time, Sage Valmiki composed the *Valmiki Ramayana*, the Sanskrit epic we now consider the original *Ramayana*.

When Valmiki completed his work, he sought feedback and shared his *Ramayana* with Hanuman. During this meeting, Valmiki happened to see parts of Hanuman's *Ramayana*. Upon reading it, he was astonished by its brilliance and felt disheartened. Valmiki reportedly exclaimed in sorrow that all the effort he had put into his *Ramayana* seemed insignificant compared to Hanuman's work. The poetic beauty and spiritual depth of the *Hanumad Ramayana* left him feeling as though his work would be overshadowed.

Hearing this, Hanuman immediately decided to destroy his *Ramayana*. In an extraordinary display of humility and detachment, he obliterated all traces of his work, stating that his intention was never to seek glory but to let the *Valmiki Ramayana* flourish. This act demonstrates Hanuman's profound humility and ability to relinquish his efforts without attachment.

In another version of the legend, Hanuman completed the *Hanumad Ramayana* and presented it to Lord Rama as an offering. Hanuman shared with Lord Rama that he had documented his first-hand experiences of Rama's life in this work. Upon hearing this, Lord Rama's initial response was one of humility. He is said to have remarked, "Do I need this? I am no one great. I am just an ordinary being."

Lord Rama then posed a second, pointed question to Hanuman: "When this work is known as the *Hanumad Ramayana,* who will receive the glory - me or you? Are you seeking praise for yourself, or is this truly about praising me?"

Hearing this question from his spiritual master, Hanuman immediately recognized the potential for his ego to arise. Without hesitation, he destroyed the *Hanumad Ramayana*, obliterating all traces of it. His actions reflected his unwavering dedication to Lord Rama and his refusal to allow personal pride to interfere with his devotion.

These stories remind us of the importance of humility, detachment, and the ability to recognize and overcome ego. Hanuman's actions in these episodes, and in so many stories of his life, teach us that true devotion is not about seeking recognition or personal gain but about offering oneself entirely to the service of the Divine.

There is also a belief that the great poet Kalidasa stumbled upon fragments of the *Hanumad Ramayana* etched on stone tablets. He is said to have interpreted and glorified some portions of it, further attesting to its extraordinary beauty and depth. Unfortunately, it is our loss that we do not have the *Hanumad Ramayana* in its original form today.

Nevertheless, the point to focus on is Hanuman's humility, devotion, and unwavering attitude of selflessness and egolessness. Hanuman could let go of the *Hanumad Ramayana* instantly because his sole intent was to ensure that no glory should come to him. He believed all glory and praise should be directed solely towards Lord Rama.

This is why, as the verse suggests, "When I seek you, I attain Lord Rama." By following Hanuman's example and embodying his qualities, we are led toward the ultimate goal of realizing the Divine.

A Sanskrit verse is often recited during sandhya vandanam, the daily prayers traditionally performed by a brahmachari (a seeker of knowledge). The verse goes:

ākāśāt patitaṃ toyaṃ yathā gacchati sāgaram |
sarva deva namaskāraḥ keśavaṃ pratigacchati ||

The water that falls from the sky (every drop of rain) finally
heads towards and merges with the ocean. Similarly,
every form of worship and prostration finally is towards
Keshava (Lord Krishna's name), the Divine.

For a spiritual seeker, this verse is a regular reminder during their prayers. It reflects the understanding that all glory, recognition, and praise directed toward oneself or any form must ultimately be offered to the source of that glory - the Supreme Divine or the guru who guides and empowers us.

Through this repetition, the seeker cultivates humility and remembers "I am but an instrument." Every accomplishment and praise that comes to us must ultimately be directed to the guru and the Divine, who are the true source and controllers of all actions.

That's why we say, "It was Amma's grace that it happened." While sometimes this statement may feel mechanical, it is an important reminder: You are just an instrument. This acknowledgment is a powerful means of overcoming our ego. I recall an experience from a few years ago during the brahmacharya/sannyasa diksha (initiation) ceremony, when we were given monastic robes by Amma. I have a close friend, a fellow brahmachari whom I consider a dear brother and have known for years. We are of similar age and have spent countless hours together during Amma's tours, sharing fun and meaningful moments over the years.

That evening, after the diksha ceremony, he approached me and touched my feet, as is the tradition. I felt deeply uncomfortable. It wasn't the dynamic we had ever shared, and it didn't feel right. Spontaneously, I told him, "You don't need to touch my feet. That's not the bond we have." His response, though delivered jokingly, was profoundly insightful. He said, "Who cares to touch your feet? I didn't bow down to you. I bowed down to the robes that Amma gave." It was a simple yet profound reminder: The respect we receive is not ours — it belongs to the guru, Amma, and the Divine. Anything directed toward us — respect, praise, or admiration — is for the higher power we represent. The moment we forget this is when ego begins to take root.

Whenever we find ourselves in situations where our ego is tempted to grow, we should remind ourselves: This is not for me. This is for Amma. This is for my guru. This is for the Divine. This is for my Lord. Redirecting everything we receive toward its rightful source is one of the most effective ways to curb our ego.

At various satsangs and programs I attend, it's heartwarming when people share words of appreciation and encouragement. They might say they thoroughly enjoyed the program, the talk was great, or the bhajan was moving. However, such comments can easily inflate one's ego if not handled mindfully. As a spiritual aspirant, one mechanism I follow to keep my ego in check — though I am far from egoless — is constantly reminding myself of the undisputable fact that the very reason people attend these programs is not because of me. They come because of Amma. Imagine if a flyer simply announced that such and such a Swami/Brahmachari would be singing bhajans today. You're all welcome!" How many would turn up? Likely no one. After all, who even knows or cares about a random Swami? Why would they come to hear my bhajans or talks? Only when the program is associated with Amma, her disciples, or her ashram do people feel drawn to attend.

This reminds me of an example often shared in Kerala during temple festivals. Beautifully decorated elephants march through the streets carrying the deity's idol on their backs. People crowd around, bow, and show reverence to the elephant. But does this respect genuinely belong to the elephant? Not at all. It's because the elephant carries the deity's symbol that people bow. The same elephant, walking unadorned down the street on an ordinary day, wouldn't receive much attention. Maybe a few kind souls might feed it bananas, but most wouldn't give it a second glance. The reverence comes only because of the divine symbol on its back.

Similarly, as emissaries of Amma, any glory or praise we receive is not ours. It belongs to Amma, to the divine force acting through us. Every time we remember this, it becomes a powerful antidote to ego. If we fail to remind ourselves, our ego can easily creep in and block our spiritual growth.

The verse serves as such a profound reminder for spiritual aspirants. Just as every praise directed at Hanuman ultimately belongs to Lord Rama, every praise we receive should mentally be redirected to our guru, Amma, or the Divine. Practicing this consistently is one of the best ways to grow spiritually. Otherwise, the ego will continue to inhibit our growth.

Nullifying Problems Accumulated from Several Births

The second part of the 33rd verse underscores the idea of multiple births: Janama janama ke dukha bisaraavai. It highlights how the pains, challenges, and complications accumulated over countless lifetimes, rooted in our karma, are ultimately dissipated.

What holds us in this endless cycle of birth and death? At its core, it is our ego. In its various manifestations, the ego leaves things unresolved, and these unresolved aspects necessitate further births to address them. This is the essence of karma - the idea that our thoughts, desires, and actions, stemming from ego, create karma that must be resolved in future lifetimes.

When we break down the ego, it isn't just a singular entity within us. It manifests through likes and dislikes, self-centric thoughts and actions, preconceived notions, and desires/expectations. These collectively materialize our ego. Acting solely based on our preferences and self-interest incurs karma, which binds us to the cycle of rebirth. Each birth becomes an opportunity to address, resolve, and dissipate this ego. Instead of accumulating more karma due to our ego, the focus of each birth should be to dissolve the ego as much as possible. This can be achieved through our efforts to let go of desires, self-centered thoughts, and likes/dislikes.

One of the easiest and most effective ways to achieve this is through the path of bhakti. When we attribute everything to the guru or to the Divine, we shift the focus away from ourselves. This process naturally helps us overcome ego more effectively.

We've discussed examples of various asuras. These are beings bound by their ego and karma. In the stories we've explored throughout this book, their liberation often comes through their ultimate surrender and grace from the Divine. The Lord, in these stories, "kills" the asura. This act of slaying, far from being punitive, is metaphorical. It is more like punctuating the sentence of life with a period or comma so that life continues meaningfully on to the next birth. It represents an act of compassion by the Divine to free the asura from the curse, allowing them to transcend their accumulated karma and ego. The asura's liberation comes from their repentance, acknowledgment of their wrongs, and efforts to nullify their ill deeds.

Similarly, over many births, through devotion and divine grace, we, too, can transcend this cycle of birth and death, overcoming the ego and finding liberation. We move closer to liberation and realizing our True Self by overcoming the ego and resolving our karma.

A good example from the *Bhagavata Purana* is the episode of Gajendra Moksha, where the distinguished elephant Gajendra attains liberation through the grace of Lord Vishnu. It is said that Gajendra was once a king named Indradyumna, a capable and accomplished ruler with many abilities. However, he was also arrogant about his achievements.

One day, when Sage Agastya visited him, Indradyumna failed to offer the respect customary in receiving a sage. He didn't even rise to greet Agastya, an act considered an essential expression of reverence. Agastya, recognizing that Indradyumna's ego was hindering his spiritual growth, cursed him, saying, "May you be born as an elephant, carrying a massive body that symbolizes your ego. Let that body cause you great trouble." As a result, Indradyumna was reborn as Gajendra, a royal elephant and the leader of a large herd. Despite his new form, he lived a life of luxury, surrounded by multiple elephant queens and followers. He remained unaware of the curse and the purpose of his birth, wholly immersed in his royal lifestyle. Sage Agastya had foretold that this birth would ultimately lead to liberation, but Gajendra had forgotten this.

One day, while Gajendra was bathing in a lake with his herd, a crocodile suddenly grabbed his leg and refused to let go. Although Gajendra was mighty, his strength proved futile. As the struggle continued, his followers and queens abandoned him one by one, unwilling to risk their lives. Left alone and unable to free himself, Gajendra realized his might was useless. A memory from his past life flashed in his mind at that moment. Indradyumna, despite his arrogance, had been a devotee of Lord Vishnu. Remembering this, Gajendra called out to Vishnu with heartfelt devotion. Instead of fighting the crocodile with strength, Gajendra plucked a lotus flower from the lake, extended it with his trunk, and offered it to Lord Vishnu in complete surrender, praying, "I offer this to you, my Lord. Please protect me." Moved by Gajendra's sincere devotion and surrender, Lord Vishnu appeared and rescued him. Vishnu killed the crocodile, freeing Gajendra from its grip. Vishnu then blessed Gajendra, liberating him from the curse and granting him moksha (liberation).

The crocodile, too, had a backstory. He was once a celestial being (gandharva) named Huhu. Arrogant due to his abilities, Huhu had disturbed a sage performing his daily rituals in a river. Angered by this disrespect, the sage cursed him, saying, "May you be stuck in this water body as a crocodile." Later, out of compassion, the sage added that Lord Vishnu would eventually liberate him. When Vishnu killed the crocodile, Huhu was freed from his curse and restored to his celestial form as a gandharva.

This story illustrates how we accumulate karma driven by our ego over many births. For Gajendra and Huhu, their ego caused their suffering. Liberation was only possible through sincere bhakti and the grace of the Divine. For us, too, each birth provides an opportunity to lessen the burden of karma. By letting go of ego, desires, self-centered thoughts, and attachments, we move closer to freedom from the cycle of birth and death. The story of Gajendra and Huhu reminds us that divine grace and sincere devotion can help us transcend even the most challenging situations, ultimately leading us to liberation.

Here again, surrender and bhakti are not about giving up or giving in. The Divine, the Lord, or the Guru do not need our devotion, respect, or praise. They are already complete and content within themselves - that is the reason they are referred to as Sadgurus. Rather, bhakti is for us — to help us develop humility and replace our ego with something more transformative.

Attaining the Divine Abode

The 34th verse speaks of life's final moments. It conveys that if, at the very last breath, one remembers Hanuman — chanting his name and holding him in their thoughts — one ascends to the Abode of Raghuvar, the dwelling of Lord Rama, or the ultimate state that Lord Rama embodies. This verse beautifully emphasizes that in the final moment, remembrance of God becomes the guiding light, leading one toward a higher state of divinity and ultimately unity with the Divine.

Chapter 8 of *Bhagavad Gita* says:

anta-kāle cha mām eva smaran muktvā kalevaram
yaḥ prayāti sa mad-bhāvaṁ yāti nāstyatra sanśhayaḥ ||5||

*In the last moment (time of death), one who
relinquishes the body remembering me achieves my
bhava (nature); there is no doubt about that.*

yaṁ yaṁ vāpi smaran bhāvaṁ tyajatyante kalevaram
taṁ tam evaiti kaunteya sadā tad-bhāva-bhāvitaḥ ||6||

O son of Kunti, all that one remembers while giving
up the body at the time of death, one attains that state,
always absorbed in the remembrance of it.

Amma says remembering the Divine at the very last moment is not as simple as it sounds. In that critical moment, when life slips away, our instincts take over. If we haven't cultivated the habit of remembering the Divine, it's unlikely that we'll recall the Divine's name in that fleeting instant. To ensure that the Divine's name comes naturally to us in the final moment, we need to make it a habit. Better yet, it should become our very nature. There's a popular saying, which Amma often echoes, that emphasizes this same idea:

Our thoughts influence our words,
Our words lead to actions,
Our actions shape our habits,
Our habits define our character,
And our character becomes our destiny.

The two verses above from the *Bhagavad Gita* highlight this principle. The first verse says that if one remembers the Divine in the final moment, one will ascend toward the Divine's nature. The second verse explains how this can be achieved: One can remember in the final moment only what they have contemplated throughout their life. This constant contemplation determines one's destiny.

Every thought, word, and action — however insignificant it may seem — contribute to shaping who we are. Therefore, Amma advises us to practice shraddha (faith and focused attention) in every aspect of life. By doing so, we can gradually integrate this awareness into our nature, ensuring that the remembrance of the Divine happens spontaneously when it matters most.

There's a famous story about the Mughal Emperor Akbar, who ruled the Indian subcontinent and had a renowned court of ministers celebrated for their intelligence, knowledge, and wit. Among them, one minister stood out: Birbal, known for his quick thinking, sharp intellect, and profound wisdom.

One day, a scholar visited Akbar's court and challenged the assembly of intellectuals, saying, "I've heard of your greatness and your unmatched intellect, but let me test it. I am fluent in many languages, so well that I speak each as if it were my mother tongue. Can you determine what my true mother tongue is?" The challenge intrigued the court, and the ministers and scholars took turns debating with the scholar, trying to discern his mother tongue. However, the scholar was exceptionally skilled, and prepared for such challenges, and none could succeed in identifying his native language. He mocked the court, saying, "Is this the famed court of Akbar that I've heard so much about? How shameful that not one of you could solve this simple challenge!"

At this point, Birbal had not yet arrived. When he entered the court, Akbar turned to him, saying, "Birbal, it's now up to you to defend the reputation of my court. Can you discover his mother tongue?" Birbal replied, "Of course, Your Majesty, but I'll need until tomorrow morning to provide the answer." The scholar smirked and said, "Ah, I see! Even Birbal is stalling and preparing to admit defeat." Birbal calmly responded, "I've neither admitted defeat nor given up. I simply need until tomorrow morning to prove my point."

The scholar reluctantly agreed, and the court adjourned. The following day, the court reconvened. Birbal confidently declared the scholar's mother tongue. The scholar was stunned and visibly impressed. He asked, "Birbal, how on earth did you figure it out? You truly have remarkable abilities!" Birbal smiled and explained, "It was quite simple. I didn't need debates or clever arguments to uncover the truth. Last night, I waited until you fell asleep and entered your chamber. Using a feather, I tickled your nose and woke you abruptly. Startled and annoyed, you shouted in anger. And in that unguarded moment, when you had no time to think, you yelled in your mother tongue. That's how I confirmed it." He concluded, "No matter how much you train or prepare, when you lose control of your senses during a testing moment, your true nature reveals itself automatically."

Similarly, what will emerge from us when the moment of death comes? What will we chant, remember, or contemplate? It will reflect what we have cultivated as our nature throughout our lives. We cannot artificially decide, "Oh, I'll think of the Divine in my final moments, no matter what I do now." That is not how it works. We need to begin training for that right here, right now. Only then will we be prepared to focus on the Divine in our final moments.

Amma often shares a story related to Ajamila from the Srimad Bhagavatam. Ajamila was a shrewd and selfish businessman who lived an unrighteous, adharmic life. In his pursuit of wealth, he resorted to unethical deeds to prosper. He was deeply attached to his youngest son, whose name happened to be Narayana — the name of Lord Vishnu. Lying on his deathbed at the end of his life, he called out, "Narayana!" in desperation, addressing his son. But because he uttered the name of Lord Vishnu, even unknowingly, the messengers of Lord Vishnu came instead of the messengers of Yama (the lord of death). They took him to Lord Vishnu's abode, and he attained liberation. It is important to note that Ajamila didn't outsmart the law of karma; rather he had accumulated enough merit in his earlier births that, despite living a less virtuous life, a single utterance of Lord Vishnu's name was enough to grant him liberation.

On that note, Amma also shares a humorous story of another businessman who, inspired by Ajāmila, devised a similar plan. This man was selfish and unrighteous but thought he could secure liberation by naming his sons after Lord Vishnu. He named his three sons Keshava, Narayana, and Madhava, hoping that when his end came, he would call out one of their names and attain liberation. Years later, on his deathbed, he called out, "Keshava! Narayana! Madhava!" All three sons came rushing to him, worried about their father. Seeing them gathered around him, the businessman became frustrated and said, "You fools! Why are you all here? If you're here, who is taking care of the business?" Those were his final words and thought before passing away.

As part of the fun in the telling, Amma invites us to reflect on what his next birth might have been. Since his last thoughts were filled with frustration and the word "fool," he was likely reborn as one. This story serves as a reminder: what we hold in our hearts and minds at the moment of death is shaped by how we live our lives. If we live with devotion and righteousness, we will naturally think of the Divine in our final moments. But if our mind is filled with worldly concerns or negativity, that will dictate our next birth. It's not enough to try and trick the system — our true nature and thoughts will always prevail.

Elevated to Being a True Devotee

The 34th verse emphasizes that we will attain Raghuvarpur, the abode of Lord Rama (raghuvar) when we live a life dedicated to practicing devotion and righteousness. This verse reminds us that leading a spiritually oriented and dharmic life doesn't necessarily mean we won't have another birth. Instead, it could mean that we are born into a much better and more meaningful life — one that is conducive to spiritual growth. That's why the verse says we will be born as a Hari Bhakta, a devotee of Lord Vishnu, and in an environment surcharged with devotion.

This reminds me of the children growing up in Amma's ashram now. I was also brought up in the ashram. Still, I feel the children today are utilizing Amma's divine presence and the spiritually charged environment much more effectively than I did when I was young. To be born and grow up in such an environment is a great blessing, likely the result of good deeds from previous births. These children are reaping the benefits of an atmosphere that naturally helps them let go of their ego and grow spiritually.

When we say Raghuvarpur, or Vishnu Loka, the abode of Lord Vishnu, it isn't someplace high above the clouds. I used to think heaven was up in the clouds when I was little. In the *Ramayana* TV series, heaven was always shown as being surrounded by clouds. So as a child, whenever I flew on an airplane and it went above the clouds, I'd frantically look around to see if I could spot any devas walking on the clouds. Of course, I never did! Heaven is not a physical place. It's right where we are, and we create it through bhakti. The more we let go of our ego, the more heavenly our surroundings become, transforming our environment into Vishnu Loka.

This verse beautifully conveys that as we practice devotion in this life and maintain it in our last moments, our next life will naturally be in an environment that is even more spiritually conducive. Through this process, life after life, we inch closer to liberation, ultimately reaching a state where we no longer need to be born again. It's up to us to create the heaven we aspire to attain — not something we must wait for. We can manifest it right here and now through our choices and how we live our lives.

A young seeker once approached a mahatma, a realized master who lived in a quiet monastery at the edge of the forest. "Where is heaven?" the seeker asked. "How do I find it?" The mahatma handed him a small clay lamp, its gentle flame flickering in the early dusk, and gestured toward a path leading into the forest. "Take this lamp," the mahatma said. "Walk down this path and keep going until the flame goes out. When it extinguishes, you will find heaven."

The seeker bowed, filled with anticipation, and set off down the path. He walked through the night, holding the lamp carefully in his hands. But to his surprise, the flame never dimmed. As he walked, he came across a man who had lost his way in the dark. The seeker helped him back to the road. A little farther along, he found a frightened child crying alone beneath a tree. He stayed with the child until a caretaker came. Later, he saw a stray dog, limping and hungry. He shared his food and gently tended to its wound. The road seemed never-ending — and still, the lamp showed no sign of extinguishing.

As the sky began to lighten, he was surprised to find the path looping back to the monastery. The mahatma was waiting for him. "Did you find heaven?" he asked. The seeker looked down at the lamp in his hands. "It never went out," he said. "But I did find heaven. I saw it in the grateful eyes of the lost man, in the relief of the frightened child, in the quiet satisfaction of the dog. And I realized I don't have to wait for the light of my life to extinguish to reach heaven. The path to heaven loops back to where I began — my own self."

The mahatma smiled. "Exactly. Heaven is not something to be found elsewhere; it is something you create where you are."

So, that is the heaven, the Vishnu Loka or Raghuvarpur, that we must strive to enter. What stops us from creating heaven within and around us? Again, it is our ego. And how do we overcome that ego? Bhakti is the way. Bhakti is the most effective and accessible path to dissolve the ego and open the doors to true happiness and liberation. Let us reflect on the example set by Lord Hanuman as a devotee and imbibe it to the best extent we can. Following his example, we can cultivate bhakti, displace our ego, and transform our lives and surroundings into the heaven we long to dwell in.

Insights on the Path of Bhakti from verses 33 & 34

- A true devotee revels in the ultimate state of Oneness.
- Bhakti expends all that we have accumulated through several births.
- A true devotee doesn't need to be elevated to heaven, instead creating heaven wherever he or she is.

Verses 35, 36 and 37

The path and the Deity - the ultimate
Seeking true happiness
True victory - attaining the Supreme Truth

aura dēvatā chitta na dharayī ।   और देवता चित्त न धरई।
hanumata sēyi sarva sukha karayī ॥ 35 ॥   हनुमत सेई सर्व सुख करई॥

aura - other; dēvatā - deity; chitta - mind; na - not;
dharayī - focus/invest; hanumata - Lord Hanuman; sēyi
- with; sarva - all; sukha - happiness; karayī - create;

There is no need to focus the mind on any other form; one will
attain all the happiness by just serving Lord Hanuman.

saṅkaṭa kaṭai miṭai saba pīrā ।   संकट कटै मिटै सब पीरा।
jō sumirai hanumata bala vīrā ॥ 36 ॥   जो सुमिरै हनुमत बलबीरा॥

saṅkaṭa - difficulty; kaṭai - removed; miṭai - removed; saba
- all; pīrā - suffering; jō - one who; sumirai - remember;
hanumata - Lord Hanuman; bala - strong; vīrā - courageous;

Sorrow and difficulties will be gone, and all suffering
will be removed for the one who always remembers
Lord Hanuman, the mighty & brave one.

jai jai jai hanumāna gōsāyī ।   जै जै जै हनुमान गोसाई।
kṛpā karahu gurudēva kī nāyī ॥ 37 ॥   कृपा करहु गुरुदेव की नाई॥

jai jai jai - victory, victory, victory; hanumāna - (to) Lord
Hanuman; gōsāyī - the revered one; kṛpā - grace; karahu
- do; gurudēva - revered guru; kī nāyī - as/like;

*Victory to you, O master of the senses. Show mercy on
us like how a Sadguru (spiritual master) does.*

The 35th verse states that the mind need not be invested in any other
deities or forms of the Divine but solely in Hanuman. The verse
emphasizes that focusing on the form of Lord Hanuman alone is
sufficient to bring all forms of well-being, happiness, and fulfillment.
The 36th verse underscores that all hurdles and obstacles will get
obliterated; all forms of suffering disappear when one remembers or
remains devoted to the brave and mighty Lord Hanuman. The verse
reassures us that true devotion to Hanuman removes every sankat
(obstacle) and pira (suffering), bringing peace and relief. The 37th verse
proclaims victory to Hanuman, revered as the epitome of devotion
and courage, and one who facilitates the Guru's grace (Kripa) upon us.

Devotion to Lord Hanuman - Are Other Deities Inferior?

The 35th verse underscores the importance of single-minded devotion.
By directing one's thoughts and energy entirely toward Hanuman, one
can experience fulfillment and joy. This focused devotion will help us
tackle and overcome whatever problems we face. Hanuman's form
embodies strength, humility, and unwavering service to the Divine,
making him a perfect focal point for spiritual practice and inner peace.

There is a simple yet profound story involving the astrological
planets Rahu and Surya (the Sun). Surya is always radiant,
shedding light and life force upon the world. However, Rahu — known
for his rivalry with Surya — would often cast his shadow over him,
attempting to dim his brilliance. Rahu, known for his deceptive nature,
would camouflage himself among celestial bodies, making it nearly
impossible to locate him. This allowed him to evade detection and
continue troubling Surya. Being Hanuman's preceptor (guru), Surya

once sought Hanuman's help as Rahu's persistent interference hindered Surya's duty of sustaining life on Earth. Hanuman, determined to protect his guru, began searching for Rahu everywhere but could not find him. Making use of his golden lustre (discussed in the chapter on verse 4), Hanuman increased the intensity of his golden hue and began expanding in size, growing larger and brighter with divine radiance. Unable to remain hidden in the presence of such brilliance, Rahu was finally revealed and tried to flee. But Hanuman, being the son of the Wind God, was swift and unstoppable. He captured Rahu and demanded that he cease troubling Surya. Helpless, Rahu agreed and promised to act only according to cosmic law and to never again diminish Surya's brilliance for personal gain.

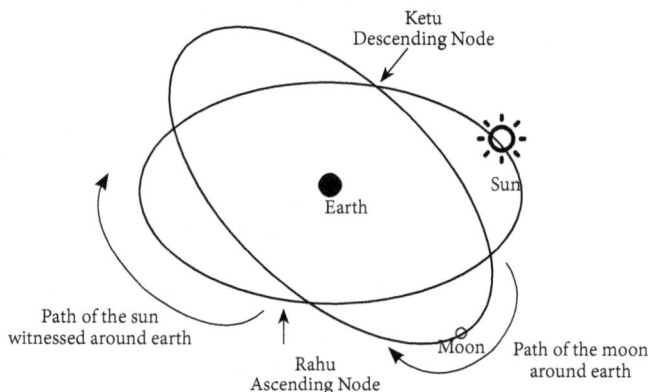

Though the story may seem mythological or even trivial on the surface, it carries deep symbolism. In Indian astrology, Rahu and Ketu are considered shadow planets. They don't have physical form; rather, they represent two significant points on the lunar path where the Moon's orbit intersects the Sun's path around Earth. A solar eclipse occurs when the Sun and Moon align precisely at one of these intersection points. According to traditional astrology, during a solar eclipse, Rahu and the Sun appear in the same house in the horoscope. Hence, Rahu is symbolically seen as eclipsing the Sun, casting a shadow that can affect the natural rhythm of life. Solar eclipses often bring about a sudden shift in the environment, and as per Indian tradition, people are advised to engage in chanting, prayer, and spiritual practices during that time to mitigate any potential negative effects.

In this light, the story conveys a deeper message in a vivid, symbolic way: When the eclipse of Rahu casts darkness over the mind and life, it is best to invoke the Hanuman within us - the force of devotion, discipline, and virtue. The golden lustre of inner goodness dispels the darkness of confusion and negativity. Just as Hanuman protected Surya, our inner devotion and spiritual practices protect the light (Surya) within us from being overshadowed by inner doubt, fear, and ignorance (Rahu).

Now, one may ask - if Surya needed Hanuman's help, does that make Hanuman greater than Surya? Does this imply that Hanuman is superior and other deities are inferior? This question arises not only here but across many religions, traditions, and faiths, where some proclaim their God as the only true God, dismissing all others. How do we understand such claims?

This verse seems to convey a similar message — that focusing solely on Hanuman is sufficient. While the statement is valid, it must be understood with wisdom and a spiritual perspective. To illustrate this, let us reflect on this question: Who is the greatest mom in the world? Many of us would undoubtedly say, "My mom." Why? Because our bond, our connection, and our experiences with her have shaped our lives. Our mom is the greatest for each of us, but this in no way diminishes the greatness of others' moms. We honor and dedicate ourselves to our mom for what she has done for us, but that doesn't make other moms any less significant. Similarly, dedicating ourselves to a particular deity doesn't mean other forms of the Divine are inferior. It simply reflects our personal connection and experiences with that form.

Speaking of moms, this reminds me of a little joke. Three kids were boasting about their moms.

The first said, "My mom is the greatest. She spends all her time in the kitchen, cooking me delicious meals."

The second chimed in, "That's nothing. My mom is even greater! She works all day and still comes home to cook amazing food for me."

The third boy said, "Your moms are good, but mine is the best. She has trained my dad so well that he cooks for us."

For each one of us, our mom is the best. Likewise, whether it is within Sanatana Dharma or other religious and spiritual traditions, the purpose of scriptures isn't to prove the supremacy of one deity over another, and expressions of one-pointed devotion shouldn't be read as such. For example, Lord Shiva is portrayed as the ultimate in the *Shiva Purana*, with all other forms supporting him. Meanwhile, the *Vishnu Purana* elevates Lord Vishnu, presenting every other deity as being in service to him. These scriptures cater to the devotion and connection of a specific group of followers, providing a text that helps them relate deeply to their chosen deity. Sanatana Dharma is vast and accommodating. It allows individuals to choose a deity they resonate with the most based on their temperament and mental inclination. Each text reinforces the greatness of that particular deity to strengthen the devotee's conviction and commitment. This doesn't mean other forms are inferior; the purpose is to help the devotee focus and grow. And finally, the higher texts within Sanatana Dharma enlighten us to go beyond all these forms, recognizing that all these forms are manifestations of the same One Divine.

The Shvetashvatara Upanishad (Chapter 11) states:

eko devaḥ sarva bhūteṣhu gūḍhaḥ

The Divine is only one, hidden in all the forms and beings.

Think of it like choosing a field of study in college. If you join law school, you're made to believe that law is the best field and where you should dedicate your efforts. This doesn't mean medicine or engineering is inferior. Similarly, someone in medical school is taught that medicine is the most noble profession, while an engineering student is inspired to believe that engineering is the way forward. Without this conviction, no student can truly excel in their chosen field. Now imagine if someone joins law school in the first year, then decides midway that law isn't good enough and switches to engineering in the second year, only to abandon that for medical school in the third year. At the end of it all, they are neither a lawyer, an engineer, nor a doctor. By constantly shifting focus, they achieve nothing.

Once we choose a path, it is best to dedicate ourselves to it wholeheartedly, believing it to be the best for us. That's the essence of this verse — not to put down other paths but to affirm that our chosen path is ideal for us and to focus on it with dedication and faith to grow spiritually. The same goes for the path we take in life. For example, I've chosen the path of being a monk, and I firmly believe that being a monk is the best path. If I start doubting that, thinking that other paths are better, I'll falter at some point. Similarly, if someone has chosen the path of a householder, they should consider the householder's life the best. Otherwise, they won't be able to do justice to it or live it fully. This approach applies universally: Once we commit to a particular path — whether it's in life, in worship, or any pursuit — we must consider that path, that deity, or that object of focus as the ultimate. This mindset fuels our enthusiasm and drive, helping us to remain steadfast and to move forward with confidence.

The 66th verse of Chapter 18 of *Bhagavad Gita* says:

sarva-dharmān parityajya mām ekaṁ śharaṇaṁ vraja
ahaṁ tvāṁ sarva-pāpebhyo mokṣhayiṣhyāmi mā śhuchaḥ

Relinquishing all the dharmas (principles, priorities, etc.), take refuge in me alone. I will liberate you of all the misdeeds; have no fear.

Some may interpret this to mean that Krishna is saying he alone is the ultimate form of God and that worshiping any other deity is a waste of time. But that's a limited way of understanding the verse. When Krishna says "me," he doesn't identify himself solely with his physical form. Instead, he identifies with the Supreme Truth. In the 15th chapter of *Bhagavad Gita* Lord Krishna explains himself to be the Purusha - the Ultimate Being. By saying, "Take refuge in me," he guides us to surrender to the Divine in its ultimate sense.

It's perfectly valid for a Krishna devotee to see Krishna as the greatest. For that devotee, Krishna should be the greatest. But this doesn't mean that other forms of the Divine are inferior. One can say, "My deity is the greatest," but the problem arises when one says, "Your deity is inferior." All these forms of the Divine are manifestations of the same Supreme Being. Focusing exclusively on one form and declaring it the only valid form demonstrates a lack of understanding.

The same question often arises when discussing gurus. Some wonder, "Is my guru better than someone else's guru? Should I follow another guru?" Some refer to this tendency to compare or seek other gurus as guru shopping. It's not a productive or spiritually beneficial approach. I recall an incident several years ago when two persons I know, each devoted to different gurus, got into an argument. Initially, they were both extolling the greatness of their respective gurus. But soon, the discussion devolved into pointing out the supposed shortcomings of the other's guru. It became less about glorifying their own gurus and more about criticizing the other's. The entire discussion was fruitless, and, more importantly, it showed that neither of them truly understood their gurus' teachings. A faithful follower of any guru would not engage in such arguments.

Once you recognize a true Sadguru, it's essential to dedicate yourself to that guru. Consider that guru as the ultimate guiding light for your spiritual journey. Each guru, like each deity, may have different methods of conveying the same universal truth. Why? Because we all have different mental dispositions and life circumstances, a guru tailors their guidance to suit their disciples. Some gurus may emphasize bhakti yoga (the path of devotion), and others may focus on karma yoga (the path of selfless action) or jnana yoga (the path of knowledge). Certain gurus may have unique practices or mannerisms, while others emphasize simplicity. These differences are meant to cater to the needs of their disciples, not to create divisions.

Amma gives a beautiful analogy: Jumping from one guru to another is akin to digging shallow wells in multiple places without ever reaching water. Imagine digging a borewell and committing to dig 20 feet every day. If we keep switching locations, digging 20 feet here, 20 feet there, and so on, we will never reach water. But if we stay in one spot and dig consistently, we will eventually reach the source. Similarly, spiritual growth requires consistent dedication to one guru.

The same principle applies to the deities we worship. When we dedicate ourselves to Lord Hanuman or Amma, for instance, we should focus on Hanuman or Amma as the ultimate form of the Divine. This does not mean we're dismissing other forms of God but rather committing wholeheartedly to a specific path. Without that dedication and conviction, spiritual growth becomes fragmented and unsteady. This is the essence of the 35th verse: Focus on Hanuman or Amma as the ultimate, and let that devotion guide you on your spiritual path.

Devotion Begets Happiness

The 36th verse highlights the attitude of dedication and devotion one must cultivate toward Lord Hanuman. It emphasizes that when one fully dedicates oneself to Hanuman with true devotion, all problems dissipate, and all forms of suffering are eradicated, leading to happiness.

In this regard, there is a folk tale: One day, Hanuman was walking down a busy street when he heard a heated argument coming from a nearby sweet shop. Curious, he stepped closer and found an old shopkeeper surrounded by a group of children. The man was clearly upset at the boys, as they hadn't paid in full for the sweets they had taken.

Hanuman gently diffused the situation and sat beside the shopkeeper. "Tell me," he asked, "why are you so worked up over something so small?" The shopkeeper sighed deeply and poured his heart out. "How can I not be upset?" he said. "I'm getting old. My wife is permanently ill. Who will care for her if something happens to me? Meanwhile, I can't find a good match for my daughter. My son isn't educated because I don't have the money to send him to school. Business is slow. We barely have enough to survive a few days. And now, these boys didn't even pay for their sweets. How can I not be upset?"

Hanuman listened patiently. He gathered from the conversation how lovingly the man cared for his wife, how hard he worked to support his children, and how sincerely he ran his humble store. After a moment, Hanuman said, "I see that you're doing everything you can to face your challenges. You're not sitting idly - you're doing your part. Then why burden your heart with so much stress?" The shopkeeper replied quietly, "I don't know. I try my best, but I'm constantly worried about what the future holds." Hanuman offered him a simple remedy. "You're already doing your duty," he said. "Now, add one small practice. Every time you feel stressed, sit quietly for just a few moments. Close your eyes and chant 'Ram… Ram… Ram…' - just nine times. Then say to Lord Rama, "I've done what little I can. I offer the rest to you. These are your problems now, not mine.' And then continue with your day." The shopkeeper was skeptical. "And how is that going to help?" Hanuman smiled. "Just try it. But do it sincerely, every single day. Then wait and see."

A month passed. Hanuman returned to the sweet shop and found a very different scene. The shopkeeper was cheerful, smiling, and laughing with the same group of boys who had once upset him.

"Looks like a miracle has taken place," Hanuman said, smiling.

The shopkeeper laughed. "Yes, indeed."

"Did your wife recover?"

"No. Her condition is still the same."

"Then your daughter must be married?"

"Not yet."

"Your son has started school?"

"Still waiting."

"Then perhaps business is booming?"

"It's improved a bit, but nothing major."

Hanuman paused. "Then what miracle are you talking about?" The shopkeeper's face softened. "The miracle," he said, "is in my mind. Nothing big has changed outside, but I have changed. Though it didn't seem to help initially, I still sincerely chanted 'Ram, Ram, Ram' and offered my worries to the Lord, at first just because you made me promise I would do it. But after a few days, I felt the burden slowly lift. I no longer felt alone. My heart felt lighter." He continued, "Because of that peace, I'm able to care for my wife more with more patience. I manage my store with a clearer head. I'm saving more for my son's education. I'm searching for a match for my daughter without desperation. And just yesterday, one of those boys' fathers came by and offered a generous contribution to the store, saying I brought joy to his child. Every day feels like a miracle now."

Hanuman smiled. "That is the miracle of true bhakti. It doesn't always change the world around us — it changes how we face it. A peaceful mind is a powerful mind. And when that happens, happiness follows you like a faithful servant."

Hanuman blesses us by helping us recognize and tap into our true potential, enabling us to overcome what might have felt like intractable and overwhelming problems. He grants us the strength to confront the ego within, which drains our true potential, and to rise above it, allowing happiness to flourish naturally.

Let us understand that when we say "devotion begets happiness," it doesn't mean that because we are devoted to Hanuman or Amma, they bestow happiness upon us. It is not transactional. Rather, through devotion, we reflect on their qualities, such as Hanuman's humility, devotion, strength, and selflessness, or Amma's love, compassion, patience, and acceptance, which inspires us to imbibe those qualities in our lives. This is the real purpose of devotion. By developing these qualities in ourselves, we can eliminate many problems in our lives. Most of our issues stem from rigid mindsets, self-centered thinking, and attachment to likes and dislikes. If we let go of these, many of our problems will disappear. For those that don't, we will gain the strength to face them with something approaching equanimity.

For instance, consider communal living in the ashram or sharing a room during a trip to Amritapuri. These situations can feel like challenges if we cling to our preferences and comfort zones. Similarly, not getting a chance to sing in a satsang or hearing someone gossip about us can seem like significant problems if our ego dominates our consciousness. However, when we cultivate humility and selflessness, such concerns lose their grip on us.

Amma continues with unwavering conviction to serve the world despite having overcome unimaginable challenges and sometimes ridicule. That is the state we should aspire to reach. Dedication to Hanuman or Amma doesn't mean relentlessly praising them; rather, it means dedicating ourselves to developing their virtues - humility, devotion, egolessness, and strength. Once we embody these qualities, our problems diminish naturally, and we can live with peace and purpose.

Victory to Hanuman

The 37th verse says, "Victory, victory, victory to Lord Hanuman." But does Lord Hanuman need us to declare his victory? What exactly does it mean to call someone victorious? What is true victory?

The concept of victory here is not about external conquest but the triumph of truth. This resonates with the proclamation made in the Mundaka Upanishad:

satyameva jayate nānrtam

Truth alone triumphs, not otherwise.

Even the Indian national emblem displays this motto. Truth, in its purest form, is victorious over falsehood. When we speak of Hanuman's victory, we refer to the Supreme Truth and reflect on the ultimate state of Oneness.

In a state of Oneness, there is no duality — no separation between me and you, between truth and falsehood. Duality creates division, but in the ultimate singular state, only Truth exists. This state of Oneness is what Hanuman, Amma, or any spiritual master embodies. The question of victory arises only when there are two to compete. Realized beings have already attained the state of Oneness and need no proclamation of victory. When we chant their victory, we are reminding ourselves of the state they have achieved and the path we must strive to follow. The actual battle to win is within us. It is the conflict between our higher self and ego — our likes, dislikes, and self-centered attitudes. Chanting "Jai Jai Hanuman" or any such mantra becomes a war cry, urging us to rise above our inner negativities and ego.

Amma often mentions this during her satsangs. When we chant "Mata Rani Ki Jai" (Victory to the Divine Mother), she advises us to visualize two things: White flowers of peace showering onto the earth and spreading harmony, and the victory of positive qualities within us over our inner negativities — the Divine triumphing over the demonic within.

No matter how much we try to grow spiritually, the grace of the guru (guru kripa) is essential. The 37th verse of the *Chalisa* emphasizes this: kripa karahu gurudeva ki nayi. The guru is the one who holds our hand and guides us on this journey. Without the guru's grace, the path becomes arduous. The guru helps us remain humble, providing a constant anchor to ground us. In our battle against ego, the guru is our greatest ally. The guru creates opportunities, offers verbal guidance, and sets an example to help us resolve our ego. By staying connected to the guru, we are reminded to embody humility, a critical trait for spiritual growth.

Chanting "Victory to Hanuman" or "Victory to the guru" signifies our aspiration to triumph over ego, guided by the guru's grace. This grace is indispensable in our spiritual journey. It completes and perfects our efforts.

Insights on the Path of Bhakti from verses 35, 36 & 37:

- Verse 35

  ○ For a devotee, the form or deity chosen is the ultimate inspiration and goal. We should try to become one with that.

  ○ However, it is essential to recognize that every other form is a reflection of the same Divine and should be respected accordingly.

- Verse 36

  ○ Devotion and dedication fetch us true happiness. There is no room for suffering in that state.

- Verse 37

  ○ True victory is realizing the Supreme Truth — a state of oneness with the Divine and with all of creation — while letting go of our ephemeral and limited ego identity.

Verses 38, 39 and 40

Constant practice and remembrance
The attitude of selflessness and humility
Make the heart deserving of the divine dwelling

jō śata vāra pāṭha kara kōyī ।   जो सत बार पाठ कर कोई।
Chūṭahi bandi mahā sukha hōyī ॥ 38 ॥   छूटहिं बंदि महा सुख होई॥

jō - one who; śata - hundred; vāra - times; pāṭha kara - does
recite; kōyī - anyone; chūṭahi - freed; bandi - bound; mahā
- great/ultimate; sukha - happiness; hōyī - becomes;

*One who recites this text 100 (numerous) times will
be freed of all bondages and find supreme bliss.*

jō yaha paḍai hanumāna chālīsā ।   जो यह पढ़ै हनुमान चालीसा।
hōya siddhi sākhī gaurīsā ॥ 39 ॥   होय सिद्धि साखी गौरीसा॥

jō - one who; yaha - this; paḍai - read/learns; hanumāna
chālīsā - the forty verses in praise of Lord Hanuman; hōya
- become; siddhi - perfect/abled; sākhī - witness; gaurīsā
- Lord Shiva, the Lord of Gauri (Mother Parvati);

*One who reads and imbibes these verses on Hanuman
will attain spiritual perfection and success. None other
than Lord Shiva is the witness to this statement.*

tulasīdāsa sadā hari chērā ।
kījai nātha hṛdaya maha ḍērā ॥ 40 ॥

तुलसीदास सदा हरि चेरा ।
कीजै नाथ हृदय महँ डेरा ॥

tulasīdāsa - Saint Tulasidas; sadā - ever; hari - Lord
Vishnu; chērā - servant; kījai - do; nātha - Lord;
hṛdaya - heart; maha - my; ḍērā - abode;

*Tulasidas (the composer of these verses) will forever
be a disciple of Hari (the Divine – Lord Vishnu). O
Lord!! Please make my heart your abode.*

Verses 38 and 39 emphasize the repeated chanting of the *Hanuman
Chalisa* and its profound benefits. These verses highlight how one who
recites the *Hanuman Chalisa* is freed from all bondages that weigh
them down, ultimately attaining bliss and happiness. Through this
practice, these verses are saying one reaches a state of perfection. The
39th verse further reinforces this claim by stating that none other than
Lord Shiva serves as the witness to this truth. Finally, in the 40th verse,
Tulasidas signs off by humbly referring to himself as the "servant" of
Lord Rama (Vishnu), underscoring the importance of humility in the
path of devotion.

Chanting the Chalisa as a Regular Practice

The 38th verse stresses chanting the *Hanuman Chalisa* 100 times to be
free from bondages and obtain happiness. Here, the number 100 should
not be taken literally. Rather, the emphasis is on constant chanting, an
essential aspect of spiritual practice on the path of bhakti. Constant
chanting and remembrance are integral to the path of devotion.

Let's begin our analysis of the concluding verses with the story
of Ratnakara, the forest dweller who was transformed into Sage
Valmiki. Ratnakara was a forest dweller who hunted to make a living
and had a family to care for. However, hunting alone wasn't enough to
support his family, so he began robbing travelers and, eventually, killing
them. His actions became increasingly unrighteous and sinful. One

day, Sage Narada was passing through the forest when Ratnakara ambushed him, demanding all his possessions. Narada asked why he was committing such acts, and Ratnakara explained that he had no choice but to provide for his family. Narada asked, "Will your family, who benefits from your actions, also share the consequences of your sins?" Confident, Ratnakara said they would. On Sage Narada's insistence, he went to his family to ask this question. None of them agreed to share in the fruits of his misdeeds, to his dismay. This revelation shook Ratnakara. He returned to Narada, distraught and confused. Recognizing this as a turning point, Narada introduced him to the path of devotion and instructed him to chant the name of Lord Rama. However, due to the weight of his sins, Ratnakara could not even utter the name "Rama." Understanding his difficulty, Narada advised him to chant the name "Mara" in reverse instead. When repeated continuously, "Mara mara mara mara mara…." naturally transformed into "Rama."

Valmiki became so immersed in this practice that he sat in penance for ages, engrossed in chanting. During this time, an anthill (valmika) grew around him. Narada eventually returned and woke him, freeing him

from the anthill. Thus, Ratnakara was transformed into Valmiki, who eventually composed the epic *Ramayana* as the Adi Kavi (the first poet).

This story beautifully illustrates the transformative power of constant chanting and remembrance. Even a simple, seemingly meaningless word like "mara" can lead to profound change when chanted with sincerity and dedication. This is what the 38th verse of the *Hanuman Chalisa* highlights - the importance of constant repetition and its ability to bring about positive change.

If we have paid attention to the archana book published by our ashram, with which we chant the *Lalitha Sahasranama*, the 1,000 names of the Divine Mother, there is a significant quote from Amma at the back. This quote states:

"Devi, the Divine Mother, always protects those who chant the 1,000 names with devotion every day. They will never face a shortage of food and basic necessities and will also gain spiritual growth."

It's important to not only chant it daily but to chant it with devotion, as Amma emphasizes. This combination of regularity and heartfelt devotion is key to reaping its benefits. It is not just about mechanically chanting it but, importantly, doing it with the right attitude, imbibing the qualities like patience, understanding, sincerity, and dedication.

Bhagavad Gita, Chapter 12, verse 9 states:

atha chittam samādhātum na śhaknoṣhi mayi sthiram
abhyāsa-yogena tato mām ichchhāptum dhanañjaya

If one isn't able to fix the mind unwaveringly at me,
then through abhyasa (constant practice), one could
still attain me, O Dhananjaya (Arjuna)

Here, Lord Krishna speaks about bhakti and the qualities of a true devotee. In this context, he explains that a true devotee is one whose mind is steadfastly and unwaveringly focused on him and his divine qualities alone. However, Krishna acknowledges that not everyone can maintain such unwavering focus. Thus in the above verse, he offers an alternative path. The Lord is telling us here that we need not despair if our minds don't naturally gravitate toward the Divine — we can overcome any shortcomings and negative tendencies in our mind through constant, sustained spiritual practice, thereby reaching the ultimate state through a combination of effort and divine grace.

In our daily lives, especially in moments of tension or emotional triggers — when negative emotions arise or we feel the urge to react impulsively — chanting a mantra can be transformative. For example, when we are triggered by an email and feel ready to respond sharply, instead of reacting immediately, we can pause and chant our mantra 54 times or 108 times. By the end of the chanting, we will likely notice a shift in our attitude or perspective.

Chanting isn't merely about repeating the mantra a specific number of times but doing it with understanding, awareness, and devotion. This process calms the mind and gradually aligns it with the divine qualities the mantra represents. However, without the right attitude or understanding, chanting mechanically is unlikely to yield the desired results. What makes chanting truly fruitful is the intention and attitude with which it is done. When we are instructed to chant 100 or 1,000 names repeatedly, it's not just about the repetition itself; it's about using the repetition as an opportunity to reflect deeply on the qualities and teachings conveyed by the text time and again.

For instance, if we read the *Hanuman Chalisa* once through, or even read this book and explore the verses one at a time, we may grasp inspiring lessons from Hanuman's qualities. However, it's natural for these insights to fade from our memory over time. By chanting repeatedly, we revisit and reflect on Hanuman's qualities repeatedly, making it easier for them to stay with us and eventually become part of our nature.

This principle applies to learning almost anything. Whether typing on a computer, playing a musical instrument, or mastering a sport like tennis, repetition is key. The more we practice, the more natural and second nature it becomes. Similarly, repeated chanting helps us internalize the teachings and qualities of the Divine.

This process also explains why Amma says that chanting the 1,000 names of the Divine Mother daily will ensure we never face a shortage of food or necessities. As we chant and reflect on names that describe the Divine Mother — such as one who is unaffected by external circumstances, humble, and content with the least of everything — we naturally begin to embody these qualities ourselves. As we adopt a mindset of humility and contentment, we find satisfaction even with minimal resources, and our problems start to feel less overwhelming.

Similarly, by regularly chanting the *Sahasranama* or the *Hanuman Chalisa* and genuinely reflecting on the inspiring qualities therein, our attitudes and perceptions begin to shift. This regular practice can help us see challenges differently, enabling us to find meaning or growth even in adversity.

And here's the profound truth: If done with the right mindset and dedication, you don't necessarily need to chant 100 times. Even a single, heartfelt recitation can be enough to create a meaningful transformation. Since we are in the process of developing that attitude, chanting numerous times remains critical for us.

A popular Sanskrit verse — a conversation between Lord Shiva and Goddess Parvati — that is often chanted alongside the *Vishnu Sahasranama* (1,000 names of Lord Vishnu) goes like this:

sri rāma rāma rāmeti rame rāme manorama
sahasranāma tattulyam rāma nāma varānane

Reciting "Rama Rama Rama" is so blissful and
rejoicing to the mind. It is equivalent to chanting the
thousand names, O pleasant-faced one (Parvati)!

Here it is said that chanting the name of Lord Rama three times is equivalent to reciting the *Sahasranama* (the 1,000 names). However, what is truly emphasized here is how we chant Lord Rama's name. Chanting must be imbued with devotion and mindfulness, bringing us bliss. If we chant mechanically, it will unlikely bring any transformation or joy. Simply chanting his name three times and thinking, "I've completed my 1,000 names for the day," misses the point entirely. The goal is to deeply internalize what Lord Rama represents - the values and qualities he embodies. When we truly imbibe these qualities and call out to him, even chanting his name three times with such sincerity becomes as potent as chanting it 1,000 times.

Continuing with the 39th verse of the *Chalisa*, it states that one who reads or learns it attains siddhi - perfection. In the chapter on the 31st verse, we discussed how Lord Hanuman is described as the bearer of the ashta siddhis (the eight forms of perfection) and nava nidhis (the nine forms of precious treasures). We delved into how Hanuman attained these through his devotion, humility, selflessness, and unwavering dedication.

The 39th verse suggests that we, too, can attain siddhi by learning and internalizing the *Hanuman Chalisa*. This is because as we engage with the *Chalisa*, the assumption is that we also begin to understand and embrace the qualities that Hanuman embodies. Only by genuinely imbibing these qualities — such as devotion, humility, and selflessness — can we aspire to reach a state of perfection. Without this understanding or effort to internalize its teachings, simply reading or reciting the *Hanuman Chalisa* likely won't yield the desired transformation. It's not just about recitation; it's about reflection and implementation. A profound verse from the text *Padma Purana* states that one who chants mantras or performs rituals without understanding their meaning is like a foolish donkey, unaware of the value of the sandalwood it bears on its back.

Shiva Stands Witness to the Statement

In the last part of the 39th verse, we encounter the phrase, "sakhi gaurisa" - Lord Shiva is the witness to all of this. Here Tulasidas makes a definitive assertion: If you read the *Hanuman Chalisa*, you will attain the state of perfection, and none other than Lord Shiva bears witness to this truth.

The Divine, as the ultimate witness, observes everything we do in three profound ways:

- Literal omniscience: The Divine is omniscient and omnipresent. Many of us have experienced how Amma seems to read our minds or respond to our unspoken thoughts. This omniscience is an inexplicable yet undeniable aspect of the Divine's presence, reassuring us that we are constantly guided and seen.

- Through the laws of nature: The Divine also watches us through the principles of nature. Every action we take is recorded and inevitably met with consequences, like the law of gravity, which ensures that a ball thrown upward will return. Nature operates as an impartial witness, balancing and compensating for our deeds.

- Through our conscience: Perhaps the most immediate and personal witness is our conscience. This inner awareness evaluates and holds us accountable for our actions, serving as an ever-present reminder of right and wrong.

Shiva also symbolizes the ultimate state of chit (consciousness) and ananda (bliss). In the *Nirvana Shatkam*, Adi Shankaracharya beautifully expresses this idea with the refrain shivoham - "I am Shiva." This signifies our true essence as the embodiment of consciousness and bliss, free from the illusions of the physical and mental realms.

When all physical elements dissolve, what remains is the soul - the true witness, often referred to as Shiva. In this sense, Shiva, as sakshi, also points to our conscience, which is ever-aware and reflective. Thus, the verse reminds us that we are always observed and guided, whether it is the Divine in its cosmic form, the laws of nature, or our inner conscience. This awareness should inspire us to act with sincerity, integrity, and devotion.

A story similar to what Amma shares: There was a king searching for a successor between his two sons. He wanted to determine which of them was more capable and deserving of taking on the responsibility of ruling the kingdom. To test them, he gave each of them a bag filled with valuables and instructed them: "Go and hide this somewhere — hide it so well that no one can find it or know where it is." Both sons accepted the challenge and set out. Days passed, and finally, the elder son returned, jubilant and confident that he had succeeded. The king asked, "What took you so long, and where did you hide the valuables?"

The elder son replied, "I tried to find a place where no one was watching me, where no one could ever discover where I hid it. I went to the town, but there were too many people. I went to the forest, but the animals and trees were there. Then I traveled to the desert, but even there, I saw reptiles and plants. Finally, I found a cave with no one around. I dug a pit, placed the bag inside, covered it up, and camouflaged the area so no one could find it. I'm confident it's hidden well."

The king was quite impressed with the elder son's resourcefulness. However, the younger son had not returned yet. The king waited many more days, but the younger son did not show up. Finally, several weeks later, he returned, unsuccessful and with the bag still in his possession. The king asked him, "What happened? Why did it take you so long, and why couldn't you hide the bag?" The younger son replied, "I went to the town, but there were too many people, so I knew it wasn't safe. Then I went to the forest, but I realized the animals and trees were watching me. I traveled to the desert, but reptiles and plants seemed to bear witness even there. Finally, I found a cave. It seemed perfect because no one was around. I started digging a pit and placed the bag inside. But as I was covering it up, I realized something — I was watching it. No matter where I went or how I tried to hide it, I was always there, observing. You asked to hide it where no one would know, and that was impossible." This story beautifully illustrates the idea that our conscience is always present, always watching, no matter where we go or what we do. The phrase sakhi gaurisha in the 39th verse could also be interpreted this way: our conscience constantly stands witness, observing us. Whatever we think, say, or do — our thoughts, words, and actions are always under the scrutiny of our own conscience.

Ever Remaining a Servant

The 40th verse begins with Tulasidas signing his name, but not in a boastful manner. He doesn't end by proclaiming, "Look at this splendid masterpiece of *Hanuman Chalisa* that will be revered for centuries!" Instead, he humbly declares, "I am nothing but a servant of Lord Vishnu." Tulasidas refers to himself as Hari chela - not even a servant in the grand sense, but the humblest of them, like a minion. This act highlights the profound attitude of humility of a true devotee.

This tradition of signing one's name with humility is seen across many saint-poets. For instance, Saint Tyagaraja, one of the trinity of South Indian Carnatic classical music composers, included his name in his compositions. However, his name always appeared in the context of his devotion to Lord Rama - phrases like "Tyagaraja, who bows down to Mother Sita" or "Tyagaraja, devoted to Lord Vishnu." His signature was never about self-promotion but a constant reminder to remain humble and dedicated.

Similarly, we touched earlier on the example of Mirabai, a princess from the Rajput family of Northwestern India, who renounced her royal luxuries and lived a saintly life dedicated to Lord Krishna. In her compositions, the name Meera often appears, but always in the context of devotion - for example, Meera ke Prabhu Giridhara Nagar (Meera's Lord is Giridhara, the lifter of Govardhan Hill). By signing her name this way, Mirabai subtly conveys that any praise attributed to her should instead remind us of the greatness of Lord Krishna.

Saint Tyagaraja (18 century)
One of the trinities of
Carnatic classical music
Signed his name as a devotee of Rama

Mirabai (15th century)
Rajput princess
Was ever devoted to Krishna
"Mira ke Prabhu Giridhar Nagara."

Saint Tukaram (17th century)
Saint from Western India
Devoted to Vitthala and Lord Vishnu
"Tuka mhane..." - Tuka says .... (and dedicated it to the Lord)

Another example is Sant Tukaram, a 17th-century saint from Maharashtra. In his Marathi compositions, he often included the phrase Tuka mhane (Tuka says), followed by a message of devotion or humility, such as "Devote yourself to God," or "Let go of ego and attachments." This simple yet profound act of signing his name with a spiritual message reinforced the values of humility and selflessness.

One might wonder why these saints signed their names instead of leaving their works anonymous. Their names and a message of humility make a deeper impression. Seeing their names reminds us of their devotion and inspires us to emulate their qualities. The act of signing becomes a service, not a self-promotion, especially when the signature carries a lesson in humility and devotion.

As always, the Divine doesn't need our praise. The act of praising is for our benefit - to reflect on the qualities of humility, surrender, and devotion that we must imbibe. These qualities, exemplified by saints like Tulasidas, Tyagaraja, Mirabai, and Tukaram, bring peace into our lives and help dissolve many problems rooted in ego and self-centeredness. The more humility we cultivate, the simpler and more harmonious life becomes.

While writing this book, I felt a firm conviction that displaying my name as the author would go against the very message it conveys. Initially, it was credited as "written by an aspiring devotee." However, when I brought this to Amma's attention, she was clear that I should include my name. Amma explained that, firstly, without an author's name, the book might seem orphaned. Secondly, having an author allows readers to connect with someone as they absorb the book's message in the context of the author's experience and perspective. Following Amma's guidance, I added my name, though know I am merely a medium - while any mistakes or omissions are my own, anything of value you find in this commentary on the *Hanuman Chalisa* has come from my Guru - Amma, who is the true author of this book.

Amma reminds us: Whenever we experience the creation, we should remember the Creator and be thankful to the Creator.

This applies not just to the entirety of creation but even to the most minor details, such as the food we eat. Amma often says that when we eat food, we should remember the person who cooked it and be thankful to them. On Tuesdays in Amritapuri Ashram, when Amma serves food, and everyone is about to eat, after chanting Brahmarpanam (food prayer), Amma reads out the names of those who sponsored the food. This has been a tradition for decades. Amma constantly reminds everyone: "Remember the Creator before you experience the creation. Be thankful to those who made this possible — send out a positive thought to them — and then relish the food." In the context of *Hanuman Chalisa*, it also emphasizes remembering the composer, Tulasidas, along with his message of humility. By doing so, we not only appreciate the creation but also internalize its deeper spiritual message, making our experience all the more meaningful.

Let us reflect on Amma's words from *Awaken Children*, Vol 1, page 144, wherein she underscores that God, rather, becomes the servant of a true devotee:

Mother: Yes, He is the servant of His true devotee. A true devotee is one who takes everything as God's Will, both bad and good. In reality, there is nothing bad for him. Everything is seen as good and beautiful for a true devotee because, for him, all is God, so there is nothing to hate. Something is good, and something else is bad only for a person who has likes and dislikes. But in the case of a real devotee, there are no likes and dislikes. He sees God's divine hand behind every experience and every act. For such a person, is there anything that could be called 'bad'? If he hates or dislikes something, it is the same as hating God, which is unnatural to him. In his world, there is only love. To such a devotee, God is his servant.

Mother suddenly entered an abstracted mood and, as if from another world, She said, "Children, Mother is the servant of every one of you. I do not have a particular dwelling place of my own. I dwell in the heart of all of you."

Making our Heart the Divine Abode

This leads us to the next part of the verse, where Tulasidas says, "I am the servant of Lord Vishnu," and then prays, "O Lord, make my heart your dwelling." This sentiment resonates deeply, especially as Amma often speaks about the Divine dwelling in our hearts.

But what does it truly mean when we say, "The Divine dwells in our heart?" If we were to take a CT scan, would we see Lord Hanuman, Lord Rama, or Amma within us? As thrilling as that idea might be, that's not how it works. When we say, "Let the Divine dwell in my heart," we emphasize the need to make our hearts worthy of the Divine's presence.

In other words, we are called to transform our hearts into an abode of divine qualities. It means cultivating the virtues inspired by the divine figures we revere. When we develop these positive qualities within ourselves, our heart naturally becomes the dwelling place of the Divine. The Divine is, after all, the embodiment of all these virtues. Therefore, to make our heart the Divine's shrine, we must consciously nurture and embody these qualities. In doing so, we transform ourselves, and our heart truly becomes the abode of the Divine.

An excerpt from *Awaken Children*, Vol. 3, page 116, can help us reflect on Amma's words in this context:

Just as a mother does to her child, the Holy Mother expressed love and affection to the boy as she conversed with him. She asked about his age and his grades in school. The Mother said, "It seems that you are very mischievous. What will be the end result of all these mischievous deeds? You will end up in trouble for them, won't you? Therefore, my child, you should study diligently and grow up as a good boy. Okay?"

The boy enthusiastically nodded his head in agreement with what the Mother had said.

The boy: Amma, I would like your address.

Amma: Mother has no such thing as an address.

The Mother took the diary from the young boy and started writing on one of the pages:

"Darling Children,

Your happiness is Mother's health. Let Children's attitude of selfless service last forever. The compassion that we show towards the poor and needy is the real duty towards God. That is real service. God does not need anything from us. What can we give to the Ever-Full One? The whole universe belongs to Him. The sun does not need a wax candle. An electric bulb does not need a kerosene lamp. These orphaned children are equal to God. God dwells in those who have the attitude, "I have nobody else." Eternally blessed and blissful are those who look after them selflessly. Let Children's selfless service be everlasting, darling Children."

This reflection is quite apt as it highlights the attitude we should cultivate towards the Divine. When we say, "I am of service to the Lord," Amma often reminds us that serving the poor and needy is the best way to serve God. When we develop an attitude of selflessness — helping others and giving to those in need — God naturally resides in our hearts. These two passages from Awaken, Children! beautifully summarize and elaborate on the essence of the 40th verse we just explored: Tulasidas, ever at the service of Lord Vishnu, prays, "O Lord, make my heart your abode, make it your shrine."

Insights on the Path of Bhakti from verses 38, 39 & 40:

- Verses 38 and 39
  - O Constant practice and effort is critical in the path of devotion
  - O Equally or more important is the attitude with which we practice
- Verse 40
  - O Ever behold the attitude of a humble servant, embracing selflessness in all that we do.
  - O Make our heart deserving of the Divine to dwell.
  - O We should make ourselves the abode of divine qualities like patience, love, compassion, humility, understanding, and acceptance.

The Concluding Doha (couplet)

Humility is the way
Becoming deserving of divine grace

pavana tanaya saṅkaṭa haraṇa
maṅgaḷa mūrati rūp ।
rāma lakhana sītā sahita
hṛdaya basahu surabhūp ॥

पवनतनय संकट हरन,
मंगल मूरति रूप ।
राम लखन सीता सहित,
हृदय बसहु सुर भूप ॥

pavana - wind; tanaya - son; saṅkaṭa - problem and worries;
haraṇa - remover; maṅgaḷa - auspiciousness; mūrati -
embodiment; rūp - form; rāma - Lord Rama; lakhana - Brother
Lakshmana; sītā - Mother Sita; sahita - along; hṛdaya - heart;
basahu - dwell, settle; sura - demi-god; bhūp - ruler/king;

*O Son of the Wind God, the remover of difficulties, the embodiment
of auspiciousness, greatest among the Gods, please reside in our
hearts along with Lord Rama, Lakshman, and Mother Sita.*

The last couplet of the *Hanuman Chalisa* marks the conclusion of the
text. Typically, the forty verses are chanted with a rhythm, but this
couplet, or doha, is recited without rhythm, serving as a reflective
conclusion to the 40 verses. As mentioned earlier, a doha traditionally
consists of two lines; in this case, it provides a fitting end to the
Hanuman Chalisa.

Son of the Wind God

The verse begins with the reference to Hanuman as the son of the Wind God (pavan tanaya); we recall how the second verse of the *Hanuman Chalisa* introduces him as Anjani Putra (son of Mother Anjani) and Pavan Suta (son of the Wind God). Hanuman is often referred to as the son of Vayu Deva due to this divine intervention that led to his birth, even though his biological father is Kesari. This connection highlights Hanuman's divine origin and his destined role in supporting Lord Rama's endeavors.

From a spiritual perspective, when we talk about Vayu (wind or air), it represents an essential element for the existence and sustenance of life on Earth. From breathing — prana, the life force within us — to maintaining the balance of the environment, air is vital. Without air, imbalance and void are inevitable, leading to the cessation of creation as we know it. Air, or wind, thus plays a crucial role in the harmony of life, and as the son of Vayu, Lord Hanuman embodies the traits of Vayu Deva. He could traverse vast distances instantly, demonstrating the speed and freedom associated with wind. However, there's a more profound symbolic trait of Vayu that Hanuman carries: simplicity and immense power.

Air surrounds us, subtle and often unnoticed. It is humble and selfless, with no distinct color, shape, taste, or smell to boast about. We can displace it with our movement; it accommodates and adjusts without resistance. We can even confine it into a Ziploc bag. Yet, when it displays its might through a tornado, typhoon, or hurricane, this very air can uproot the tallest of trees, topple massive buildings, and leave an indelible impact. The simplicity and humility of air transform into unparalleled force when required.

Similarly, Hanuman is the humblest of the humble, selflessly serving Lord Rama. But when the time demands, he is also the mightiest of the mighty, displaying unparalleled strength and courage. This duality is a powerful lesson for us, especially as spiritual seekers on the path of bhakti.

As devotees, we must strive to be humble and self-effacing, like the gentle breeze, adapting and serving without ego. Yet, when dharma calls — when it is time to uphold righteousness — we must not hesitate to exercise our strength, potential, and power with unwavering conviction and courage. As Lord Hanuman exemplifies, balancing humility with strength is a guiding principle for anyone walking the path of devotion.

At the same time, it is essential to note that when we talk about dharma, it should not be something we define selfishly. Defining dharma is a complex process and requires careful discernment. It is easy to justify our actions by claiming they align with dharma. Still, we must ensure that our understanding of dharma in a given situation is accurate and not driven by self-interest. When we say, "exhibit your might," we sometimes take that instruction in isolation and forget the essential aspect of dharma. Exercising our strength and power should always be rooted in what is genuinely right and appropriate in that moment, and it should be the benefit of all, and not just ourselves. It should not be motivated by self-interest. We must be mindful and reflect on what dharma demands before taking action. Lord Hanuman was the perfect example of acting with discernment and wisdom.

Embodiment of Auspiciousness

The following line in the concluding doha refers to Hanuman as "mangal murati rup," the embodiment of auspiciousness. Often, we consider people, places, and situations as auspicious or otherwise. But what exactly is auspiciousness?

Auspiciousness occurs when all the factors contributing to a given situation align harmoniously. It is a state where everything seems to fall into place effortlessly. Cultural beliefs often associate certain signs or occurrences with auspiciousness. For instance, someone heading out to write an exam might consider a sneeze or tripping at the door as inauspicious signs. If the car doesn't start, some may return home, sip water, and try again, believing this resets the whole process. While such practices may be viewed as superstitious, they highlight how we interpret certain factors as aligning or not aligning with auspiciousness. When we speak of auspiciousness, we are essentially talking about the interplay of factors that influence a moment or an event. When these factors are in harmony, we perceive the situation as auspicious.

From a spiritual perspective, auspiciousness is deeply connected to grace - the divine blessing in its fullest potential. Grace could be understood as the magical combination of factors that make a situation conducive to success. Grace, however, is always present. It is never lacking. What determines our experience of auspiciousness, then, is our receptiveness to that grace. As Amma says, "We need divine grace, but we also need our own grace." This means that while divine blessings are always there, we must cultivate openness, humility, and awareness to receive and experience them fully. Auspiciousness must be understood as not merely about external circumstances, but also about our inner state and how we align ourselves with divine grace. By harmonizing our efforts with divine blessings, we allow all the factors to fall into place, creating the conditions for auspiciousness in any situation.

In the chapter discussing verses 20 and 21, we looked at the three factors influencing a given situation. As we contemplate auspiciousness and grace and near the end of our time together in reflection of the *Chalisa*, it's worth returning to these once more:

1. adhi-atmikam

These refer to aspects within ourselves: our mood, attitude, memories, humility, selflessness, selfish motives, pessimism, or optimism. All these internal factors significantly influence how a situation unfolds, not least because our reaction to a given circumstance shapes how it plays out. For example, if we approach a situation with a positive mindset, it is more likely to unfold favorably than if we approach it with negativity or doubt. This is why Amma says we need our own grace. Sometimes, we want everything to align perfectly, but our inner state can disrupt that harmony. Considering the example mentioned above, if we are heading to an exam and our car doesn't start, we may interpret it as an inauspicious sign. Even after the vehicle starts, that initial hiccup might linger in our mind, creating unnecessary anxiety. While the mind may not always be under our control, striving to cultivate inner balance and grace is essential.

2. adhi-bhautikam

These are the factors associated with people and physical objects around us. The attitude and behavior of those around us — whether they offer support, understanding, or opposition — can impact the outcome of a situation. Similarly, external circumstances, like the reliability of equipment or environmental conditions, can play a role. For instance, during the interview there may be a power cut, or one of the interviewers keeps sneezing, creating distraction, or throws up all over the table. While these factors are not entirely within our control, we can still manage or navigate them to a certain extent. They require a combination of our effort/grace and divine grace.

3. adhi-daivikam

These factors are entirely out of our control — forces beyond the physical realm. For such factors to align, we need krpa (grace). Grace alone allows these external and uncontrollable elements to fall into place harmoniously.

Lord Hanuman sets the perfect example of how to be abundant in grace. Throughout his life, he exemplified the qualities of a true devotee: humility, selflessness, dedication, acceptance, patience, and understanding. These qualities made him the embodiment of auspiciousness and a magnet for grace. He consistently demonstrated how all factors fall into place for someone with such qualities. When we say someone is the embodiment of auspiciousness, it means they are receptive to grace and help others become receptive to it. If we truly develop devotion and embody the qualities of a devotee, auspiciousness becomes a natural state. Wherever we go, we will see auspiciousness within and in the world around us.

Mahatmas such as Amma embody unparalleled joy and auspiciousness. They create an environment filled with celebration, bliss, and positivity wherever they go. Hard work, physical exertion, and effort are always involved in organizing Amma's program. But Amma's visit is still about rejoicing and celebration. Whether in North America, Europe, Africa, or India, the atmosphere around Amma is always one of divine celebration.

A relevant example from one of Amma's programs held in Washington, DC over 20 years ago comes to my mind. Though it was before my time being based at Amma's center there, the organizers recounted to me the challenges they faced in organizing the Amma program that year. The venue in Glen Burnie, Maryland, was far from ideal. The program was scheduled at the very last moment, and no better venues were available. They had to settle for a random event hall that was unclean, filled with mold, and had a dark and inauspicious atmosphere. The wedding party that had used the hall right before left it in disarray with bottles of alcohol lying around. There was another wedding to be held on one side of the hall, which would set anything but a conducive environment. Volunteers and organizers were disheartened — how could this space host something as sacred as Devi Bhava or Atma Puja? Moreover, there was no dining space available for the attendees. Tables had to be set up outdoors. But it was unusually hot that day making it a challenge.

Despite the initial challenges, the organizers and volunteers sprang into action. Their motivation was fueled by their enthusiasm about Amma's impending arrival. They cleaned and transformed the hall, set up the stage, and prepared the venue for the program. What began as a daunting task turned into a labor of love, demonstrating the contagious effect of Amma's positivity. As the event unfolded, something remarkable happened. The wedding party, which was initially thought to be disruptive due to its loud music and celebratory noise, wrapped up unexpectedly early, well before Devi Bhava began. Even the oppressive summer heat softened, creating a pleasant and welcoming environment for outdoor dining arrangements. Factors that once seemed entirely out of control began to fall into place effortlessly

This isn't an isolated case. Every organizer of an Amma program in any part of the world will have a similar story to share, wherein the Amma factor seamlessly makes every situation conducive. Everything just seems to fall into place.

When we reflect on Lord Hanuman as the embodiment of auspiciousness, it should be with the goal of cultivating that auspiciousness and positivity within ourselves. By developing positivity and goodness within, we can automatically transform our environment. Amma often says, "To change your surroundings, change your attitude and mindset; the environment will transform on its own." Hanuman and Amma set the perfect example for us, demonstrating how to embody auspiciousness. Their inherent goodness and positivity ripple outward, transforming everything and everyone around them. When we say a place feels divine or godly, the manifestation of our inner goodness and purity radiates as divinity in the environment.

Dwell in My Heart with Rama, Sita and Lakshmana

The last two lines of the concluding doha of the *Hanuman Chalisa*, "Settle in my heart, O Lord of the Devas, along with Rama, Sita, and Lakshmana," express a plea not just for Lord Hanuman but for the divine trio of Rama, Sita, and Lakshmana to reside in our hearts. However, when we say, "Hanuman, rule my heart," it's essential to understand the deeper meaning.

In his humility and spiritual state, Hanuman has no interest in ruling anyone or controlling their actions. Hanuman is not looking to wield power over us or dictate our lives. When we say, "Hanuman, rule my heart," we truly mean that the qualities Hanuman embodies — his devotion, humility, courage, selflessness, and strength — should govern our hearts. Our thoughts, words, and actions should be guided by these virtues. In this way, our heart becomes the very abode of these divine qualities, allowing them to influence us positively. As a result, our actions benefit us and those around us.

Moreover, the verse isn't just saying, "Oh Hanuman, rule my heart." It says, "Hanuman, rule my heart along with Lord Rama, Sita, and Lakshmana." Lord Rama is an incarnation of Lord Vishnu, the Supreme in human form. His form alone is sufficient. One might argue that we only need Lord Rama's form to focus on, as he embodies all the divine qualities we aspire to reflect upon.

So why include Sita, Lakshmana, and Hanuman alongside Lord Rama? Why do we need their presence when Lord Rama alone is enough? Typically, whenever Lord Rama is depicted, we see Sita, his consort; Lakshmana, his devoted brother; and Hanuman, his loyal devotee, by his side. Their inclusion is not just incidental but deeply significant.

Lord Rama's form alone symbolizes the ideal virtues and divine qualities. However, the presence of Sita, Lakshmana, and Hanuman reminds us of the attitudes we, as devotees, should cultivate towards the Divine. Including Sita, Lakshmana, and Hanuman in our invocation expands our understanding. While Lord Rama's form inspires us to reflect on the Divine's greatness, the other three figures teach us how, as devotees, to shift our attitude toward the Divine. As we grow spiritually, our focus shifts from merely admiring Lord Rama's qualities to embodying the attitudes exemplified by Sita, Lakshmana, and Hanuman.

Amma says that if we want to grow spiritually, we need three key qualities: complete awareness (shraddha), devotion and dedication (bhakti), and faith (vishwasam). These qualities are beautifully represented by Hanuman, Lakshmana, and Sita, respectively.

Mother Sita represents vishwasam (faith). Lord Rama embodies the Supreme Soul (Paramatma), while Mother Sita is an indispensable part of the Supreme Soul, symbolizing the individual soul (jivatma). Ultimately, the jivatma and the Paramatma are one and the same. The jivatma in us is an infinitesimal part of the Paramatma, and the entire spiritual journey is about realizing this oneness.

In the *Ramayana*, Lord Rama was exiled to the forest for 14 years. Mother Sita, however, was not bound by this punishment. She could have stayed back in Ayodhya, in the comfort of the palace, sympathizing with Lord Rama and waiting for his return. But instead, she chose to accompany him, saying, "Wherever my husband goes, I will go too." This decision was not easy. The forest promised endless hardships far from the comforts of home. Today, people struggle to adjust to even minor changes in their surroundings, let alone such a drastic shift. Imagine leaving your home and living in the wilderness for over a decade, exposed to wild animals, venomous reptiles, and harsh conditions. Yet, Mother Sita embraced these challenges willingly, trusting that she would remain safe and happy as long as she was with Lord Rama.

Her unwavering trust and faith in Lord Rama that he would safeguard her exemplifies vishwasam. This faith is a cornerstone of the spiritual path. Mother Sita's story teaches us that true faith allows us to face the most challenging situations with strength and assurance, knowing that the Divine will always protect and guide us.

Lakshmana, Lord Rama's younger brother, also had no obligation to go into exile. He was neither banished to the forest nor sentenced to endure the hardships of exile. Yet, from a young age, his mother, Sumitra, instilled in him the values of unwavering devotion and service to his elder brother. She nurtured him to be a loyal younger brother, ready to support and stand by Rama. Lakshmana fully embodied these teachings. His devotion and dedication were unwavering. He could not fathom letting Lord Rama face hardships alone. With immense determination, Lakshmana accompanied Rama, not out of compulsion but pure love and selfless commitment.

His actions beautifully demonstrate the essence of bhakti. Lakshmana's example reminds us that true devotion encompasses steadfast dedication and commitment, regardless of the challenges that arise.

Finally we come to Hanuman. Throughout all the verses we have discussed in the *Hanuman Chalisa*, Hanuman emerges as an amalgam of all these qualities — devotion, dedication, understanding, broad-heartedness, and more. These are the very attributes we refer to as shraddha.

We've touched on this before: While shraddha can be loosely translated as awareness, it encompasses much more. Ultimately, acting with shraddha means approaching anything we undertake or any situation we face with:

- Complete concentration: Being fully present and undistracted.
- Faith and trust: Having trust in the people and circumstances involved, and, most importantly, faith in ourselves — believing "Yes, I can do this."
- Respect: Respecting the people, things, and efforts involved, as well as our abilities.
- A positive attitude: Practice patience and kindle the attitude of acceptance in whatever way the situation may unfold.
- Being aware and conscious: Being aware of what lies within and around us and responding appropriately.
- Discrimination between what is right and otherwise: All these qualities enveloped in true knowledge/wisdom, with the proper discernment of dharma.

When all these qualities are combined, we can say we acted with true shraddha. Hanuman exemplifies this shraddha in its fullest form.

He fully and beautifully embodies all these qualities, which is why he perfectly represents this principle. His qualities have a strong foundation in jnana (knowledge/wisdom), that of true discernment. Throughout the *Hanuman Chalisa*, we have repeatedly seen how Hanuman's actions reflect this unwavering shraddha.

Without bhakti and vishwasa, we won't get the benefit no matter how much grace is showered upon us. Amma often gives the analogy of sunlight: Sunlight may fall on our home, but if we keep the windows closed or draw the curtains, the sunlight will never enter. Similarly, grace is always present and available, but we can only tap into its potential when we cultivate these essential qualities within ourselves. This is the significance of the four forms in the image — taken together, they represent a complete and balanced spiritual relationship: the Divine complemented by shraddha, bhakti, and vishwasa.

Grace is like a hundred-dollar bill. Imagine taking such a bill to a place so remote that the people there have never interacted with modern civilization and saying, "I have a hundred dollars; I can do whatever I want with it!" Do you think it would work? If we hand that bill to someone in such a remote place, they might not even recognize it or know what it is. We wouldn't be able to buy food or anything else with it. For the hundred-dollar bill to be useful, we must convert it into the local currency. Only then would it have practical value in that specific setting.

It's not that the hundred-dollar bill lacks value — it holds its worth no matter where we are in the world. But for it to work in that particular context, it must be translated into something usable. Similarly, grace is grace. It's abundant, valuable, and always present. There is no diminishing of its worth. However, for grace to be effective in our lives, we must "convert" it into actionable qualities relevant to our situation. That "conversion" happens through shraddha (awareness), bhakti (devotion), and vishwasa (faith).

Lord Rama, representing divine grace, is always there. But to access and make use of that grace, we need to awaken Sita (vishwasa), Lakshmana (bhakti), and Hanuman (shraddha) within ourselves. This is why, in this context, there's greater emphasis on the devotee rather than the Divine. The Divine is ever-present. This is taken for granted. The awakening of the devotee within us is critical for our spiritual growth. Without that, even the the most abundant grace remains untapped and unused.

A folklore tale associated with an episode in *Ramayana* provides a beautiful perspective on the relationship between the Divine and the devotee. The story takes place when Lord Rama and his vanarasena (army of monkeys) reach the southern shores of India, on their way to rescue Sita.

Lord Rama assigns Nala, the architect of the monkey kingdom, and his twin brother Nila to design and build the bridge to Lanka. Nala and Nila take up the challenge and begin constructing the bridge. However, they face a significant obstacle — rocks typically sink when thrown into water. They need to make the rocks buoyant to float and form the bridge.

The next day, Lord Rama visits the construction site and sees the team throwing rocks into the ocean. To his amazement, these rocks are floating. Intrigued, he observes Nala, Nila, and Hanuman working together to process the stones in some way before tossing them into the water. Curious, Lord Rama decides to test it himself. He picks up a rock and throws it into the ocean, but it sinks immediately. Yet, all the rocks handled by Hanuman and his team continue to float. Rama is puzzled. He approaches Hanuman and asks, "How are you making the rocks float? What are you doing to them?" Hanuman humbly responds, "All we do is inscribe your name on the rocks, Lord. It floats when your name is on the rock, and we toss it into the water."

The story highlights an interesting question: Lord Rama, the embodiment of the Supreme Divine, could not make the rocks float, but his devotee Hanuman could. Does this mean Hanuman, the devotee, is superior to the Lord? This story is a reminder of the unique bond between the Divine and the devotee. It emphasizes the power of devotion and faith. Hanuman's unwavering faith and dedication imbued even lifeless rocks with the ability to float, showcasing how the Lord's name, when chanted or invoked with pure devotion, can overcome all odds. While Rama represents the divine grace, which is always available, Hanuman's devotion activates and manifests that grace in a tangible way.

Critically, the story does not suggest that the Lord is inferior to the devotee but rather highlights the importance of the devotee's role in expressing and utilizing divine power. The story emphasizes the importance of the path, the role of devotion, and the need for faith and surrender to reach the Divine. In the path of devotion, the devotee's faith and selfless dedication allow the Divine to act through them, creating miracles and transforming the seemingly impossible into reality.

In the *Srimad Bhagavatam*, Sri Krishna states:

> ahaṁ bhakta-parādhīno
> hyasvatantra iva dvija
> sādhubhir grasta-hṛdayo
> bhaktair bhakta-jana-priyaḥ

I am subjugated by my devotee, and I am not independent.
Oh Brahmin! My heart is controlled by a Sadhu (one who lets
go of ego), and my devotees' devotees become dear to me.

We are not discounting the fact that the Divine is the ultimate. However, in this context, when we are trying to develop devotion, what is most important now is devotion itself. It's like this: If I travel from Washington, DC to New York, my ultimate goal is to reach New York.

That is the destination. But what is crucial for me at this moment? My bag is essential; everything I need for the journey and beyond must be packed. I need a vehicle to get there, which is equally essential, as is the road I take. Without these, I cannot reach New York.

New York remains the ultimate goal. There is no question about that. But right now, the bag, the car, and the road are the most critical things I need to get there. Similarly, Lord Rama is the ultimate goal, the supreme destination. However, to reach him, what becomes most important for a devotee right now is bhakti — the path that leads to him.

That's why, in the story, Lord Rama cannot make the rocks float, but Hanuman can. And how is Hanuman able to do it? By invoking Lord Rama's name, not through his name or anything else. The rocks float because of Lord Rama's name. There's no diminishing the fact that the Lord is the Supreme or the ultimate goal. The story emphasizes the importance of the path, the role of devotion, and the need for faith and surrender to reach the Divine.

The forms of Lord Rama, Hanuman, Sita, and Lakshmana represent this path. They embody the qualities and stages necessary to reach the Lord. When we go to a temple, we see Lord Rama's and Lord Hanuman's idols worshiped similarly. This is because Hanuman attained oneness with Lord Rama through his devotion. It is not that Hanuman became greater than Lord Rama or that Lord Rama became equal to Hanuman. Instead, Hanuman realized his oneness with the Supreme Soul, so we worship him as much as we worship Lord Rama.

The image of Lord Rama, Lakshmana, Sita, and Hanuman is not just a depiction of the Divine but, perhaps most importantly, represents the expansive path of bhakti yoga. It reminds us that devotion, faith, humility, and selflessness are essential on our spiritual journey. This is the essence of bhakti yoga. This is the essence of the message conveyed in the *Hanuman Chalisa*.

Insights on the Path of Bhakti from the concluding verse:

- A true devotee should be the humblest of the humble but not a weakling; use our might to uphold righteousness.

- Become the embodiment of auspiciousness through our thoughts, words, and deeds.

- The path of devotion can be summarized as the combination of shraddha (awareness), bhakti (dedication), and vishwasa (faith).

Afterword

In one sense, the path of devotion could not be simpler. Yet, as we begin to walk it, we discover it to be as deep as the ocean and as infinitely vast as space. A logical understanding and a practical attitude can help us navigate this path effectively. Lord Hanuman stands as a shining example of practical devotion practiced with discernment, with the verses of the *Hanuman Chalisa* beautifully illustrating how he embodied these qualities in various situations.

To walk this magnanimous path, Amma often advises us to cultivate a combination of shraddha (awareness born of right understanding through jnana - knowledge/wisdom), bhakti (devotion and dedication), and vishwasa (trust and faith). These qualities are essential for navigating this profound journey of spiritual pursuit.

Though simple in essence, the path of bhakti may at times feel otherwise as we walk it. This sense of complexity or simplicity does not stem from the nature of the path itself, but from our own attitude. When approached with sincerity, selflessness, humility, and acceptance, the path remains simple. It becomes complicated when clouded by self-centeredness, attachments to likes and dislikes, preconceived notions, desires, and expectations. The true deciding factor in our experience treading the path of bhakti yoga is our ego.

If we are determined to carry the baggage of ego throughout the journey, it will only weigh us down. But if we place that ego at the holy feet of our Guru, our most beloved Amma, or our chosen deity, we can travel lighter, with greater ease and comfort.

The ball is in our court — it is up to us whether to keep the path simple or complicate it.

May Amma's divine grace guide us through this transformative journey.

Aum.

A letter to Amma

To end this book on a lighter note, I would like to share with you a letter I placed in Amma's room a few years ago. Make sure you read till the end. It read:

My most beloved Amma,

I write to you today with a heart filled with a strange mixture of love, and confusion. I don't quite know how to say this. I've carried this in the folds of my heart for far too long, and it aches now to stay hidden.

Amma.... I've fallen in love.

I am very sorry, Amma. I really don't know how to handle this. I have known her when I was in India, but, after moving to the US we began to grow closer. Perhaps being physically away from you drew me close to her. Though she isn't particularly attractive from outside, Amma, she is a treasure chest of grace and beauty within. She always follows Amma everywhere you travel – India and abroad. The more I got to know her, the more deeply I am drawn to her. I feel like knowing her more and more. I've reached a stage wherein it has become difficult to let go of her. It feels like I can't live without her, Amma. If at all I've a future birth, I pray that it is with her. Amma, I am confused. The more I know her, I feel like I have so much more to know. Only your Grace can help me achieve her and be a good match for her. Please help me, Amma.

Your beloved son,

Ramanand

P.S. Amma, by the way – her name is Bhakti. You definitely know her very, very well.

This letter would have served its purpose if, all this while, you thought I was referring to a girl. I am sorry, I was actually speaking of Bhakti – Devotion. Please do read the letter once more now and it may make better sense.

Scan to chant along

Hanuman Chalisa
40 verses dedicated to Lord Hanuman,

the epitome of Devotion, the greatest inspiration for a spiritual aspirant

śrī guru charaṇa sarōja raja
nijamana mukura sudhāri ।
baraṇau raghuvara bimala jaśu
jō dāyaku phalachāri ॥

श्रीगुरु चरन सरोज रज
निजमनु मुकुरु सुधारि ।
बरनउँ रघुबर बिमल जसु
जो दायकु फल चारि ।

Cleansing the mirror of my mind with the dust from the Lotus-feet of the guru, I describe the unblemished glory of Lord Rama, which bestows four fruits of Righteousness (Dharma), Wealth (Artha), Pleasure (Kama), and Liberation (Moksha).

buddhihīna tanujānikai
sumirau pavana kumāra ।
bala buddhi vidyā dēhu mōhi
harahu kalēśa bikāra ॥

बुद्धिहीन तनु जानिके,
सुमिरौं पवन-कुमार ।
बल बुद्धि बिद्या देहु मोहिं,
हरहु कलेस बिकार ॥

Humbled, realizing that this body lacks wisdom, I pray to Lord Hanuman to bless me with strength, intelligence and knowledge and cure my tendencies and internal conflicts.

jaya hanumāna jñāna guṇa sāgara ।
jaya kapīśa tihu lōka ujāgara ॥ 1 ॥

जय हनुमान ज्ञान गुन सागर ।
जय कपीस तिहुं लोक उजागर ॥

— 301 —

Victory to Hanuman, who is the ocean of Wisdom and Virtues.
Victory to the king of Monkeys, who illuminates the three worlds.

rāmadūta atulita baladhāmā । añjani putra pavanasuta nāmā ॥ 2 ॥	रामदूत अतुलित बल धामा। अंजनि-पुत्र पवनसुत नामा ॥

You are the messenger of Rama (to Sita). You are the abode of incomparable power. You are also known by the names - 'Anjani Putra' (Son of Anjana) and 'Pavana suta' (son of wind god).

mahāvīra vikrama bajaraṅgī । kumati nivāra sumati kē saṅgī ॥3 ॥	महावीर विक्रम बजरंगी। कुमति निवार सुमति के संगी ॥

O mighty and valorous one, whose body is as strong as vajra (the precious stone/diamond). Please remove the negativities of my mind, for you are the companion of those with a pure heart.

kanchana varaṇa virāja suvēśā । kānana kuṇḍala kuñchita kēśā ॥ 4 ॥	कंचन वरन विराज सुवेसा। कानन कुण्डल कुंचित केसा ॥

One with golden effulgence, resplendent in your grand attire. Adoring beautiful earrings and curly hair.

hātha vajra au dhvajā virājai । kāndhē mūñja janēvū sājai ॥ 5 ॥	हाथ बज्र औ ध्वजा बिराजै। काँधे मूँज जनेऊ साजै।

Vajrayudha (a special mace made out of the powerful Vajra) and flag are shining in your hand. The sacred thread made of Munja grass adorns your shoulder.

śaṅkara suvana kēsarī nandana । tēja pratāpa mahājaga vandana ॥ 6 ॥	शंकर सुवन केसरीनंदन। तेज प्रताप महा जग वन्दन ॥

O partial incarnation of Lord Shiva, giver of joy to King Kesari. Your great majesty is revered by the whole world.

vidyāvāna guṇī ati chātura । rāma kāja karivē kō ātura ॥ 7 ॥	विद्यावान गुणी अति चातुर। राम काज करिबे को आतुर ॥

All knowledgeable one, the one full of virtues, sharp-minded one, you are always eager to serve Lord Shri Rama.

prabhu charitra sunibē kō rasiyā ǀ	प्रभु चरित्र सुनिबे को रसिया ǀ
rāmalakhana sītā mana basiyā ǁ 8 ǁ	राम लखन सीता मन बसिया ǁ

You enjoy listening to Lord Rama's stories and divine plays; Lord Rama, Lakshman and Sita verily reside in your heart.

sūkṣma rūpadhari siyahi dikhāvā ǀ	सूक्ष्म रूप धरि सियहिं दिखावा ǀ
vikaṭa rūpadhari laṅka jarāvā ǁ 9 ǁ	विकट रूप धरि लंक जरावा ǁ

You assumed the smallest of the forms as you visited Mother Sita. Then, assuming a gigantic form, you burnt down the capital of Lanka.

bhīma rūpadhari asura saṃhārē ǀ	भीम रूप धरि असुर संहारे ǀ
rāmachandra kē kāja saṃvārē ǁ 10 ǁ	रामचंद्र के काज संवारे ǁ

Assuming the all-powerful form you slayed the demons. Your efforts facilitated and helped achieve Lord Rama's task.

lāya sañjīvana lakhana jiyāyē ǀ	लाय सजीवन लखन जियाये ǀ
śrī raghuvīra haraṣi uralāyē ǁ 11 ǁ	श्रीरघुबीर हरषि उर लाये ǁ

You brought the whole mountain peak containing Sanjeevini (medicinal herbs to bring back to life) to save Lakshmana's Life. Lord Rama embraced you in joy.

raghupati kīnhī bahuta baḍāyī ǀ	रघुपति कीन्ही बहुत बड़ाई ǀ
tuma mama priya bharata sama bhāyī ǁ12 ǁ	तुम मम प्रिय भरतहि सम भाई ǁ

Lord Rama had high praises for you. He exclaimed, "You are dear to me like my brother Bharata."

sahasa vadana tumharō yaśagāvai ǀ	सहस बदन तुम्हरो जस गावैं ǀ
asa kahi śrīpati kaṇṭha lagāvai ǁ 13 ǁ	अस कहि श्रीपति कंठ लगावैं ǁ

Lord Rama embraced you, saying, "May the thousand-headed serpent Adishesha sing of your glory."

sanakādika brahmādi munīśā |
nārada śārada sahita ahīśā || 14 ||

सनकादिक ब्रह्मादि मुनीशा।
नारद सारद सहित अहींसा॥

Sanaka and other Sages, Lord Brahma and other Gods, Narada, Devi Saraswati and Seshnag (the king of the serpents)...

jama kubēra digapāla jahāṃ tē |
kavi kōvida kahi sakē kahāṃ tē || 15 ||

जम कुबेर दिगपाल जहां ते।
कवि कोविद कहि सके कहाँ ते॥

Yama, Kubera, Dig-paalakas (protectors of each of the directions), poets, and singers; all fall short of praising you to the fullest of your greatness.

tuma upakāra sugrīvahi kīnhā |
rāma milāya rājapada dīnhā || 16 ||

तुम उपकार सुग्रीवहिं कीन्हा।
राम मिलाय राज पद दीन्हा॥

You helped Sugriva (the king of the monkey kingdom – Kishkinda). You made him friends with Rama which gave him his kingship back.

tumharō mantra vibhīṣaṇa mānā |
laṅkēśvara bhayē saba jaga jānā || 17 ||

तुम्हरो मंत्र विभीषन माना।
लंकेश्वर भये सब जग जाना॥

Vibhishana humbly heeded your advice. The whole world knows he became the king of Lanka because of your advice.

yuga sahasra yōjana para bhānū |
līlyō tāhi madhura phala jānū || 18 ||

जुग सहस्र योजन पर भानू।
लील्यो ताहि मधुर फल जानू॥

You flew towards the Sun, which is thousands of Yojanas (precise distance measurement) away, mistaking it for a sweet fruit.

prabhu mudrikā mēli mukha māhī |
jaladhi lāṅghi gayē acharaja nāhī || 19 ||

प्रभु मुद्रिका मेलि मुख माहीं।
जलधि लांघि गये अचरज नाहीं॥

*Carrying Lord Rama's ring for Mother Sita in your
mouth, you jumped and flew over the ocean to Lanka.
It is no surprise that you could achieve this feat.*

durgama kāja jagata kē jētē ǀ	दुर्गम काज जगत के जेते।
sugama anugraha tumharē tētē ǁ 20 ǁ	सुगम अनुग्रह तुम्हरे तेते॥

*Even the impossible tasks in the world become
possible because of your grace.*

rāma duārē tuma rakhavārē ǀ	राम दुआरे तुम रखवारे।
hōta na ājñā binu paisārē ǁ 21 ǁ	होत न आज्ञा बिनु पैसारे॥

*You are the doorkeeper of Lord Rama's royal court.
No one can enter it without your consent.*

saba sukha lahai tumhārī śaraṇā ǀ	सब सुख लहैं तुम्हारी सरना।
tuma rakṣaka kāhū kō ḍara nā ǁ 22 ǁ	तुम रक्षक काहू को डरना॥

*One who takes refuge in you will always have happiness
beside them. Why fear you are there to protect us?*

āpana tēja samhārō āpai ǀ	आपन तेज सम्हारो आपै।
tīnōṃ lōka hāṅka tē kāmpai ǁ 23 ǁ	तीनों लोक हांक तें कांपै॥

*Only you can match your might. All three worlds
would tremble in front of your power and force.*

bhūta piśācha nikaṭa nahi āvai ǀ	भूत पिसाच निकट नहिं आवै।
mahavīra jaba nāma sunāvai ǁ 24 ǁ	महाबीर जब नाम सुनावै॥

*Evil forces can't even come to the vicinity when and where the
chanting of your name can be heard, O supremely courageous one!!*

nāsai rōga harai saba pīrā ǀ	नासै रोग हरै सब पीरा।
japata nirantara hanumata vīrā ǁ 25 ǁ	जपत निरंतर हनुमत बीरा॥

Diseases will be cured, and pain and suffering will be healed when a devotee constantly repeats the supremely brave Hanuman's name.

saṅkaṭa sē hanumāna chuḍāvai ।   संकट तें हनुमान छुड़ावै।
mana krama vachana dhyāna jō lāvai ॥26॥ मन क्रम वचन ध्यान जो लावै ॥

Hanuman will rescue those who meditate upon him through their thoughts, actions, and words from troubles and tribulations.

saba para rāma tapasvī rājā ।   सब पर राम तपस्वी राजा।
tinakē kāja sakala tuma sājā ॥ 27 ॥   तिनके काज सकल तुम साजा।

Ruling over all is Rama the tapasvi - the greatest of the ascetics. Through Your devotion to him You assist in all the tasks taken up by such a great being.

aura manōratha jō kōyi lāvai ।   और मनोरथ जो कोई लावै।
sōyi amita jīvana phala pāvai ॥ 28 ॥ सोई अमित जीवन फल पावै ॥

Whoever brings their many desires and wishes to you, are showered with boundless life as fruit (of their action)

chārō yuga partāpa tumhārā ।   चारों युग परताप तुम्हारा।
hai prasiddha jagata ujiyārā ॥ 29 ॥ है परसिद्ध जगत उजियारा ॥

Your splendor proliferates all the four ages (yugas); your fame and greatness illuminates the whole world.

sādhu santa kē tuma rakhavārē ।   साधु-संत के तुम रखवारे।
asura nikandana rāma dulārē ॥ 30 ॥ असुर निकंदन राम दुलारे ॥

You are the guardian of the sages and good-hearted ones. You annihilate the demonic forces. You are most dear to Lord Rama.

aṣṭhasiddhi nava nidhi kē dātā ।   अष्ट सिद्धि नव निधि के दाता।
asa vara dīna jānakī mātā ॥ 31 ॥   अस वर दीन जानकी माता ॥

You are the bestower of the 8 Siddhis (supernatural powers) and 9 Nidhis (divine treasures). Mother Sita granted you the boon to be so.

rāma rasāyana tumhārē pāsā l	राम रसायन तुम्हरे पासा।
sadā rahō raghupati kē dāsā ‖ 32 ‖	सदा रहो रघुपति के दासा॥

You have a special potion with ingredients for perfect devotion to Lord Rama. You are ever greatly devoted to Lord Rama.

tumharē bhajana rāmakō pāvai l	तुम्हरे भजन राम को भावै।
janma janma kē dukha bisarāvai ‖ 33 ‖	जनम-जनम के दुख बिसरावै॥

Singing your glory, ridding ourselves of the pain and suffering of many lives, we can reach Lord Rama himself.

anta kāla raghuvar purajāyī l	अन्त काल रघुबर पुर जाई।
jahā janma haribhakta kahāyī ‖ 34 ‖	जहाँ जन्म हरि-भक्त कहाई॥

He who sings your glory at the end of the life attains Lord Rama's abode. For all births, he or she will be devoted to Lord Rama.

aura dēvatā chitta na dharayī l	और देवता चित्त न धरई।
hanumata sēyi sarva sukha karayī ‖ 35 ‖	हनुमत सेई सर्व सुख करई॥

There is no need to focus the mind on any other form; one will attain all the happiness by just serving Lord Hanuman.

saṅkaṭa kaṭai miṭai saba pīrā l	संकट कटै मिटै सब पीरा।
jō sumirai hanumata bala vīrā ‖ 36 ‖	जो सुमिरै हनुमत बलबीरा॥

Sorrow and difficulties will be gone and all sufferings will be removed for one who always remembers Lord Hanuman, the mighty and brave one.

jai jai jai hanumāna gōsāyī l	जै जै जै हनुमान गोसाई।
kr̥pā karahu gurudēva kī nāyī ‖ 37 ‖	कृपा करहु गुरुदेव की नाई॥

Victory to you, O master of the senses. Show mercy on
us like how a Sadguru (spiritual master) does.

jō śata vāra pāṭha kara kōyī | जो सत बार पाठ कर कोई।
Chūṭahi bandi mahā sukha hōyī ‖ 38 ‖ छूटहिं बंदि महा सुख होई॥

One who recites this text a hundred (numerous) times will
be freed of all bondages and will find supreme bliss.

jō yaha paḍai hanumāna chālīsā | जो यह पढ़ै हनुमान चालीसा।
hōya siddhi sākhī gaurīśa ‖ 39 ‖ होय सिद्धि साखी गौरीसा॥

One who reads and imbibes these verses on Hanuman
will attain spiritual perfection and success. None other
than Lord Shiva is the witness to this statement.

tulasīdāsa sadā hari chērā | तुलसीदास सदा हरि चेरा।
kījai nātha hṛdaya maha ḍērā ‖ 40 ‖ कीजै नाथ हृदय महँ डेरा॥

Tulasidas (the composer of these verses) will forever
be a disciple of Hari (the Divine – Lord Vishnu). O
Lord!! Please make my heart your abode.

pavana tanaya saṅkaṭa haraṇa पवनतनय संकट हरन,
maṅgaḷa mūrati rūp | मंगल मूरति रूप।
rāma lakhana sītā sahita राम लखन सीता सहित,
hṛdaya basahu surabhūp ‖ हृदय बसहु सुर भूप॥

O Son of the Wind God, the remover of difficulties, the embodiment
of auspiciousness, the greatest among the Gods, please reside
in my heart with Lord Rama, Lakshman, and Mother Sita.

Putting Bhakti into Actual Practice
A Quick Reference Guide

This is a summary of the practical takeaways we can draw from Lord Hanuman, the epitome of devotion, who exemplified bhakti through the 40 verses of the *Hanuman Chalisa*. It highlights the practical essence of bhakti — focusing on its application and practice, moving beyond the flowery and philosophical interpretations often associated with it.

What do we learn about practicing bhakti yoga from Hanuman, as seen in *Hanuman Chalisa*? How do we do that through the lens of Amma's teachings?

- Doha - prelude verse
  - The guru is an indispensable part of our spiritual pursuit, and the guru's grace is critical. Even the insignificant dust on the guru's feet is significant for the disciple.
  - The mind is like a mirror reflecting our true self if cleansed and conditioned correctly.
  - Acknowledge and understand the limitations of our physical existence; seek the strength, intellect, and knowledge to grow.

- Verse 1
  - Remain open to learning from all sources, whether seemingly significant or insignificant.
  - Our conduct should be such that we illuminate all three worlds with our virtues.

- Verse 2
  - Be the messenger of the Lord or the guru (Amma). Set the right example.
  - Exercise mental strength and face every situation with confidence.

- Verse 3
  - Everyone has positives and negatives.
  - Our strength is in:
  - Confronting the negative tendencies of our mind
  - Befriending our positive tendencies

- Verse 4
  - Constant chanting of the mantra - remembrance and imbibing the qualities of the deity/guru is an essential part of spiritual progression.
  - Defining our beauty - we become good-looking by looking at the goodness in others.

- Verse 5
  - Be self-sufficient and independent.
  - The primary factor determining our strength and fame is our own inner qualities. What others think and say about us is superficial.
  - Ever be a beginner, humble as a student, ready to learn and grow even more.

- Verse 6
  - Selfish motives can turn even our best efforts into unfavorable outcomes.
  - Be truthful to yourself - deceiving the conscience is meaningless and unfruitful.

- Verse 7
  - Act per what the guru and scriptures teach us.
  - Dedicate your actions to the guru/lord. Even mundane actions become meaningful then.

○ Work smarter, not harder - assess the context of the situation with wisdom before taking action, considering the bigger picture.

● Verse 8
  ○ Rather than just glorifying the Lord/guru through stories, draw inspiration, imbibe those qualities, and live as an example. That is true worship.

● Verses 9 and 10
  ○ Face every situation with full might but with the understanding that what finally fetches victory is humility.
  ○ Our strength should empower us, not make us arrogant.
  ○ Adapt to any situation; be prepared to display humility or toughness as the circumstances require.

● Verses 11, 12 and 13
  ○ Be prepared for the guru to point out our ego often and seldom praise us.
  ○ However, our thoughts, speech, and actions should be such that they deserve the guru's praise.
  ○ Strive for the divine embrace - becoming one with the Lord - established in the state of non-duality.

● Verses 14 and 15
  ○ Praise and ridicule may come our way. Let them be the means to make us even more humble.
  ○ Humility makes us receptive to grace.
  ○ Grace, in a situation, is simply the seamless alignment of all factors to achieve the desired outcome.
  ○ Our self is the most significant factor - be established in the Self!

● Verses 16 and 17
  ○ Good company is critical for spiritual and materialistic growth.
  ○ The company of a realized being (mahatma) takes us to an exalted state.

- Verse 18
  - Whatever our goals, always aspire for the ultimate knowledge of the Supreme.
  - "Seek, learn, and grow" should always be our attitude.
  - Strive to be deserving of divine grace, allowing it to flow into us and consume the ego completely.

- Verse 19
  - Chanting the name of the Divine helps us stay focused and present in all that we do.
  - Recognize the strengths we have.
  - Be determined to reach the goal but do not be obsessed with it. Flexibility is critical.
  - Have the attitude of no compromise when it comes to our inner negativities and negative tendencies.

- Verses 20 and 21
  - Bhakti helps obtain grace, making even impossible deeds easily possible
  - Grace can be threefold - our own grace, grace of the surroundings (things and people), and grace of the factors beyond.
  - To practice bhakti is to practice all possible good qualities in every moment (dedication, selflessness, understanding, acceptance, broad-mindedness, patience, etc.)
  - Bhakti facilitates us to the ultimate abode, the highest state of oneness.

- Verse 22
  - Surrender to the guru/Divine
  - That doesn't mean we give up or give in.
  - Do all actions giving our very best and with the right attitude. Then develop the attitude of acceptance, acknowledging that many factors are beyond our control.
  - Remove self-centered thoughts from the equation.

- Verse 23
  - Be self-confident.
  - Only we have the power to decide how we want to feel.
  - Others (people and things) can be triggers, but the decision on how to think and feel is on us.

- Verse 24
  - Devotion and surrender are for the brave. There is no room for fear.
  - Faith and trust dispel fear.

- Verses 25 and 26
  - Devotion is the medicine for the most significant disease of all - our ego.
  - Devotion brings bliss and helps overcome difficulties and suffering.
  - Practice shraddha in every thought, word, and action that we perform.

- Verse 27
  - A true master does not sit on a throne, executing orders; rather they exercise penance and sacrifice in being of service to others.
  - A true master will be the ruler of hearts.
  - A true devotee is dedicated to realizing the master's cause of dharma and upliftment of others.

- Verse 28
  - Rather than just craving for long life or immortality, let us pray we live every day to its full potential.

- Verse 29
  - Everything in creation can be perceived as a function of time. The ultimate state of devotion goes beyond time.
  - The fame and following that a true devotee achieves will benefit others.

- Verse 30
  - Devotion is about upholding our goodness and overcoming our negativities.
  - Living selflessly for others' benefit makes one dear to the Lord/guru.

- Verse 31
  - Through true devotion, one can attain the eight supreme abilities and the nine wealths of virtues.

- Verse 32
  - The greatest wealth for a devotee should be the divine name and spiritual practice.

- Verses 33 and 34
  - A true devotee revels in the ultimate state of Oneness.
  - Bhakti expends all that we have accumulated through several births.
  - A true devotee doesn't need to be elevated to heaven, instead creating heaven wherever he or she is.

- Verse 35
  - For a devotee, the form or deity chosen is the ultimate inspiration and goal. We should try to become one with that.
  - However, it is essential to recognize that every other form is a reflection of the same Divine and should be respected accordingly.

- Verse 36
  - Devotion and dedication fetch us true happiness. There is no room for suffering in that state.

- Verse 37
  - True victory is realizing the Supreme Truth — a state of oneness with the Divine and with all of creation — while letting go of our ephemeral and limited ego identity.

- Verses 38 and 39
  - Constant practice and effort are critical in the path of devotion
  - Equally or more important is the attitude with which we practice

- Verse 40
  - Ever maintain the attitude of a humble servant, embracing selflessness in all that we do.
  - Make our hearts deserving of the Divine to dwell.
  - We should make ourselves the abode of divine qualities like patience, love, compassion, humility, understanding, and acceptance.

- Doha - ending verse
  - A true devotee should be the humblest of the humble but not a weakling; use our might to uphold righteousness.
  - Become the embodiment of auspiciousness through our thoughts, words, and deeds.
  - The path of bhakti in its fullness is the perfect blend of shraddha (awareness), bhakti (devotion), and vishwasa (faith).

Amma says "Grace is ever flowing towards us like the sunlight falling on a house. We need to become deserving of receiving it through our thoughts, words, and deeds, like opening the window of the house to let sunlight in."

Bhagavad Gita Chapter 12
Bhakti Yoga - the path of devotion

mayyeva maná ādhatsva mayi buddhim niveśhaya
nivasiṣhyasi mayy eva ata ūrdhvaṁ na sanśhayaḥ || verse 12 ||

Focus your mind upon Me alone and invest your intellect in Me.
Thereafter, you will always revel in Me. There is no doubt about it.

atha chittam samādhātuṁ na śhaknoṣhi mayi sthiram
abhyāsa yogena tato mām ichchhāptuṁ dhananjaya || verse 13 ||

If you are unable to focus your mind steadfastly on Me,
you can still be dear to me through abhyasa - constant
effort, my remembrance, and practicing restraint.

abhyāse-pyasamartho-si mat karma paramo bhava
mad-artham api karmāṇi kurvan siddhim avāpsyasi || verse 14 ||

If you are unable to practice abhyasa - (constant effort and
remembrance), then just try to engage in action for Me.
Thus selflessly serving Me, you shall achieve perfection.

atha etad-api-aśhakto-si kartum mad-yogam āśhritaḥ
sarva karma phala tyāgaṁ tataḥ kuru yatātmavān || verse 15 ||

If you are unable to do even that, performing action
devoted to me with refuge, then try to renounce the fruits
of your actions and be established in the self.

"Parabhakti (supreme devotion) is pure Vedanta. The true devotee sees everything as pervaded by God. He does not see anything except God everywhere. When a devotee says, 'Everything is pervaded by God,' the Vedantin says, 'Everything is pervaded by Brahman.' Both are one and the same."

Awaken Children Vol 1 Page 54